The Moon Rises from the Ganges

EUGENIO BARBA

The Moon Rises from the Ganges
My Journey through Asian Acting Techniques

Edited, introduced,
and with an appendix by LLUÍS MASGRAU
Photo selection and captions by RINA SKEEL
Translated from Italian by JUDY BARBA

Holstebro – Malta – Wrocław
London – New York
2015

ICARUS Publishing Enterprise is a joint initiative
of Odin Teatret (Denmark), The Grotowski Institute (Poland)
and Theatre Arts Researching the Foundations (Malta)

Cover design and layout Barbara Kaczmarek
Typesetting Tadeusz Zarych
Index Monika Blige

Published by
Icarus Publishing Enterprise and Routledge
www.icaruspublishing.com
www.routledge.com

The Grotowski Institute
Rynek-Ratusz 27, 50-101 Wrocław, Poland

Routledge
2 Park Square, Milton Park, Abingdon, OX14 4RN, UK
711 Third Avenue, New York, NY 10017, USA
Routledge is an imprint of Taylor and Francis Group, an informa business

ISBN 978-0-415-71929-2 (paperback)
ISBN 978-0-415-71928-5 (hardback)

Printed and bound in Poland by JAKS

Contents

IV. COHABITATION: THE PERFORMERS' VILLAGE

POSTSCRIPT

INTRODUCTION

Eugenio Barba and traditional Asian theatres

BY LLUÍS MASGRAU

► Volterra, 1981. Part of the day at ISTA – the International School of Theatre Anthropology – was spent watching the demonstrations by the individual performers. The purpose was to compare ways of thinking, technical procedures and the working terminology in the different performance genres. Here, the Swede Ingemar Lindh demonstrates Étienne Decroux's corporeal mime. It is interesting to notice the concentration of Katsuko Azuma (nihon buyo) watching in the background.

East and West in twentieth-century
theatre culture

In his impressive *Eurasian Theatre*, Nicola Savarese (2010) describes the flow of exchanges between actors, dancers, mimes, and singers that unfolded with alternating frequency between East and West from ancient times to our day. However, the facts show that during many centuries the Western and Eastern theatres were two worlds apart with no direct and deep contact. The constraints of geography transformed the Asian theatres into a reality accessible only to travellers and adventurers. It was not until the end of the nineteenth century and beginning of the twentieth that the first direct exchanges between Asian and Euro-American stage artists took place with mutual repercussions on each other's craft.

The beginnings were a few tours of actors-dancers, especially from Cambodia, Java and Annam (Vietnam), within the framework of World and Colonial Exhibitions, as well as the presence of Chinese traditional theatre on the West Coast of the USA (San Francisco). But it was the tour of the Japanese Kawakami Otojiro and Sada Yacco in 1899 in USA and subsequently in Europe that provoked the first interest and enthusiasm in Western audiences and among theatre professionals. This first-hand acquaintance, marked by the unfamiliarity Americans and Europeans alike had of Asian theatres, generated curiosity and surprise as well as a host of debates and misunderstandings.

The first Asian performances seen in Europe and America were appreciated mainly for their exotic aesthetics, their theatricality and gorgeous costumes. The actors' achievements – with rare exceptions – went unperceived. The critics of the time mentioned the actors' power of expression but didn't analyse the inner logic and merit of their technique. A deep ignorance existed on this question. Nicola Savarese puts this problem in its cultural context when he writes:

> The reason for this ignorance is familiar: it lies in the ancient and deep-rooted schism between *body* and *soul*, much emphasised by the Christian message, which defined the body as the source of instinct and animal satisfactions, and the soul as the cradle of spirituality and noble aspirations. [...] One of the consequences of this culture of division, still in full force in the nineteenth century, was an undervaluing not only of the culture of the body but also of every notion of body technique. Consequently, artistic techniques, whether practised by actors or dancers, were not

taken into consideration outside the most strictly limited professional contexts, and sometimes not even then.

(Savarese 2010: 398)

It was only at the beginning of the twentieth century that the significance of corporality in theatre and dance became a topic for discussion.

In addition, another significant factor dominated European culture: the division between dance and theatre as two completely different performative universes. In the West, the debate on the appropriate corporal culture for the stage took place first in the dance milieu and later in that of the theatre. It is not strange then that the Asian actors' performances had more consequences at first for dancers than for actors and directors. The realism reigning in European theatre, with its narrative demands and dispersed acting technique neglecting an autonomous corporal stage language, constituted a context in which the Asian performers' skill appeared distant an unusable. But the same performers represented a powerful incentive for those dancers who tried to renovate their art. Cléo de Mérode, Ruth Saint-Denis, Loie Fuller, Ted Shawn, and even Nijinski were inspired by Eastern forms in their attempt to disrupt the traditional codes of Western classical dance.

At the beginning of the twentieth century, in an atmosphere of renewal and search for expressive forms as alternatives to realism and naturalism, a few directors and pedagogues became keenly interested in the traditional Asian theatres and tried to acquire more information about their actors-dancers. Little by little this knowledge became a reference in the effort to create new teaching methods aiming at a 'total actor' skilled in all the expressive means: dancing, singing, reciting, improvising, and even writing. Together with ancient theatre forms (Greek tragedy, commedia dell'arte and the neglected and scorned popular circus, cabaret, and the whole theatrical patrimony which Meyerhold called by the Russian name of *balagan*), Asian theatres were a source of inspiration – with a pre-eminent role, according to Savarese (2010: 448) – for the practice and theories of the protagonists in the theatre's Great Reform.[1]

---

[1] Barba uses this term coined by the influential Polish director Leon Schiller in the 1930s to define the period of profound mutations in European theatre from the beginning of the twentieth century until the Second World War. In a little more than three decades, the European theatre's unitary model disappeared, and modern theatre, as we think of it and practise it today, took shape. These structural and anthropological changes were the consequence of the experiments, teaching methods and visions starting from the generation of Edward Gordon Craig, Adolphe Appia, Konstantin Stanislavski, Vsevolod Meyerhold and Jacques Copeau to that of Erwin Piscator, Bertolt Brecht, and Antonin Artaud.

The Asian theatres provided examples of long-lasting living traditions as opposed to the extinct European forms such as Greek theatre, commedia dell'arte, Elizabethan theatre, and that of the Spanish Golden Century. In addition, the Asian theatres made use of a theatricality rooted in rigorous and demanding acting skills. Finally, a third reason explains the fascination of the European reformers for Asian genres: they conveyed a sophisticated artistic quality, which was alien to Western settings, a radical otherness.

We should keep in mind that the European theatre reformers were not simply looking for a new aesthetic alternative to naturalism. They were eagerly searching to escape from the professional mentality of their time, the uses, customs, and practices of a craft that was the expression of a transient culture marked by commercialisation, spectacularism, and the star system. For this reason they were not merely satisfied with performances that filled the theatres. Their needs pushed them towards a theatrical model that went beyond all this. The minor and more overwhelming theatre revolutions in the twentieth century took place in laboratories, studios, ateliers, workshops, small schools, artistic communities, and enclaves where the foundations of an autonomous and influential theatrical culture were laid (Cruciani 1995 and Schino 2009). Almost all these micro-cultures – which in time would change the features of Western theatre – pointed to a new type of actor. Here the model of the traditional Asian performer found fertile ground: it was an effective example of the 'total' actor.

It was not a question of imitation. During the whole twentieth century the Western reformers confronted the Asian theatres to extract stimuli capable of nurturing their own practices and theories. They knew how to extricate ideas, analogies, technical resources, and fertile misunderstandings which, blended with other influences in the crucible of their obsessions and research, gave place to new forms and actor models. Edward Gordon Craig, Alexander Tairov, Vsevolod Meyerhold, Jacques Copeau, Charles Dullin, Antonin Artaud, Bertolt Brecht, Jerzy Grotowski, and Eugenio Barba are among those who experienced this encounter with Asian theatres in the search for a new actor. Each case was different and followed its own individual path, but, until Grotowski, this confrontation was characterised by three factors defining a specific horizon and the possibilities that derived from it.

First, until the beginning of the 1960s, the interest in Asian performers didn't imply a journey to their land in order to get acquainted with their art in its cultural context. The contact took place within the short stays of Asian companies in Europe and North America during Colonial and World Exhibitions, or within the framework of tours bound by commercial, practical, ideological, and economic demands. These alien contexts, very different from the original ones, altered some fundamental aspects of the Asian theatricality and favoured a host of misinterpretations.

Another factor, deriving from the first, was that direct knowledge of Asian performers was very limited. Edward Gordon Craig saw Sada Yacco in London in 1900 and Hanako in Florence in 1907. Stanislavski and Meyerhold had also the opportunity to appreciate the art of these two Japanese actresses. In 1928, Meyerhold saw the kabuki company of Sadanji Ichikawa – the first to perform outside Japan – on tour in the Soviet Union (in Leningrad and Moscow). Two years later, in 1930, Meyerhold attended another kabuki performance in Paris, that of the Dotombori Theatre from Osaka led by Tokujiro Tsutsui, also seen by Charles Dullin. This company came from the USA and, after a stop in Paris, performed in London, Berlin, Stockholm, Copenhagen, Milan, and Rome. Brecht saw the Company in Berlin. Meyerhold saw the fragments of Peking Opera that the company of Mei Lanfang presented during the Theatre Congress in Moscow in 1935.[2] Mei Lanfang had previously performed in the USA in 1930 (New York, Chicago, San Francisco, and Los Angeles). Stanislavski, Tairov, Eisenstein, Brecht, and many other directors saw the work demonstration by this famous Chinese artist. Craig, who also participated in the Congress, accompanied Mei Lanfang to *The Princess Turandot*, Yevgeni Vakhtangov's legendary performance from 1922, which was still playing in 1935. Artaud witnessed a show of Cambodian dances at the National Colonial Exhibition of Marseille in 1922. Later on, in 1931, he discovered Balinese theatre in Paris in the Dutch pavilion of the Colonial Exhibition. These were accidental encounters, limited to single performances or fragments of these and, therefore, not sufficient to foster the study of the acting processes or the logic inherent to the performances' preparation.

Acquaintance with the Asian performers' working methods, with their technical procedures and apprenticeship – this is the third factor – took

---

[2] In the eighteenth century, the Jesuits gave the name of 'opera' to Chinese theatre forms because of the predominant role of music and song. In recent years, the experts employ more and more the term *xiqu* to refer in general to Chinese traditional sung theatre, and *jingju* to refer to one of its traditions, the Peking Opera. The term *huaju* (spoken theatre) denotes performances based upon Western models. In this book I will keep to the terms 'Chinese theatre' and 'Peking Opera' since they belonged to Barba's cognitive and imaginative universe and were used by him in his texts.

place mainly through books, in other words via an intellectual path. In some paradigmatic cases, such as with Brecht and Artaud, seeing the performances was neither preceded nor followed by any reading. In fact, Brecht and Artaud were not much interested in the Asian theatres as such. The Asian actors-dancers were an enlightenment, a sudden inspiration illuminating and encouraging personal inclinations and ideas which the two creators had long carried in their mental baggage. In other cases, the study was real and even passionate, but it was carried out in an indirect way through books and iconography. Until the 1950s – and this was another obstacle – books and articles on traditional Asian theatres were not written by theatre specialists but by philologists or by people who, due to their occupation (diplomats, missionaries, merchants), had lived for years in Asia and had become interested in local performances. The experience of the French playwright Paul Claudel is an exception. He was the French Consul in various towns in China (1895–1909) and the Ambassador in Tokyo (1922–28). During his stays in these two countries he became interested in their various traditional theatre forms and left a few competent texts with his impressions.

Due to these circumstances, knowledge on Asian actors-dancers was fragmentary and prone to misinterpretation. Savarese quotes Meyerhold, who summarises this situation perfectly:

> 'I knew Kabuki theatre from the theoretical point of view, from books and iconographical material, I knew kabuki theatre technique, but when I finally watched one of its performances, it seemed to me that I had read nothing, knew nothing about it.'
>
> (Meyerhold in Savarese 2010: 531)

The arrival of Asian performers in Europe and the USA unleashed a two-way influence. The discovery of a theatrical reality so different from its own became a stimulus both for the Euro-American and for the Asian stage. The case of the couple Kawakami Otojiro and Sada Yacco is emblematic. The performances of the Japanese actresses Sada Yacco and Hanako unleashed a huge debate and deserve a short comment. Particular circumstances in Japan turned Sada Yacco and Hanako into actresses who toured in Europe. They took advantage of their experience as geishas and performed in one-act plays with historical Japanese plots made comprehensible to Western audiences. When they went back to Japan, Sada Yacco and Kawakami (her director and partner in life) did the opposite: they adapted plots from the Western repertory (for example *Othello* and *Hamlet*) to Japanese taste and sensibility.

Sada Yacco's and Hanako's basic technique was a mixture of buyo dance (taken from kabuki) used by the geishas, as well as martial arts. It was far from being a traditional theatre technique. Craig was not so enthused by Sada Yacco's and Hanako's performances since he considered them to be a falsification of kabuki. Other Western spectators, less informed than Craig, believed that these were genuine examples of kabuki. Savarese contextualises the situation by explaining:

> Kawakami and Sada Yacco's performances were an imitation of *kabuki*: but an imitation is not necessarily a forgery, just as an operetta is not a 'little opera' or a 'fake opera', but simply a 'small-scale opera', the renewal of the model in a different light style. It may therefore be said that, in the world of Japanese theatre, geisha dances were (and still are today) an 'imitation' of *kabuki* dances, or that *kabuki* itself is an 'imitation' of *nō*. In other words, a model developed over time, at levels of expression, technique, culture, and economy different from those of the original.
>
> These different levels of imitation of *nō* theatre, which is the original model, are still visible. They are apparent when we watch the same story being performed in the styles of *nō*, *kabuki*, and *Nihon buyō* (Japanese dance), which has incorporated also the geisha dances. These are three *styles*, or rather, three *different levels* of art, each having its own particular artistic formulation, its own prestige, and its own public of passionate followers.
>
> (Savarese 2010: 345)

The wave of renewal that swept over European theatre during the first thirty years of the twentieth century weakened as a result of Nazism and Stalinism, and, later, the Second World War. The new theatre culture shaped by the protagonists of the Great Reform was destroyed or fell into lethargy. We had to wait until the 1950s to find the first signs of a renewed interest, thanks to the publication of books on traditional Asian theatres by Western scholars who also had a close bond with theatre practice. These were mostly American and British, who, after living in Asia because of the Second World War, taught in universities in the USA and trained generations of students, filling them with a passion for Asian performances. Faubion Bowers, who was General Douglas MacArthur's personal interpreter, wrote *Japanese Theatre* (1952), *The Dance in India* (1953) and *Theatre in the East* (1956). Bowers was in charge of the US Censorship Office in occupied Japan just after the Second World War, and he saved kabuki theatre from a total prohibition since its performances were judged to be imbibed with 'feudal' and militaristic ideology (Okamoto 2001). Earle Ernst published *The Kabuki Theatre* (1956). The British Adolphe Clarence Scott lived for several years in China and Japan working for the British Council and published *The Kabuki Theatre of Japan* (1955), *The Classical Theatre in China* (1957) and *Mei Lan-Fang, Leader of the Pear Garden* (1959). In 1960, René Sieffert translated Zeami's *The Secret Art of Nô* into French (1960). Another American scholar, Leonard Pronko, wrote *Theatre East and West: Perspectives towards a Total Theatre* (1967).

After the Second World War, the first European director to show an interest in traditional Asian theatre was Grotowski. India's philosophies and religious systems were one of his passions and influenced the development of his personality as well as his theoretical formulations. Nevertheless, in the beginning, Grotowski's eagerness towards India didn't include its traditional theatres. His *mise-en-scène* of *Shakuntala*, the Sanskrit text by Kalidasa, at the Theatre of the 13 Rows in 1960 was a result of his knowledge of Indian literature and gave him, above all, an alibi to move the actors away from a realistic style. Grotowski made his actors use positions of hatha yoga (which he himself practised) and let the speech be enhanced by suggestive intonations derived from the sonority of mantras. The choice of the classical text *Shakuntala* corresponded less to an attraction to the traditional or popular forms such as kathakali or yakshagana (totally unknown in the West at that time) and more to the challenge of implementing a 'theatrical theatre' that Grotowski and Ludwik Flaszen had postulated in their first programmatic texts.

Two years later, in 1962, Grotowski spent a month in the People's Republic of China with an official Polish delegation, where he had the opportunity to see Peking Opera at first hand, to visit some drama schools and to speak with specialists from the milieu (Osiński 2014: 95–105).

By that time, the direction of his theatrical experiments had changed. After *Akropolis* (1962), by the Polish symbolist Stanisław Wyspiański, Grotowski established in his theatre the practice of training, apart from performances and rehearsals, in which his actors deepened their technical knowledge through exercises. In this way, the Theatre of the 13 Rows, known for the daring *mise-en-scène* of avant-garde texts by Jean Cocteau and Vladimir Mayakovski, took the first steps towards its transformation into the history-making Laboratory Theatre.

Grotowski was the first European director who went to Asia and saw *in situ* traditional Chinese performances. Undoubtedly, this first-hand knowledge reinforced his predisposition to theatricality and contributed to the development of some aspects of his actors' training (Osiński 2014: 95–105). One year later, in 1963, Eugenio Barba, his Italian assistant, travelled to

India for six months and brought back information about kathakali exercises. Grotowski introduced some of them in his training. However, Grotowski's interest in Asian theatres faded in his later trajectory, while his fervour towards Hindu philosophies remained intact.

This historical outline – unavoidably schematic and incomplete – is necessary when approaching Eugenio Barba's accomplishments and putting into perspective his contribution to the dialogue between Western and Asian theatres. It stops in 1963 when Barba starts to develop his relationship with Asian theatres. Later on, directors such as Peter Brook, Ariane Mnouchkine, and Bob Wilson, among others, were contributing to enlarge the Western dialogue with traditional Asian theatres.

Journey of learning

Eugenio Barba was interested in the Asian cultures, mostly for their philosophies and religions and less for their theatres. In 1955, as a young immigrant working as a welder in Oslo, he came upon Romain Roland's book *Ramakrishna's Life*. The discovery of this mystic, one of the main exponents of the cultural renaissance in nineteenth-century Bengal, led to other readings on the various developments of Hinduism and Buddhism and motivated Barba's first journey to Asia. In 1956, only twenty years old, he signed up as a sailor on a Norwegian merchant ship bound for India and the Far East. His goal was to visit a temple on the Ganges built for Ramakrishna by a rich widow in Dakshineswar near Calcutta, where, as Roland recounted in his book, the Hindu ascetic daily descended the stairway to make his ablutions in the river (see 'The steps on the river bank' in Part IV). After this first journey, Barba persevered in widening his knowledge on Hinduism. Six years later, when he arrived at the Theatre of the 13 Rows in Opole, Poland, this common interest was the main point of contact with Grotowski (Barba 1999a: 48).

Barba's fascination with Asian cultures and their views of the world – one that has enthralled him throughout his life – has never been a strategy for extending the limits of his Italian background, enriching it through a dialogue with foreign cultures. Already at this early stage, it wasn't an intercultural dialogue that moved Barba, but a deeper existential need. Before dealing with theatre, the East was for Barba an opportunity to break the bonds with his Italian and European background and to build the uprooted identity of an emigrant. This would become one of his persistent obsessions, probably the most significant: to let roots grow out of the need not to belong in any one place but to shape an ideal homeland made of values and without borders. Barba defined this process by expressions such as 'to sink roots in the sky' or 'the conquest of difference' (Barba and Watson 2002: 234–62).

When, in January 1962, after a year at the Warsaw theatre school, Barba joined the Theatre of the 13 Rows, Grotowski had just begun his iconoclastic *mises-en-scène* of Polish classical texts, which, in less than a decade, made him into an influential theatre reformer. Grotowski had just finished *Kordian* (1962) by Juliusz Słowacki and was on the verge of starting on *Akropolis* (1962) by Wyspiański with Barba as his assistant. In the course of rehearsals, Grotowski introduced in his theatre a regular training with various types of exercises which were not directly connected to the preparation of the performance. In August of that same year Grotowski travelled to China, and, in June 1963, Barba went on a second trip to India, this time in search of 'professional secrets'. Barba knew nothing of the existence of the traditional Indian theatres, since, at that time, there was very little information about them in Europe. After stopping in Delhi, Bombay, and Madras, he ended up, almost by chance, in Cheruthuruthy, a village in Kerala, home to the most important school of kathakali, the Kerala Kalamandalam. For three weeks he lived with the pupils of the school, attending from dawn to late evening their daily training, and saw several kathakali performances (see 'In search of theatre' in Part I).

When Barba returned to Europe, he wrote a long essay on kathakali, which at the time was published in its totality or partially in French (1965), English (1967), Italian (in three parts, 1967, 1968, 1969) and Danish (1974). Barba's text contributed to drawing attention to kathakali, until that moment unknown in Europe, and to awaken an interest in it (see 'The kathakali theatre' in Part I).

Barba's stay at the Kerala Kalamandalam had long-lasting consequences. This experience marked deeply his professional personality, and he refers to it again and again in his writings. Beyond the forms, the aesthetics, the training, and the kathakali actor's dramaturgy, what genuinely impressed Barba was the ethos of those boys who got up every day at dawn to do their exercises for hours in silence. This ethos didn't spring from ideals or personal obsessions, but from the discipline, the meticulousness, and the humility with which those young boys learned the demanding technique of their tradition. The whole sense of their doing theatre seemed to be encapsulated in their submission to the tradition of which they were a part.

Barba had studied at the official theatre school in Warsaw, and he knew the atmosphere of the European theatres. He came from a context in which the professional practice was often adulterated by self-centred conceit, intellectual justifications, ideological discussions, debased attitudes, political ideas or commercial demands. The experience at the Kerala Kalamandalam showed him that technique is an embodied ethic – the craft's foundation. An incorporated technique is impregnated by values and norms, something that later Barba defined as professional ethos. No theatrical adventure could do without that dimension of the craft. The absorption of a technical knowledge implies a resistance that forces the student to take a position and materialise personal motivations into a concrete behaviour.

The sojourn in Kerala and the 'discovery' of kathakali constituted for Barba an authentic *Wanderlehre*, a journey of learning and a displacement of his criteria that implemented his professional education. Thus, Barba, at the very beginning of his apprenticeship, experienced the encounter with an Asian theatre.

Inspiration

In October 1964, Barba founded Odin Teatret in Oslo, Norway, with a group of youngsters who had failed to be admitted to the State Theatre School. Two years later, in June 1966, he and his actors emigrated to Denmark and settled down definitively in Holstebro, a small town of 16,000 inhabitants in north-west Jutland. Until the beginning of the 1970s, they concentrated on the growth of a personal technique. In these first years, the value and the need of a technical insight constituted Barba's main professional compass. This need was amplified by the fact that they were autodidactic. Above all, there was the challenge of proving an artistic competence which, in the beginning, they didn't possess due to their rejection by the official theatre milieu.

In the process of building his actor-model, Barba leaned on what he had learned with Grotowski. At the same time, he read books by the theatre reformers and attempted to personalise and integrate in the Odin training the teachings of Stanislavski, Meyerhold, Vakhtangov, Dullin, the pantomime of Marcel Marceau, and classical ballet. In the solitude and isolation of Holstebro, the books of the great reformers were an anchor, a refuge, and a stimulus of the first order. In the theatre culture that Barba was forging for himself and his actors, the influence of Asian theatres was to be found side by side with the appeal of the European tradition of the Great Reform.

In spite of the experience in Kerala – short and related to one tradition – the diversity of the Asian theatres continued being for Barba and his actors a distant, mythical reality, which inspired them through pictures and the few books available at that time. *Ukiyo-e* prints of kabuki performers or A.C. Scott's book on Mei Lanfang (1959) encouraged them to invent exercises of a training that drifted away from Grotowski's and already contained features of its own.

The vocal training was also populated by Asian suggestions and references: how could they reach the sonorous range and the impact of a noh actor or a Balinese arja performer? At this stage, one can see Barba's intention to avoid the imitation of the Asian forms and use them as an incentive to create their own exercises. His approach to the Asian actors' knowledge was not very different to that of the great European reformers. Basically, they shared the same lack of a direct and deep knowledge (see 'The most disparate metals' and 'A dreamed and reinvented Arcadia' in Part II).

This stimulation in the Odin training was enhanced by Barba's readings on this subject. In 1964, he began publishing the four-monthly *Teatrets Teori og Teknikk*, a journal in Danish, Norwegian, and Swedish, mostly about actor's technique from the Great Reform as well as from Asian theatres. Issue no. 15, in 1971, was exclusively about acting in China and Japan. Barba wrote several articles of various lengths: on kabuki, on Chinese actor training, on Mei Lanfang, about comparing the Russian formalists' research to Brecht's *Verfremdung* and Zeami's *hana*, the actor's 'flower' (see 'Mei Lanfang' and '*Priem ostrannenija, Verfremdung, hana*' in Part II). The following number, from the same year, was a special issue in book form: a Danish translation of René Sieffert's French translation of Zeami's writings. In 1974, issue no. 21 was entirely devoted to kathakali and to various theatre and dance forms in Bali.

To remedy its professional isolation, to survive economically and to witness practical examples of theatrical knowledge, Odin Teatret, from the very year of its establishment in Denmark in 1966, began a pioneering practice which in time became common throughout Europe: that of inviting actors and directors to Holstebro to give practical seminars for professionals from all over Scandinavia. A host of young and less young artists, more or less known, some of whom became the theatre protagonists of the following decades, were invited to teach: Jerzy Grotowski, Otomar Krejča, Dario Fo, the brothers Carlo and Romano Colombaioni, Étienne Decroux, Jacques Lecoq, Jean-Louis Barrault and Madeleine Renaud, Joseph Chaikin, Julian

Beck and Judith Malina with their Living Theatre. Barba and his actors saw at first hand how these artists thought and worked during their creative and teaching processes, living with them during the seminar, asking them all sorts of questions, and absorbing the glow of their artistic identity.

In the early 1970s, Barba took a further step in his relationship with Asian theatres when he invited renowned traditional masters to international seminars in Holstebro.[3] This initiative must be seen in the context of a time in which Asian performances were a rarity in Europe and America – Asian actors had never led seminars or presented work demonstrations.

Odin Teatret opened the 1972 seminar with grandeur. It included Japan's most important theatre genres: the noh company of Hideo and Hisao Kanze, kyogen with the Nomura family, a selected group of kabuki actors led by Sojuro Sawamura, and Shuji Terayama's contemporary avant-garde group Tenjo Sajiki. More than sixty artists, who never mingled in their own country, travelled together and defied their reciprocal prejudices during their work demonstrations and performances at the Odin. This huge enterprise was made possible thanks to collaboration with the Venice Biennale. It was the first and only time that a European seminar gathered such a number of genres and different classical and contemporary Japanese actors.

In 1974, the seminar involved Balinese and Javanese theatre forms, with thirty-five artists, among whom the Javanese choreographer Sardono Waluyo Kusumo and the Balinese masters I Made Pasek Tempo and I Made Djimat.

In 1976, the Odin devoted its seminar to some of the genres from India. Once again, the idea was to gather masters and musicians of different styles who were not accustomed to observing their respective work processes in their own country. The Scandinavian participants were able to attend work demonstrations and performances of the highest level: Shanta Rao, one of the protagonists of the renewal of Indian classical dance, one of the first women from a Brahmin family to take up professionally bharatanatyam and the first woman to learn kathakali; Uma Sharma, a dancer of kathak; Krishna Namboodiri (whom Barba knew from his first journey to Kerala) presented kathakali. Barba also invited the young Sanjukta Panigrahi with her husband Raghunath, whose artistic mastery was transforming a regional dance, the odissi, into a classical one.

---

[3] Barba has always called his Asian collaborators 'masters', an attempt at translating the Indian *guru*, the Japanese *sensei* and the Chinese *ta shi* which means teacher, an older person who masters the craft.

▶ Holstebro, 1972. The American-Canadian professor Frank Hoff watching Hideo Kanze (noh) during a demonstration in Odin Teatret's white room at the Japanese seminar.

▶▶ Holstebro, 1974. The dancer-choreographer Sardono Kusumo teaching Balinese children who participated in his performance. Among his main collaborators were I Made Pasek Tempo and I Made Djimat, both from Bali, who, after 1980, became part of the ISTA staff.

▶ Holstebro, 1976. Shanta Rao during a demonstration in Odin's black room at the Indian seminar. She was forty-six and a legend in her country. Born to an upper caste, she embraced a career as a bharatanatyam dancer and was the first woman to study kathakali.

▶▶ Holstebro, 1976. Sanjukta Panigrahi. Her talent was decisive in transforming the odissi from a regional to a classical dance. At the Odin seminar she expected just to give a performance. Consequently, she refused to do anything as alien as a working demonstration. After seeing Shanta Rao's exposé of her technical biography, Sanjukta agreed to do the same. With the years, she excelled at showing the various layers of technical knowledge hidden behind the levity and splendour of her dance.

Through these encounters with Asian traditional actors/dancers, Barba gained first-hand insight, which he combined with information from books. From an ethical point of view, Barba felt an affinity with these representatives of century-old traditions, and he didn't hesitate in September 1977 to invite Hideo Kanze (noh), Krishna Namboodiri (kathakali), and the Balinese I Made Bandem and his wife Swasthi Widjaja with their daughters to the Encounter of Third Theatre in Bergamo, Italy. These Asian masters were later often welcomed by Third Theatre groups all over Europe, especially in Italy. Jerzy Grotowski, whom Barba had invited to the Encounter, saw their demonstrations and included Namboodiri and Kanze in his symposium 'The Art of the Beginner' in Warsaw (4–7 June 1978).

When Odin Teatret began to arrange the Asian seminars, Barba and his actors had about ten years of experience behind them. They had accumulated a remarkable technical know-how that impregnated their performances. *Ferai* (1969) and *Min Fars Hus* (*My Father's House*, 1972) had been internationally acclaimed, and the critics spoke of a new actor-model. The presence of Asian performers in Holstebro played a fundamental role as an inventive stimulus to compare the technical efficacy of actors from different genres. Once again, it was not a question of interculturalism but of finding personal paths towards artistic autonomy (see 'A dreamed and reinvented Arcadia' in Part II).

But the encounters with the Asian performers at the Holstebro seminars had another consequence. Barba wove a web of professional complicity, in some cases involving deep friendship with some of the Asian masters who became close travelling companions when, in 1979, Barba founded the International School of Theatre Anthropology (ISTA).

Beneath the skin: levels of organisation and recurring principles

Towards the end of the 1970s, Barba glimpsed another way to relate to traditional Asian performers. When, in 1963, he came back from India, he was haunted by the question 'How was it that kathakali actors affected him as a spectator although he knew nothing about their theatre tradition?' He was not an expert in their acting conventions, nor did he grasp the stories and the inherent religious content. Nevertheless, those actors had the capacity to hold his attention and to enthral him with the intense 'life' they radiated. The young Barba was disturbed by his failure to explain the peculiar communication between him and the kathakali actors.

Now, after fifteen years' work with his actors and countless professional experiences, Barba began to modify his view of Asian performers. Some of his actors were the cause of this change.

In January 1978, Barba set in motion one of those 'earthquakes', which, over the years, he regularly provoked in order to revitalise his group. This time, he barred his actors from working in the theatre for three months: they were paid but were free to do what they wanted.

Some of them used the opportunity to travel and learn. Iben Nagel Rasmussen, Silvia Ricciardelli, and Toni Cots went to Bali, where they learned basic baris and legong dances. Toni Cots also studied topeng (mask theatre) and the martial art pencak silat. Tom Fjordefalk went to India to learn kathakali. The rest of the actors chose other destinations. Roberta Carreri and Francis Pardeilhan went to Brazil and learned capoeira and the Candomblé dance of the Orixás. Else Marie Laukvik visited Haiti. Julia Varley and Tage Larsen learned ballroom dances – waltz, paso doble, and cha-cha-cha – in the small town of Struer, 15 kilometres from Holstebro. Torgeir Wethal planned to study flamenco in Spain, but gave up the idea and remained at home.

Back at Odin Teatret, Toni Cots and Tom Fjordefalk kept on working with the Balinese and kathakali forms, structuring their new knowledge into work demonstrations. Watching the daily training of these two actors, who alternated Asian elements with those of Odin, Barba no longer saw their diversity but became aware of the analogies that existed under different technical 'skins' (see 'The museum of the theatre' and 'Beneath the skin' in Part III).

This new way of seeing and the resulting questions and doubts became the field of research at ISTA. From then on, the contact and collaboration with the Asian performers increased through their presence at ISTA sessions and Barba's frequent sojourns in Asia in order to follow the creative and teaching process of certain masters. This fieldwork deepened his knowledge of the specific nature of the various apprenticeships for the Asian performers and their way of thinking with the body-mind.

In 1980, Barba produced the first hypotheses concerning his new field of research (see 'Knowing with the mind and understanding with the body' in Part III). Its focus was the analysis of scenic behaviour through which actors and dancers from various genres and traditions build their scenic presence. Right from the start, Theatre Anthropology developed in two directions:

What is ISTA?

Eugenio Barba established ISTA, the International School of Theatre Anthropology, in 1979 as a situation of exchange for theatre practitioners and scholars whom he had met and befriended. There they could mutually show, compare and discuss their technical and creative processes. ISTA was meant as an inspiration for the invited 'friends' as well as for directors and actors from the Third Theatre groups. The Asian performers were accompanied by their ensembles of up to ten people, including the musicians, in order to present the magnificence of their tradition in a real performance after dissecting in depth the technical steps leading to these results. Participation was free, but after the seventh ISTA in Wales (1992), the participants paid a symbolic fee. ISTA sessions ended with a public two-day symposium and performances by the different masters. The necessary funding was provided by the organisers who were mostly theatre groups but also established cultural institutions and a prestigious festival.

What Barba at first expected to be a single meeting with technical exchanges between theatre friends, evolved into ISTA and, thanks to its continuity, into a unique milieu of pure research. No results had to be achieved in order to be applied or shown publicly. During a session, much time was dedicated to scrutinising an actor's performance, his or her scenic figure. The individual performers recreated the learning phases of their first day of work, showing or recounting in detail the corrections and advice of their teachers. They presented a performance with costumes and music, then they showed the same thing without music, then also without costumes so that participants became aware of the particular postures and orchestration of tensions in the performer's scenic anatomy. The performances showed clearly that the styles were different, but the demonstrations by the performers about the technical foundations of their individual styles also showed clearly that similar principles were used by all of them to reach this diversity. Barba defined 'theatre anthropology' as the study of these recurrent pre-expressive principles.

▶ Holstebro, 1986. ISTA's artistic staff during the fourth session: 'The Female Role as Represented on the Stage in Various Cultures'. [1] Hemant Kumar Das (India); [2] Jagdish Prasad Varman (India); [3] Desak Made Suarti Laksmi (Bali); [4] Gangadhar Pradhan (India); [5] Katsuko Azuma (Japan); [6] Mei Baojiu (China); [7] Ni Made Wiratini (Bali); [8] Kanichi Hanayagi (Japan); [9] Swasthi Widjaja Bandem (Bali); [10] Iben Nagel Rasmussen (Odin Teatret); [11] Gautam (India); [12] Sanjukta Panigrahi (India); [13] Tracy Chung (Taiwan); [14] Kanho Azuma (Japan); [15] Ni Putu Ary Widhyasti Bandem (Bali); [16] Yvonne Lin (Taiwan); [17] Pei Yanling (China); [18] K.N. Vijayakumar (India); [19] Helen Liu (Taiwan); [20] Raghunath Panigrahi (India); [21] Kelucharan Mahapatra (India); [22] Takae Koyama (Japan); [23] Shizuko Kinea (Japan); [24] M.P. Sankaran Namboodiri (India).

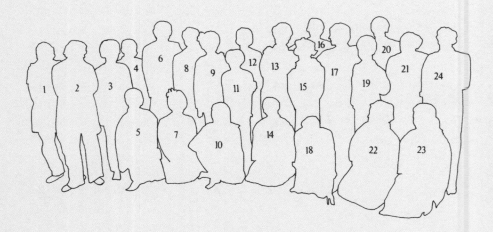

a theoretical one and a practical one. It provided tools to conceptualise the performers' pragmatic knowledge while, at the same time, formulating useful indications and technical procedures to guide the practical work towards an effective scenic presence. Barba's hypotheses presented two innovations, which, in time, had numerous consequences.

The first of these innovations considered the performer's work according to levels of organisation. Barba took this concept from biology and physics and applied it to the theatre craft. Hence his formulation of a primary level of organisation for the performer, which he called the pre-expressive level. This level comprises the mental and somatic processes utilised by actors and dancers in order to transform their social and private presence into scenic presence; or, according to Barba's terminology, from daily to extra-daily behaviour. This way of thinking implied putting aside the historical, social, cultural, political, religious, and aesthetic aspects present in each tradition. On the contrary, it concentrated only on the mental-somatic dynamics and principles that enable the performers to mould their energy into patterns of scenic behaviour, thus establishing a sensorial and kinaesthetic relationship with the spectators.

This way of thinking generated misunderstandings and polemics, almost all related to the difficulty to understand or to accept the cognitive logic of the organisation levels. Barba has insisted on the fact that the establishment of levels of organisation is a cognitive strategy or an operative fiction.

> Obviously, the pre-expressive does not exist in and of itself. Similarly, the nervous system, for example, cannot be materially separated from the entirety of a living organism, but it can be thought of as a separated entity. This cognitive fiction makes effective interventions possible. It is an abstraction, but is extremely useful for work on the practical level.
>
> (Barba 1995: 104)

In the final result, the pre-expressive level appears to merge together with the expressive level in a complex and indivisible reality. But in the inner logic of the performer's work, the pre-expressive level is frequently clearly defined. The technical procedures of the Asian performers are an evident example of this demarcation. A similar way of thinking is also to be found in the texts of the Western reformers and in the technical procedures of their actors: for instance in Stanislavski's concept 'the actor's work on himself' (as opposed to 'the actor's work on a role'); in Michael Chekhov's insistence to distinguish between the 'what' and the 'how' in the actor's work; or in Decroux's conceptualisation of what he calls the 'manner'.

Barba is aware that he has not invented pre-expressivity. He has only given it a name and has delimited it in order to make it the field of his research. Barba has emphasised that the fact of not taking cultural, social, and historical aspects into consideration when studying the performer's work doesn't mean to deny their importance. It means simply to concentrate on the study of one level of organisation: that of scenic presence.

> For those who investigate the secrets of scenic life, to distinguish a pre-expressive level from the expressive level does not mean that one is forgetting that the value of theatre lies in the meaning which the performance in its entirety assumes and reveals. It means following the normal criteria of every scientist and every empirical researcher: to choose one's field of research; to treat it *as if* it were autonomous; to establish operatively useful limits; to concentrate on these limits and to make an inventory of them; to compare, find, and specify certain functional logics; and than to reconnect that field to the whole from which it was separated for cognitive purposes only.
>
> (Barba 1995: 105)

Barba's second innovation – derived from the first one – was the practice of approaching the performer's work in categories of principles and not technical rules. It was a question of 'seeing' through the rules characterising each tradition in order to capture and formulate the recurring principles underlying the different techniques. These 'recurring principles', according to Barba, constitute the pre-expressive level shared by different acting techniques. The advantage of envisaging the acting knowledge in categories of principles, and not of rules, resides in the fact that this knowledge can be transplanted into different performative situations. A principle is not bound to a form but to a work logic. It is an abstraction that can be applied in different ways according to the personal, aesthetic, social, and narrative necessities of each theatre practice.

In order to explore and verify the pre-expressive principles, Barba conceived ISTA as a dynamic laboratory. Active from 1980 until the present time (2015), ISTA has developed through seventeen public sessions in countries as different as Germany, Italy, France, Denmark, Great Britain, Brazil, Sweden, Portugal, Spain, and Poland. Lasting for anything from two weeks to two months, ISTA is structured in two complementary teams of collaborators under Barba's direction: actors or dancers (with their respective companies and musicians) belonging to diverse styles and traditions, and scholars coming from various countries: theatre specialists, anthropologists, semioticians, psychologists. The members of these two teams form a relatively stable core of collaborators although, logically enough, changes have taken place over time. The ISTA sessions are an occasion to gather both teams of collaborators and make them work together with a maximum of 100 participants (actors, dancers, scholars, choreographers, directors, critics, etc.). The totality of those seventeen international sessions denotes a landmark with regard to the dialogue between Western and Asian theatre.

It is interesting to note that, as a rule, it was not large institutions that sponsored and organised the ISTA sessions. Most of these sessions were possible thanks to the audacity and stubbornness of anonymous Third Theatre groups and, in some cases, of single individuals. They followed their desire to bring ISTA to their respective countries or working milieus, thus revealing the capacity to find enormous economic and organisational resources for such an event. In this way, ISTA has developed its activity in areas at the edge of the main theatre system, articulating a net of contacts and professional relationships firmly anchored in alternative values to those of the official theatre.

Barba has explained that he labelled his project a 'school' as a paradox or self-provocation (Barba 1999b: 90). In fact, ISTA contradicts all the pedagogical assumptions of a school: no stable headquarters, no teachers imparting specific subjects, no permanent students, no fixed curriculum. Rather than a school, it recalls a laboratory in which practical knowledge and theoretical reflection interact mutually in a fertile way. This is one of ISTA's attractions: a milieu favouring an exploratory attitude where practice and theory not only cohabit but end up losing their profiles and blending in a complex, dense reality. Thus, the masters' practical descriptions of the 'first day' of their apprenticeship, the work demonstrations, rehearsals, performances, lectures, comparison of specific technical aspects such as improvisation, rhythm or subscore/subtext, personal dialogues and discussions, spontaneous initiatives and experiments – all these blend and alternate during the working period from early morning to late at night. Two books are useful in becoming acquainted with the dynamics of the ISTA sessions: *The Tradition of ISTA* (Skeel 1994) and *The Performers' Village* (Hastrup 1996).

In the first sessions of ISTA, Barba concentrated mostly on Asian acting traditions, which generated the misunderstanding that these were his field of research. This misunderstanding often stems from a confusion between some historical or circumstantial aspects regarding the evolution of Barba's research and the paradigm of Theatre Anthropology itself. The field of Barba's research was the pre-expressive level, and its main goal was to explore the recurring technical principles through which a performer built his scenic presence. Thus, Barba has always considered the various acting techniques – and not only the traditional Asian ones – as a particular manifestation of embodied knowledge related to scenic presence. He does the same when approaching Stanislavski's system, classical ballet or Decroux's corporeal mime. His arguments on traditional Asian theatres are not connected to a specific analysis of them but to a study of the technical principles of their actors' pre-expressive level.

In the beginning, Barba focused on the Asian traditional theatres for two operative reasons: first because Asian performers, due to their codified systems, were able to repeat the scores from their repertoire with a striking degree of precision. This capacity made them particularly effective and reliable examples in order to explore pre-expressive principles. Second, because the Asian performers' forms are so different from the European or American ones, they are useless for Western actors unless they want to learn one of them at length and with the necessary rigour, identifying themselves with this particular tradition. Paradoxically, it is precisely this distance from the Asian acting styles that can be useful for an actor to whom these forms are alien and who has only a fleeting acquaintance with them. It is useful because the actor cannot absorb them but becomes physically aware of the pre-expressive principles that nurture them. Later, the actor will deal with these principles in order to let his own personal form grow (see 'The pedagogical paradox' in Part III).

Over the years, Barba widened his research to cover many acting and dance genres, both modern and less modern: Decroux's mime, Dario Fo's improvisation, Meyerhold's Biomechanics, contemporary Western dance, butoh, Odin Teatret's actor's dramaturgy, 'realistic' Western acting, Latin American *creación collectiva* (collective creation) or Afro-Brazilian dances of the Orixás.

In more than thirty years of activity, ISTA has undeniably furthered a systematic dialogue with Asian traditional performers conveying a first-hand insight into their work procedures. Until recently, it was common to believe that the Asian traditional techniques were not suitable to contemporary Western actors, with their specific aesthetic, narrative, ethical, and social demands. Many admired Asian theatres as artistic exploits with masterly acting. But theoretical and practical study of Asian theatres rarely appeared on the programme of theatre schools in Europe and other continents, and if so, then it was only of a historical nature. Students were introduced to the training practices of Stanislavski, Meyerhold, Decroux, Grotowski, Odin Teatret or Lecoq, but were seldom confronted with the know-how of Asian performers, since their excessive codification seemed to be impractical for the education of contemporary Western actors (see 'The ripe action' in Part III).

It is here that Barba's contribution becomes relevant. By thinking of the performer's work in levels of organisation, by circumscribing the pre-expressive level and exploring it in categories of principles, he articulated a pedagogic approach whose end was learning to learn (see 'Awareness and denial' in Part III). Within this instructive way of looking, traditional performers from Asia were a source of valid teachings. Gradually, Barba created a connection between Asian and Euro-American traditions as manifestations of the same pre-expressive knowledge. This knowledge is not related to the results of the performers' creation but to their starting points that decide their process. It does not belong to the sphere of forms, styles, and genres but to that of the performers' *bios* (life), their scenic presence.

Any performer can apply this common knowledge of the recurring principles in order to invent and build his or her own artistic identity. Barba conceived this knowledge as a kind of professional homeland and called it 'Eurasian Theatre' (see 'Eurasian Theatre' in Part IV).

Cohabitation

In the mid-1990s, Barba's association with Asian performers acquired a double character. On the one hand, he continued his line of research on pre-expressive presence within ISTA. On the other hand, he began a new phase, staging productions with Euro-American and Afro-Brazilian performers, performers from various Asian traditions as well as his own Odin actors. This started when, at the closing of an ISTA session, Barba staged a performance – named *Theatrum Mundi* – with all the master teachers. Little by little, *Theatrum Mundi* became independent and acquired its own identity as an ensemble. *The Island of Labyrinths* (1996), *Four Poems for Sanjukta* (1998), *Ego Faust* (2000), *Ur-Hamlet* (2006) and *The Marriage of Medea* (2008) are, so far, the productions that belong to this second phase.

Here, all the Asian actors/dancers perform always according to their style. Scores from their original traditional productions are selected and introduced in the context of *Theatrum Mundi*, where they acquire new meanings. This technical procedure is a challenge to the idea of a Eurasian Theatre where actors and dancers from different cultures cohabit and perform together, overcoming their respective differences yet without being stripped of their stylistic identity. The scores, the musicians, the aesthetics, and the scenic language of each one of them blend into performances with a coherence of their own. They represent an additional reason to meet and an example of cohabitation between East and West (see 'The Romanesque method' and 'Eurasian Theatre' in Part IV).

In the new millennium, it is worth noting Barba's collaboration with the Gambuh Desa Batuan Ensemble, a company consisting of thirty-two performers from Batuan, Bali, which participated in *Ur-Hamlet* and *The Marriage of Medea*. Barba's relationship with this group, from 1998 to the present time, helps us to understand how, through theatrical craft, he establishes deep affective bonds that nullify all frontiers. The Italian dancer Cristina Formaggia Wistari, a friend of Barba residing in Bali since the 1980s, was captivated by gambuh, the Balinese court theatre-dance from the fifteenth century – the oldest in the world after noh – and today in danger of extinction. In the 1990s, thanks to a scholarship from the Ford Foundation, Wistari convinced three elderly gambuh masters to train youngsters from their villages over a period of three years. After this time, she established the Gambuh Pura Desa Ensemble – later called Gambuh Desa Batuan Ensemble – which was always on the edge of collapse due to financial problems. In 1998, Barba invited this ensemble to Odin Teatret's thirty-fifth anniversary in Holstebro, where he had gathered performances from the world's oldest traditions: Japanese noh, shamanistic theatre from Korea, Western classical ballet, and gambuh. Later, Barba continued to invite the Gambuh Desa Batuan Ensemble to the ISTA sessions and to other projects. In June 2008, Wistari died suddenly of cancer. From that moment, Barba and his actors assumed financial responsibility for the gambuh school in Batuan, paying their teachers for their activity with the village children, as well as for periodic gambuh performances.

This episode indicates how Barba, still continuing his research whenever an ISTA session is possible, is responsive to the bonds issuing from professional exchange and cohabitation. From the mid-1990s, Barba's commitment to Asian theatres gravitates less around their acting traditions and techniques and rather around a few artists embodying them. Personal ties were always at the foundation of his work. But now the affective dimension comes to the fore and becomes an end. Over the years, Barba and his actors have developed an artistic milieu in which Asian masters are a fundamental part. This long-lasting collaboration has drifted towards a sense of belonging to a particular form of living the craft, at the margins of the cultural, geographical, linguistic, and aesthetic frontiers which theatre systems and traditions have established.

In this last stage, instead of a dialogue with Asian traditions, it would be more pertinent to speak of Barba's cohabitation with some of their artists. Barba's urge to keep alive this relationship with the Asian theatre is the desire to meet again artists and friends with whom he feels a bond and to meet them not only in the research context of ISTA but also during his travels and frequent shared projects (see 'The geography of illusions' in Part IV).

Conclusions

Within the historical context of the European theatre of the twentieth century, Barba's relationships with Asian performers and their technical knowledge have several specific characteristics.

First, it is worth emphasising that the interest and the contact with Asian performers took place, in Barba's case, since the very beginning of his apprenticeship. Contrary to his predecessors, for Barba, the Asian performers were not an influence which was integrated into the experience of an already shaped creative personality (although in constant process of evolution), but they were one of the primary factors through which he forged his professional identity and competence.

Second, Barba went to Asia and got a first-hand knowledge of its traditional theatres. He did countless periods of authentic fieldwork in order to get acquainted with the teaching activity of the masters who would collaborate with him at ISTA. He attended again and again their performances, immersed himself in their work context and studied in depth their performing devices and their personal methods of transmitting them to their pupils. Through this fieldwork and the many sessions of ISTA, Barba accumulated experiences of collaboration with Asian masters that for their duration, density, and variety of activities – not to mention the number of different traditions – provide an important landmark in the relationships between Western and Asian theatre (see Appendix).

Barba's ongoing contact with the Asian masters awoke in several of them an impulse to reflect upon their own technique in a different way, relating it to the technique of masters from other Western and Asian traditions (Hastrup 1996: 88–114). When speaking and writing about ISTA activity, the dialogue between Asian and Western traditions is often emphasised. Thus, one forgets that ISTA's working dynamics also favoured a mutual insight and an unprecedented dialogue between the representatives of different Asian traditions who were not accustomed to compare and expound their technique.

Third, from his first stay at the Kerala Kalamandalam school, Barba was more impressed by the technical procedures and the apprenticeship of the Asian actors/dancers than by the performances. He certainly watched many such performances in the course of his career, but the core of his curiosity and fascination was directed to what appeared like an underground reality often difficult to identify: the technical processes through which the performers elaborated the results which were later displayed before the spectators. These technical procedures lying at the craft's base appear to be buried under the expressive effects that characterise any performance; yet they are doubly hidden in the Asian traditional theatres under the performers' impressive costumes which hinder even more the perception of the corporal techniques.

Before Barba, several European theatre people showed a keen interest in the technique of the traditional Asian performers. But their encounter with them was limited to a few performances, sometimes only fragments. Barba differs from his predecessors, for his exhaustive insight into the Asian performers' incorporated know-how. The cohabitation with these performers in their home context, at the Holstebro seminars and during consecutive ISTA sessions, gave him a privileged access to the Asian performers' 'kitchen'. Barba was able to implement a technical dialogue with them, something unattainable by his predecessors.

Barba's relationship with traditional Asian theatres has had two consequences. First, it has signified the gathering together of a practical knowledge relevant to theatre teaching and, at the same time, the creation of a field of study, Theatre Anthropology, which has provided the international community with tools to approach the performer's work. Second, regarding Barba's theatre poetics, the idea of a Eurasian Theatre has resulted in the growth of what he calls a 'performers' village'. In the very heart of this village made of journeys in space and time, of encounters and re-encounters, of work situations and celebrations, of future plans and shared memories, of books and performances, of demonstrations of work and demonstrations of affection, a dynamic atmosphere has grown as well as a peculiar form of living the craft at the edges of the official theatre's trends. In this place of motley cohabitation filled with contrasts, restless artists can find stimuli, tools, and ideas for their own theatre adventure.

About editing

The Moon Rises from the Ganges is a selection of texts by Eugenio Barba reconstructing his relationship to performers from traditional Asian theatres. Weaving together stories, encounters, reflections, anecdotes, and travels, the author brings together the phases and changes in a fascination which has been a constant reference in his more than fifty-year-long professional career. The texts are from different periods. Together with well-known articles which have already become classics in Eugenio Barba's bibliography, relatively unknown and also unpublished texts are included. The result is a book that places under the microscope an important chapter of East–West dialogue in twentieth-century theatre.

Barba's oldest texts have a clear historical value inasmuch as they allow us to see his approach to Asian theatres over the course of time. For this reason, the author and I decided to preserve the original content of the texts and his personal terminology used at the time. However, in some of the most recent texts, Barba made minor changes to adapt them to the context of the book.

I have standardised the spelling of the names used to identify the various traditional Asian theatres. I have also standardised the spelling of Asian names. For Japanese names, I used the Western system of first name and then surname since Barba has always done so in his texts when referring to his Japanese friends and collaborators (e.g. Katsuko Azuma). For pre-Meiji period, I maintained the traditional Japanese order normally used by Western scholars: family name first, followed by first name (e.g. Kawakami Otojiro).

When the footnotes are my own, I indicate this at the beginning of each note to differentiate editor's notes from author's notes.

Bibliography

BARBA, Eugenio. 1995. *The Paper Canoe: A Guide to Theatre Anthropology*, trans. by Richard Fowler (London and New York: Routledge)
— 1999a. *Land of Ashes and Diamonds: My Apprenticeship in Poland, followed by 26 Letters from Jerzy Grotowski to Eugenio Barba*, trans. by Eugenio Barba and Judy Barba (Aberystwyth: Black Mountain Press)
— 1999b. *Theatre: Solitude, Craft, Revolt*, ed. by Lluís Masgrau, trans. by Judy Barba and Richard Fowler (Aberystwyth: Black Mountain Press)

BARBA, Eugenio and Ian Watson. 2002. 'The Conquest of Difference: An Electronic Dialogue', in *Negotiating Cultures: Eugenio Barba and the Intercultural Debate*, ed. by Ian Watson and et al. (Manchester: Manchester University Press), pp. 234–52

BOWERS, Faubion. 1952. *Japanese Theatre* (New York: Hermitage House; repr. Rutland, VT and Tokyo: Charles E. Tuttle, 1977)

— 1953. *The Dance in India* (New York: Columbia University Press)

— 1956. *Theatre in the East: A Survey of Asian Dance and Drama* (London, Edinburgh, Paris, Melbourne, Toronto and New York: Thomas Nelson & Sons)

CRUCIANI, Fabrizio. 1995. *Registi pedagoghi e comunità teatrali nel Novecento* (Directors, Teachers and Theatre Communities in the Twentieth Century), ed. by Ferdinando Taviani and Clelia Falletti (Rome: Editori & Associati)

ERNST, Earle. 1956. *The Kabuki Theatre* (Oxford: Oxford University Press; repr. Honolulu: University of Hawaii Press, 1974)

HASTRUP, Kirsten (ed.). 1996. *The Performers' Village* (Graasten: Drama)

OKAMOTO, Shiro. 2001. *The Man who Saved Kabuki: Faubion Bowers and Theatre Censorship in Occupied Japan*, trans. by Samuel L. Leiter (Honolulu: University of Hawaii Press)

OSIŃSKI, Zbigniew. 2014. *Jerzy Grotowski's Journeys to the East*, ed. by Kris Salata, trans. by Andrzej Wojtasik and Kris Salata (Holstebro, Malta, Wrocław, London and New York: Icarus Publishing Enterprise and Routledge)

PRONKO, Leonard. 1967. *Theatre East and West: Perspectives towards a Total Theatre* (Berkeley and Los Angeles: University of California Press)

SAVARESE, Nicola. 2010. *Eurasian Theatre: Drama and Performance between East and West from Classical Antiquity to the Present*, ed. by Vicki Ann Cremona, trans. by Richard Fowler (Holstebro, Malta and Wrocław: Icarus Publishing Enterprise)

SCHINO, Mirella. 2009. *Alchemists of the Stage: Theatre Laboratories in Europe*, trans. by Paul Warrington (Holstebro, Malta and Wrocław: Icarus Publishing Enterprise)

SCOTT, Adolphe Clarence. 1955. *The Kabuki Theatre of Japan* (London: George Allen & Unwin Ltd; repr. New York: Dover Publications Inc., 1999)

— 1957. *The Classical Theatre in China* (London: George Allen & Unwin Ltd; repr. New York: Dover Publications Inc., 2001)

— 1959. *Mei Lan-Fang, Leader of the Pear Garden* (Hong Kong: Hong Kong University Press)

SKEEL, Rina (ed.). 1994. *The Tradition of ISTA* (Londrina: FILO)

ZEAMI, Motokiyo. 1960. *La Tradition secrète du Nô* (The Secret Tradition of Noh), ed. and trans. by René Sieffert (Paris: Gallimard)

— (1971) *Den hemmelige tradition i nô* (The Secret Tradition of Noh) (Holstebro: Odin Teatrets Forlag)

An upside-down theatre geography:
Letter to a friend

Dear Lluís,

My interest in the theatres of Asia was born within the horizon of an upside-down geography. The theatre sun has always risen for me in the West, from the waters of the Moskva river that flows through Moscow and its provinces. It was the sun of the Great Reform in European theatre at the dawn of the twentieth century, with Stanislavski, Meyerhold, Vakhtangov, Eisenstein, Tairov, Granovski, Evreinov, Sulerzhitski, whose actors Vera Komissarzhevskaya, Olga Knipper, Alisa Koonen, Mariya Babanova, Michael Chekhov, Igor Ilyinski, and Erast Garin knew how to give life to an unimaginable art.

In Poland, in the early 1960s, my teachers at the theatre school, and later Jerzy Grotowski and Ludwik Flaszen, crammed their conversations with continuous references to the theatres born on the Moskva's banks. It was their yesterday, of which they knew the written tradition and legends. It also became my yesterday and today, the point from which to invent my theatre together with my Odin Teatret actors. Once more, and this should never be forgotten when it comes to my apprenticeship and that of Odin Teatret, the Russian pioneers I mentioned above have been the horizon from which I discovered my path. This horizon widened with the names of Craig and Appia, Copeau, Dullin and Jouvet, Marceau and Barrault, Brecht, Artaud, Decroux, and all the Polish directors and stage designers – dead or alive – who nurtured me during my four years in Poland in the early 1960s. I am not quoting a list of important historical names. I am revealing to you the ancestors whom I have cannibalised to satiate my hunger for memories, traces of performances, biographies, anecdotes, technical suggestions, and faded photos.

The sun that rose from the waters of the Moskva illuminated two moons. The first was legendary and distant in time: the theatre of mountebanks, of itinerant comedians, of masks and fairs – in short, the myth of commedia dell'arte.

The second moon was exotic and distant in space: the traditional Asian theatres.[4] That India about which Coomaraswamy wrote to Craig; the noh of Ezra Pound and Fenollosa, of Yeats and Claudel; the Peking Opera (as it was

---

4 Editor's note: Barba treats the various Asian acting techniques as a whole, naming them 'traditional Asian theatres'. It is obvious that their traditions, genres and techniques are different from one another, and, when trying to analyse or study them, these differences should be preserved. Thus, in this book, the

called at the time) which had enchanted Meyerhold, Eisenstein and Brecht after seeing Mei Lanfang in Moscow in 1935; the dramatic dances from the island of Bali, described in some memorable pages by Antonin Artaud – all of these were the cardinal points of an unknown theatre geography that I glimpsed in the uncertainty of my first professional footsteps.

In 1963, during my stay in India, in the steamy tropical nights I saw my first kathakali performances in the temple courtyards. A few harassing questions and an indelible memory remained with me: the humility and dedication of the students, children about ten years old, who, in solitary silence at dawn, tried and retried the basic postures and footsteps.

When I started to make theatre in 1964, first in Norway and later in Denmark, I devoted several issues of Odin Teatret's journal *Teatrets Teori og Teknikk* to the sun of the Moskva and its two shining moons. I had an ambition to map these unreachable theatre regions.

It was in 1973, nine years after Odin Teatret's creation and when my actors were already skilled in a personal stylisation, that I had the opportunity of seeing again an Asian theatre in its own context, this time in Bali. Since then, innumerable journeys and periods of study followed in many Asian countries.

I thought – and still do think – that the treasures of theatre cultures are not only made up of different aesthetics and repertoires on which the variety of artistic creations, great traditions and single artists grow. Equally important is the legacy of techniques, the embodied know-how at the basis of our craft; in other words, the professional bond that unites us, determining and safeguarding our differences.

You will wonder, dear Lluís, why I'm telling you this geographical fable about the Moskva from whose waters rose the sun of the Great Reform of European theatre, with its moon emerging from the Ganges. For me, it was not a fable but an authentic revelation. While you gather my writings on the Asian theatres and reconstruct the history of my relationships with their actors and dancers, I beg you to remember that it was not Asian theatres I was looking for but a lost theatre, as the book I wrote on Grotowski in 1963 witnesses, well before my journey to India.[5] Equally, years later, I have not searched for theatre in anthropology but for theatre anthropology.

---

label 'traditional Asian theatres' should not be understood as an attempt to erase those differences. See also my introduction: 'Eugenio Barba and traditional Asian theatres'.

[5] Editor's note: Barba refers to his book *Alla ricerca del teatro perduto* (In Search of Lost Theatre), published in Italian (Barba 1965a) and in Hungarian (Barba 1965b).

After the foundation of ISTA, the International School of Theatre Anthropology, in 1979, and in the course of its regular sessions during more than three decades, the distinct traditions and biographies were embodied in people who shared a common craft. It became more and more difficult for me to notice the differences between our respective origins and styles. We were companions on a joint expedition, fellow inhabitants of a village, scattered here and there throughout the world, who at times were reunited.

In time, the moon that rose from the Ganges ceased orientating the wanderings of my imagination from the West to the East and vice versa. Its splendour coincided with the generosity and impassioned innovative strength of a handful of artists. Among these, Sanjukta Panigrahi, particularly dear and ever mourned, and Cristina Wistari Formaggia, an Italian who devoted her life to safeguarding the fading tradition of Balinese gambuh.

With affection,

Eugenio Barba

I

Wanderlehre: Travelling to learn

▶ Talabot, the ship on which Barba sailed to the East during 1956. After passing through the Suez Canal, the ship docked at Aden, Colombo, Bombay, Cochin, Madras, Calcutta, Chittagong, Hong Kong, Shanghai, Tsing Tao, Kobe, Yokohama, Manila, Cebu, Zamboanga and sailed back to Europe. This journey, which lasted six months, was repeated again by Barba and was a sort of initiation that left deep traces in his imagination. The image of the ship appears as a recurrent metaphor in his writings, and Talabot even became the title of one of Odin Teatret's performances (1988).

In search of theme

In this text from 1966, Barba briefly evokes the story and the consequences of his journey to India in 1963. It is worth noting the anomaly of an aspiring theatre director who 'searches for theatre' in a geographically and culturally distant country in an epoch when it was difficult to travel and when European theatre people were not interested in Asian theatres.

The text is taken from Land of Ashes and Diamonds: My Apprenticeship in Poland, followed by 26 Letters from Jerzy Grotowski to Eugenio Barba *(Barba 1999: 75–76). Barba's book was published for the first time in Italian, in 1998.*

I went to Asia for the first time in 1956 at the age of nineteen, working as a sailor on a boat. My first stop was in India. At that time, theatre was far from my mind. Seven years later, I was again travelling towards India, in a second-hand car which I didn't know how to drive. This time I wanted to learn something professionally useful. I was searching for 'Indian theatre'. In New Delhi, I would finally become acquainted with it.

I was advised to meet Ebrahim Alkazi at the National School of Drama. But there, to my surprise, I found myself hearing and watching the same things they taught at the Warsaw theatre school.

Somebody said to me, 'Why don't you go to Bombay? There you will find Adi Marzban, a writer who does some interesting theatre.' More days of driving. But in Bombay too I only found plays taken from the English tradition and popular farces.

Then someone suggested, 'Why not go down south? There you really will find something quite unique!' He assured me that kathakali would not disappoint me. He was from Kerala.

So, once again, Judy climbed behind the wheel of the Land Rover, and, after crossing the whole of India, we arrived at the Kerala Kalamandalam, in the village of Cheruthuruthy.[6]

---

[6] Editor's note: Judy Jones was an English secretary working at the International Theatre Institute, UNESCO, in Paris. Eugenio Barba met her at the International Theatre Congress in Warsaw, in June 1963, and together they decided to travel by car to India. In 1965, they got married.

What I saw in Kerala is engraved for ever in my memory. The children were admitted to the school at the age of nine or ten. They started at dawn. Still numb from sleep, they began on their own to repeat again and again the laborious kathakali postures and steps. They were friendly and curious. They became my companions.

Even more than the beauty of the performances, it was my own incapacity to understand that surprised me. Why was I, a European spectator, so bewitched by these actors when I could neither understand the story they were telling, nor the meaning of their message, nor their language or the conventions? What was it that made me follow every gesture, every step, dance or deaf-mute dialogue of these actors? Was it their technique that kept me spellbound during an entire night, seated on the ground amongst a crowd who slept or continually got up to stretch their legs, or to eat or drink?

These questions constituted the true influence on me of kathakali. For years and years they have remained alive, and have then reappeared in other contexts, leading me towards an attempt at an answer that I have called Theatre Anthropology.

In mid-December 1963, I returned to my mother's home in Rome only to discover that the Italian government had, for the fourth time, renewed my scholarship to Poland. I sent a telegram to Grotowski and set off immediately for Opole.

We had a lot to tell each other. In my room or in the station restaurant Grotowski brought me up to date with everything that had happened during my absence. Zbigniew Cynkutis, who had played Kordian and then Faustus, had left the theatre, and two new actors had been engaged. The situation had not improved, political pressures had become intolerable, and, to make matters worse, money was short because the subsidies had been suspended. He explained how far they had come with rehearsals for the new production *Studium o Hamlecie* (*Hamlet Study*), why he had chosen that particular text, how he had gone about extracting the archetype, and what was the basis for the dialectic of apotheosis and derision. I described my trip to him and the performances I had seen, and I told him about kathakali and the religious ceremonies I had attended in Iran, Pakistan, and India. I had started to write down my observations on kathakali and had adapted some eye exercises for the training of the Laboratory Theatre's actors. I had taken a series of photographs of the kathakali children. They were doubtless far more eloquent than my descriptions could ever be.

上海海員俱樂部

地址：漢口路五十號

電話：一七六六二

SHANGHAI SEAMEN'S CLUB

ADDRESS: 50 HANKOW ROAD

TELEPHONE: 17662

▶ April 1956: Barba's membership card for the Shanghai Seamen's Club.
▶▶ Copenhagen, 1956: Barba (centre) together with other Norwegian members of the crew at a shipyard entrance.

▶ Barba (right) and another member of the crew, who both worked in the engines.

The kathakali theatre

From a historical point of view, this text, written by Barba after his journey to India in 1963, is important since it relates the author's first meeting with an Asian theatre tradition, but it is also the first description of kathakali to be published by a Western theatre director.

In the eyes of the young Barba, two perspectives blend. On the one hand, there is the appeal of the ritual and religious dimension of kathakali, which is also stressed in the books that Barba reads and quotes after his journey. On the other, he links this 'spiritual' perspective with a detailed analysis of technical features in the actor's preparation and performance. It is easy to trace in this second perspective the archaeology of his future comparative research into Theatre Anthropology and the actors' technical principles. The accurate muscular descriptions of the basic stances and the long list of preparatory exercises give the clear impression that the young Barba (he is only twenty-six years old and with little theatre experience) glimpses in them an essential factor whose meaning and relevance he is still unable to explain to himself. Barba is spellbound not only by the performances but above all by the conditions, the procedures and the relationships that characterise the kathakali apprenticeship, so different from that which he knows from Europe. We may also note Barba's continuous references to other forms of Asian theatres which he knew only from the few books accessible at that time.

Written in 1963 after a three-week stay at the Kerala Kalamandalam school in Cheruthuruthy, this text was first published two years later in French in two parts ('Le théâtre kathakali', Les Lettres Nouvelles, May 1965, pp. 91–103, July 1965, pp. 91–115, and October 1965, pp. 120–30). Between then and 1974, it was published in Italian and partially in English and Danish. During the 1970s and 1980s the text was published again in Italian (twice) and in French, as well as in new languages such as Polish and Spanish. Progressively the text fell into oblivion even for Barba himself. In contrast to some of his early writings, it was not published after 1994, when it appeared for the last time in Turkish. Reconsidering the text in the context of this book, Barba was astonished to find a connection between his first approach to kathakali and the pragmatic perspective he developed later through Theatre Anthropology's paradigms.

In Kerala, on the southern coast of India, kathakali, a 300-year-old ritual theatre, still flourishes. Dance and pantomime, religious sensibility and mythological tales blend in the interpretation of actors who, solely with their body, bring again to life the prowess of compassionate divinities.

This essay is neither intended as an aesthetic analysis of kathakali nor as a study of its origins or its relationship to other Indian theatre forms. Hence, the absence of Sanskrit terminology and references to classical texts on acting such as *Natyashastra* and the *Abhinaya Darpana*. My main purpose in studying kathakali was to acquaint myself with a specific technique and to examine it from the point of view of a possible adaptation to the training and acting of European performers. Thus the detailed description of the physical exercises and of certain surprising features in the Indian actor's psychic technique which might inspire and enrich the European actor's baggage of expressive means.

Tantric and agricultural rituals and folkloric manifestations, religious ceremonies and the blossoming of bhakti, the religious fervour spread by the Alvars, those 'maddened men of God' with their ecstatic songs and dances, are at the origins of many forms of dance and theatre in India. But here one should not underestimate the direct contribution of the gods. According to the Kali chronogram, Grahya Stutirgathakaith, Krishna appeared in Kalikut in Malabar, the northern part of Kerala, in 1657 and presented a peacock feather to a high priest. To celebrate this extraordinary event, the krishnattam was created, a religious dance-drama that glorified Krishna's exploits and those of his cow-herd girls, the gopies. This kind of performance soon became famous throughout the state of Malabar. The Raja of the neighbouring state of Kottakara asked the dignitaries of Kalikut to let him have a krishnattam troupe. However, because of political rivalries, the Raja's request was rejected, and he was humiliated by the affirmation that such a refined art form could not possibly be understood and appreciated in his state. The Raja decided to avenge himself and asked for the help of the impartial gods, who appeared to him in a dream, inspiring a new form of dance-drama: kathakali.

Through the generations, this drama evolved and grew: masks were replaced by an elaborate make-up; the actor, who at first enacted and recited the text later only interpreted it in silence while two singers, accompanied by two drummers, sang the text. By the middle of the eighteenth century, kathakali attained its present-day form. In literal translation, kathakali means 'acting out stories'.

The episodes are narrated by two singers and interpreted by actors through mimicry, gestures, and movements recalling acrobatics and dance. It is a real *Wort-Ton-Drama*, and Adolphe Appia mentioned it in one of his books.

The stories, borrowed from the great Indian epics *Ramayana* and *Mahabharata* and the traditional tales of the Puranas – are written in a mixture of Sanskrit and Malayalam, the language of Kerala. The performances take place in the open air, starting at sunset and lasting through the night. The stage usually measures about six square metres. Originally, the plays were performed in temples or in the courtyards of palaces. Today, performances are also shown in village squares, factories or schools to celebrate religious or historical events. As in the Greek *skene*, there is neither curtain nor scenery. Alone on the middle of the stage, a large oil lamp is both a religious symbol, similar to the altar of the ancient Greek stage, and a source of light. The only prop is a stool, used for many purposes: the actor may rest on it, climb it like a mountain, or lift it with a great show of muscle to demonstrate his strength. The two singers and the musicians stand at the back of the stage. The orchestra is composed of two types of drums, one gong, cymbals, and a kind of organ – the tambura – and plays Carnatic melodies from southern India used in the Kerala temples.

At nightfall, a loud, continuous roll of drums announces the performance. Admission is free. People come and sit on the ground. Two young actors without make-up or costume perform a religious dance, the *todayam*, asking Shiva Nataraja to bless the performance. When the dance is over, the performance starts.

Two boys appear and unfold a silk curtain which hides an actor. The roll of drums grows louder. Two hands, one of which is artificially deformed by long silver fingernails, grasps the curtain and shakes it: the actor makes his presence known. Behind the curtain, the audience can see his feet dancing frenetically to the accompaniment of shouts ranging from deep roars to shrill tremolos. From time to time, the actor lowers the curtain, and, for a fraction of a second, the audience catches a glimpse of a face deprived of human features by an elaborate make-up. These short appearances are repeated several times and are emphasised by fortissimos from the orchestra. With a brisk movement, the two boys lower the curtain, revealing the actor in his impressive costume. His body is shaking, his arms are open, his fingers kept in a symbolic pose while his legs are spread with bent knees and his feet rest not on the sole but on the outer rim. The singers start their narrative chant, and the actor begins his interpretation. He leaps, moves about, gesticulates, mimes and acts out the story through a complex kinetic alphabet which is reminiscent of both ballet and acrobatics.

The plays describe extraordinary events involving gods, demons, legendary characters, and mythological heroes. Love scenes, battles, superhuman deeds, lyrical situations, religious ceremonies, and bursts of wrath and cruelty mingle in a story in which goodness and gods always triumph over evil and demons. The subjects are as well known to the audience as the myths of the Greek trilogies were to the Athenians. The actor enacts the struggle between good and evil solely with his body. Thus, kathakali is no longer a danced drama but becomes an ancient ritual.

Acting

In Europe, we would say that kathakali acting could be roughly compared to a blend of pantomime and ballet. Through the eloquence and expressiveness of his facial mimicry, gestures, feet and body movements, the actor transports the spectators into the drama's action and atmosphere, while suggesting where it takes place. However, his technique is closer to classical Chinese Opera than to European pantomime since his means of expression have been perfected by a long tradition and codified in an alphabet of immutable signs.

The term 'ballet' should not foster misunderstandings. Western ballet unfolds a real or metaphorical story through choreography, music, and an 'exoteric' technique, allowing the spectator to grasp most of what happens on stage. Oriental theatre and dance, on the contrary, make use of a hermetic language. Gestures, movements, postures, and rhythmical sequences do not explicitly try to present a reality but represent and reconstruct it by means of bodily 'ciphers', 'ideograms' whose conventional and symbolic meaning cannot be deciphered by someone who sees such a performance for the first time. The spectator must learn this particular language – or, rather, its key-alphabet – in order to fully seize what the singer and the actor are communicating. Without this knowledge, although the Oriental actor may surprise us with his physical skill and ensnaring rhythm, his artistic effort remains a visual mishmash.

This complex alphabet of signs encompasses facial mimicry, gesticulation, and pre-established corporal kinetics. There are nine head movements, eleven ways of looking, six motions of the eyebrows, four positions of the neck. The sixty-four motions of the limbs cover the movements of the feet, toes, heels, ankles, waist, hips – in short, all the flexible parts of the body. The gestures of the hands and fingers have a narrative, 'epic' function and are organised in a system of twenty-four fixed gestures called mudras ('signs' in Sanskrit). Those mudras are the alphabet of the actor's language.

The face is the actor's emotional mirror. He conveys all his psychical processes through the action of the neck, eyes, eyelids, eyeballs, eyebrows, lips, teeth, nose, ears, chin, cheeks, and tongue. If he is struck with terror, he raises one eyebrow, then the other, opens his eyes wide, moves his eyeballs laterally and rapidly, dilates his nostrils, his cheeks tremble, and his head turns in jerky movements. In a fit of rage, his eyebrows quiver, he raises the lower eyelids, his gaze becomes fixed and penetrating, his nostrils and lips tremble, his jaws are clamped tight, and he stops breathing, causing a change in his physiognomy. These sets of facial compositions express not only emotions as well as psychic and mental reactions but also traits of character of a more permanent nature, such as generosity, pride, curiosity, and anxiety in the face of death.

The actor does not externalise his character's feelings merely in a mechanical way. The emotional impact or, rather, the truth of each facial reaction is convincing only if he engages his imagination and psychic resources. The kathakali masters teach this rule to their pupils: 'Where the hands go to represent an action, there must go the eyes; where the eyes go, there must go the mind, and the action pictured by the hands must beget a specific feeling which is reflected on the actor's face.'

It follows that the face is the emotional mirror of the actions not of another actor but of the story narrated by the actor's own hands. There is, thus, a double structure in the actor's performance: he must set in motion simultaneously two different sets of psycho-physical and technical means to depict the complementary aspects of a story – the narrative and the emotional. The narrative (his hands) tells what happens in a particular episode; the emotional (the face) expresses the character's reactions to the situation.

A similar double structure can be seen also in the acting of classical Chinese theatre. The body represents the character, while the head represents the actor who judges the actions of the character. This function of the head with respect to the rest of the body is at the origin of Bertolt Brecht's epic theory of *Verfremdung*, or estrangement.

In kathakali, on the contrary, the head represents the character's psyche, his inner world, which reacts to the outside events shaped by the hands and the rest of the body. We could say that the head is the character and the body is the world of events. Indian religious iconography condenses this complementarity in the emblematic image of the dancing Shiva Nataraja: the god's body is the cosmos with its dialectical process of genesis and destruction (hands create and feet annihilate) while the face reveals his attitude of serenity and bliss.

Let us see how this double structure is applied in a theatre situation. A character approaches a river. His hands describe the landscape with mudras: trees, boats, people. The face, through the eyes, which keep looking at the hands, indicates the reactions of the character. Suddenly, the hands tell of the appearance of a crocodile. The face, at the sight of the animal (represented by the hands), reveals the character's inner reactions: surprise, fear, desire to flee. The hands continue telling the story of how the crocodile is killed. On the actor's face the spectators can read exhaustion, disgust, and the pride of the victorious hunter. From this simple example one can imagine the concentration and imagination required from the actor to compose such inventive acting in comprehensible phases in a performance lasting eight to ten hours.

The mudras composed by the hands and fingers are visual ideograms that take the place of the spoken word. They can be classified into four groups:

1. gestures inspired by the symbolism of religious rituals;
2. mimetic, imitative or descriptive gestures that reproduce a person, a situation, a quality;
3. gestures borrowed from everyday life but highly stylised;
4. invented gestures suggesting what cannot easily be described, for example the intensity of a husband's love for his wife.

The mudras can be composed by one or both hands and are strictly connected to the movements of the body and the pre-established expressions of the face. The same mudra may mean two different, even opposing, things, according to whether the actor makes it while moving or immobile, in conjunction with a facial expression indicating courage or panic. There are twenty-four fundamental mudras, which, when combined with one another and with gestures and facial expressions, can reproduce approximately 3000 words, enough for a play. Each mudra corresponds to a word, even grammatical terms such as 'if', 'when', and 'but'.

In some cases, the actor gives free rein to his fantasy. Let us suppose that he wants to describe a woman. After composing the mudra for the word 'woman', he elaborates on the description by improvising attributes such as 'beautiful as a lotus' or 'tender as a rose petal', or 'with eyebrows like waves'. In the section 'Education and training of the actor' (pp. 59–66) we will see how this skill in improvising (*manodharma*) is indispensable for the actor.

The actor is a sculptor whose body is both the chisel and the block of marble. The mudras are not only visual ideograms with a descriptive value, but they depict plastically a process of emotional representation that engages the actor's body in a bare space which he fills with his presence and dynamism. A mountain is not just a simple gesture – a mudra. Its height can be read in the actor's eyes, in his looking, while we see his body climb the mountain – the body which is simultaneously mountain and mountaineer. This acting

▶ Kathakali Kalamandalam, 1963. Students exercising mudras and eyes.

► 1963. Sankaran Namboodiri as a student at Kalamandalam, exercising mudras and facial expressions.

►► 2000. Sankaran Namboodiri, who had become the Kalamandalam's headmaster, demonstrates mudras and a basic stance to the ISTA participants in Bielefeld (Germany).

is not descriptive, a one-dimensional and unambiguous reproduction of the character's actions. Through a dialectical dynamic, a whole universe is created and analysed with the help of only the body. The actor's skill enables the spectators to be introduced to the inner dynamics and thus to judge the inside and the outside, capturing the totality. The actor superimposes continuously the subject and the object, the world of subjective feelings and that of objective events, the action and the reaction.

The fact of expressing each word of the play through a mudra is one of the reasons for the length of a kathakali performance. A play which can be read in twenty minutes may last three or four hours on stage. The European spectators would be bored, but the Indian audience – like any Oriental one – has a quite different approach: what is important is the performer's skill and virtuosity. Each gesture, each movement, each facial expression is evaluated and appreciated by an audience of connoisseurs who do not hesitate to express their pleasure or discontent.

From the very moment he appears in front of the audience, the actor gives an impression of artificiality due to his make-up, costume, posture, and gait. Those who created kathakali seem to have made a conscious effort to erase any form of expression imitating the reality of daily life. The make-up alters the actor's individual features and transforms them into a supernatural magic mask. The costume breaks the organic harmony of the human body, and the new silhouette astonishes for its amazing architectonic proportions. The acting technique resorts to a language which does not passively replicate reality but recreates it. The basic posture deforms the actor's dynamics without hindering him. This artificiality brings to mind a gigantic, inhuman marionette. By 'artificiality', I mean artistic distortion whose extreme theatrical aspects are strengthened by several elements.

The actor's appearance before the spectators is preceded by a complex convention with a ritual value: the *tiranokku*, or the lowering of the curtain. The actor, at the centre of the stage, is hidden behind a coloured curtain held by two boys. Behind the curtain we sense, or rather we hear, his presence expressed by shouts, yells, screams, and vocalisms which are not logical statements but are reminiscent of magical incantations. This communicates to the audience the character's supernatural power and allows the actor to access the sonorous universe and the breathing (*prana*) of the character he is about to embody. The voice as a magical vibration also has an enchantment value in other theatre forms such as tjalonarang, Barong, kabuki, and noh, as well as in tantric ceremonies and rituals of 'primitive' people. All the while, below the curtain, the actor's feet can be seen executing a frenzied dance on the spot. From time to time, the two boys lower the curtain, revealing to the audience for a few seconds the beguiling face of the actor. This complicated ceremony lasts about twenty minutes, then, with a resolute, abrupt gesture, the two boys lower the curtain, and the actor is revealed to us in all the splendour of his costume, ready to enact the story.

While performing, the actor keeps his mouth shut. He breathes through his nose except when he has to use his tongue or utter terrifying screams. When this rule is suddenly broken, and the mouth is opened, the abnormality and un-humanness of the actor's facial expression are reinforced.

In addition, there is the actor's astonishing ability to dilate the eyes. The eyeballs seem to fill half the cheeks. Often the gaze is fixed, like the eyes of a statue. The animated gesticulation and the semi-acrobatic movements contrast sharply with these enormous staring eyes, as if they were contemplating nothingness. Sometimes, the eyelids are wide open, and the iris disappears in a corner of the eye while the head moves constantly and the face takes on a succession of expressions.

The eyes follow the hands constantly; the actor looks at them as if they were the very object or person they describe. The wide open eyelids show the white of the eyes, which at times is artificially coloured red, while the iris is fixed or moves intermittently. At times, the face is totally immobile, and the eyes alone do the acting. In the play *Agni-Salabha*, a butterfly burns itself in a flame, and the actor portrays this with his eyes alone.

The utter mobility of the hands and fingers is beyond description. Like a strange deaf-and-mute alphabet, their agility and compositions are mesmerising. They are at the origin of the narrative which the actor develops through his dynamics. The intertwined movements, whether fluid or jerky, together with the dilation of the eyes, are the two elements which are most reminiscent of puppets.

The movements of the various parts of the body are not synchronised and are based on a diversity of rhythms in the different limbs. For example, the legs may be moving at great speed while the hands sculpt the mudras with a slow and deliberate precision. Or the facial mimicry may be lively while the actions of the body are imbued with a serene yet austere gravity.

Like Chinese Opera and Japanese classical theatre, kathakali does not use women. Female parts are played by men. The gait, the postures, the slightest gestures of these actors manifest a deep understanding of female psychology and behaviour. However, there is nothing vulgar or ambiguous in these impersonations, and nothing that might cater to the taste of a mass audience. Such a performance is a real test of the actor's skill. Kudamaloor Karunakaran Nair, the Indian Mei Lanfang, will remain in the history of kathakali as one of the greatest interpreters of female characters.

The *kalasam* is another characteristic of kathakali. It is a kind of interluce danced by the actor at the end of each chanted verse. Its purpose is to relax the audience while giving a chance to present the actor's skill. One could also speak of an estrangement effect. The plot comes to a sudden halt; the actor, who may have been playing the part of an old man, starts a rapid and vigorous dance. The *kalasam* lasts only a few minutes, after which the actor picks up where he left off.

Another estranging element is the actor's comportment at the end of a solo. While another colleague takes over, the actor who has just finished sits on the stool on the stage, relaxes and behaves as if he were alone in his dressing room; he touches up his make-up, settles his crown on his head and rearranges the ornaments of his costume. As soon as he is needed again in the play, he undergoes a startling and sudden metamorphosis before the eyes of the audience: he gets up from the stool and turns again into the supernatural being he was previously.

All these devices melt into a way of acting aiming at the actor's dehumanization, if the adjective 'human' is understood as natural, ordinary and belonging to everyday life. The reality of the play is passed through the sieve of artificiality and stylisation. The performance's ritual value facilitates the involvement of the audience. The role of the drums is preponderant. The sonorous rhythmic background that accompanies, stresses and modulates the action is also a strong psychic stimulant, an energising means, and an emotional ploy. The spectators slip into the 'magic time' of the ritual and drift into a stream that lifts them out of the world of phenomena into the supernatural world where gods and demons confront each other in a struggle that is the archetype of our human adventure.

The costume

One of the features of Oriental theatre is its visual impact. The audience knows the play's plots; therefore, it appreciates, above all, the actor's physical virtuosity. The latter enacts a rhythmic succession of corporeal signs endorsed by a long tradition and rigorous conventions.

In all artistic fields, expressivity is closely linked to deformation. This distortion magnifies and emphasises the multiple facets of reality, decomposing and analysing them, thus shattering conditioned reflexes and mental and emotional clichés. Costumes in kathakali do not attempt to be a historical or social reconstruction; they are a means to impress the spectators through their shape, wealth, and colourfulness far removed from daily life. Costumes are helpful extensions of the actor.

Kathakali's scenic language is corporeal semantics. It must entice the eyes in order to touch the spectator's imagination and sensibility. In the course of its evolution, the kathakali masters have refined the performer's expressive instrument – the body – through a conscious deformation. Thus, all the movements acquire a deeper significance than those of daily life.

This reshaping and magnification of the body is sheer theatricality, taking the term 'theatre' in its etymological sense: something worth seeing. The make-up changes the face into a forceful mask. The stance – knees wide apart, legs bent, and the body's full weight on the external edge of the feet – makes the actor transcend his normal posture, where each single gesture and movement is composed. The costume is striking for its vivid colours and fabulous form, cleverly used by the actor as a compliant tool to achieve visual and dynamic effects. It changes, amplifies, and sometimes even minimises the actor's body, making him able to communicate simultaneously the location and its features, as well as the character's actions and his inner reactions. The costume has, rather, the function of a living prop than that of an ornament.

At first sight it looks like an enormous cage that swallows up the lower part of the actor's body and seems to hinder the slightest movement. This impression is due to the over-dimensioned skirt and to a precariously balanced headgear, typical of male characters. The bell-shaped skirt, reminiscent of the costume worn by women in Elizabethan times, ends just under the knees. Under this outer skirt, the actor wears another one, much shorter, which looks like a tutu. To give more width and volume to these skirts and to prevent them for hindering the movements of the legs, the actor winds around his abdomen a cotton belt approximately twenty-five centimetres wide and fifteen metres long, into which he stuffs short pieces of material. Previously, when the actor recited the text, the belt was used as a support for the air column that carried the voice: the compression of the abdominal muscles pushed the voice upward. A similar belt with the same function is still used today by the actors of traditional Chinese theatre.

This impression of an impractical costume disappears as soon as the actor begins to perform. The knees are bent and wide apart to keep the skirt open, emphasising the actor's movements with a graceful swing. When the actor is immobile, the skirt delimits him as an architectonic silhouette; when he moves, it becomes the trampoline from which he springs into the most complicated yet flowing movements. The costume surrounds the actor with a halo of undulations that seem to emanate from a supernatural power: the divine character's *mana*.

The actor's mastery turns what looks at first like a handicap into a suggestive tool. If he bends down, the skirt hides his ankles and feet, and he suddenly becomes a gigantic legless torso, reminiscent of the wooden images of the Indian divinities in rural ceremonies. Since his legs are always bent, when he walks normally he becomes a tall wader bird. With astonishing skill, the actor can use the skirt to suggest the gait of a young girl or that of animals, waves in the water or a narrow road full of obstacles. This integration of the costume – which is both prop and scenery, metaphor and reality – is a symbiosis of a living organism and multicoloured materials, emerging as a sudden enchanted language.

Above the huge skirt, the actor wears a white or coloured blouse which covers the upper part of his body. Its simplicity is ornamented with colourful ribbons and long scarves attached to which are small round mirrors which the actor handles during the performance. The shoulders are broadened by golden epaulets; red and green pompoms, bracelets, and necklaces adorn the neck and arms. Clearly visible small bells are attached around the ankles, stressing rhythmically the least movement. Long, silver fingernails extend the left hand, producing elegant and graceful effects but acquiring a fierce character when used by demons. Often, the latter wear fanglike false teeth, transforming their frighteningly made-up face into a hideous grimace.

From a visual point of view, the formal balance of this bulky costume is attained thanks to the large head-dress. It is a cone surrounded by a red and green disk forming a halo around the head. It looks imposing in its symbolic splendour and adds to the dehumanization of the actor. It is made of carved wood, gilded and decorated with pieces of metal and mirrors that glint at every movement of the actor's head. Sometimes peacock feathers are added to emphasise the vibrations. Thus, the exaggerated volume of the costume is compensated for by the majestic height the actor acquires thanks to this radiant crown.

It is interesting to note that the costumes of the male characters are much more elaborate than those of the female ones. This is the more surprising since matriarchy was and still is widespread in Kerala. The female costume is simple and comparatively realistic in contrast to the grandiose opulence of the male ones. It consists of a sari, which hides the legs, a bodice the same colour as the sari, usually white or a pastel shade, a veil covering the head and falling on the shoulders, necklaces and bracelets in moderate quantity. Each character has its own attributes, ornaments, and colours. Gods are embellished with more ornaments and colours; mortals are represented with a realism blended with grotesque details.

The stage is empty, except for a stool. Sometimes, precipitating into a realism that breaks with the stylisation of the performance and costume, a red liquid is used as blood in scenes of homicide or battle, or long guts made of fabric are voluptuously extracted from disembowelled demons. The costume is ornament, scenography, and multiple prop. It is worth noting:

1. the variety of bright colours that catch the eye even in the light of one oil lamp;
2. the architectonic character that shapes, like a suggestive statue, the actor's silhouette, especially in static postures;
3. its capacity to exaggerate the actor's volume (we must remember that Indians from the south are slender and not so tall);
4. its use by the actor to widen the range of corporal expressivity and dynamics.

Some of these means are shared by religious and ancient classical theatres: large masks, high-heeled cothurnus boots, and large tunics in the Greek tragedy; stiff and disproportionate costumes in Japanese noh. The magic oval of the make-up, the costume's polychromatic profusion and the majestic head-dress increase the actor's effectiveness, endowing him with an artificial expressiveness reminiscent of that advocated by one particular European theatre reformer.[7]

Education and training of the actor

The following description is based on the method used at the Kerala Kalamandalam in Cheruthuruthy, considered the best professional school of kathakali.

---

[7] Editor's note: Barba refers to Edward Gordon Craig's seminal article 'The Actor and the Über-Marionette' from 1907 (1962: 54–94), which sparked off a controversy among theatre people and influenced directors from different generations such as Meyerhold, Copeau, Decroux, and Kantor, among others.

Students are admitted after doing an exam. The candidates must be under twelve years old and are chosen on the basis of their health, beauty, musical and rhythmic aptitudes, and physical agility. They live together in the school in huts in groups of four. They have no beds, no cupboards or furniture of any kind and sleep on mats. Their personal effects are kept in a suitcase. On the walls hang pictures of gurus and gods. They eat in a communal refectory. They work every day except Sunday, from 4 a.m. to 9 p.m., with two months' holiday each year. They pay for tuition, except when the family is too poor. The full course lasts eight years, and the students are divided into two groups, being novices for the first four years. Every day, both groups go through basic exercises for legs, eyes, and face. The classes are directed by teachers (gurus), whose strict discipline inspires fear. I never saw a student beaten at the Kerala Kalamandalam, but corporal punishment is usual at other schools; the students can be forced to stay in a painful physical position for an hour or more, and the slightest breach of discipline may result in expulsion.

The students get up at 4 a.m. and begin their exercises in a hut lit by an oil lamp. No teacher is present, but silence and discipline reign. Their first exercises are gymnastics and acrobatics according to a self-imposed tempo, repeating meaningless sentences that have a definite rhythmical value. The exercises are executed collectively and include:

1. a complex salutation to the gods;
2. a rhythmic series of leaps and bends on the spot;
3. jumps forwards, backwards and sideways; the student suddenly stops at the end of a jump, one leg in the air, holding this posture for a while without losing his balance;
4. sideways opening of the legs, until the inner side of the thigh touches the ground (splits);
5. a dynamic bridge: the standing student bends his torso backward, bends his knees and, with a sudden impulse, falls backwards on his right hand, then shifts the weight of his body to his left hand and, with one more impulse, gets back on his feet; the feet do not move.

These exercises last about one hour. The following hour is devoted to training the legs. Standing in a row in the basic kathakali position, the pupils execute various steps on the spot with increasing speed: legs bent, knees wide apart, the weight on the outside edge of the feet with toes tensed inwards. These exercises help the future actor to get used to this unnatural and uncomfortable position as well as to strengthen the legs and develop their agility.

It is now 6 a.m. The pupils go for a swim in a nearby river. At 6.30, breakfast, and at 7.15 more work. Until 12.30 they repeat without interruption fragments of a play or entire scenes under the direction of their teachers. When he has completed his studies, a kathakali actor knows perfectly the totality of signs, mimicries, jumps, and mudras of all the characters (male and female, main and secondary roles) in approximately sixty plays. The pupils repeat the same fragment numerous times until their guru is satisfied. The same stern discipline applies to both young and older students.

At 12.30, lunch and rest until 3 p.m. From 3 to 5 p.m. they attend classes on the history of kathakali, biographies of gurus, religion, English, Malayalam, Sanskrit, history, and geography. From 5 to 6.30, sitting in *padmasana* – lotus position with crossed legs – they exercise the eyes and the face. After half an hour's pause, they sing religious hymns for thirty minutes, ending with one praising a guru. From 7.30 to 8.30 p.m., they practise the mudras, which are shown one by one by the teacher and which constitute the score of the scenes to be practised next day. Sitting on the floor in *padmasana*, they engage only the upper part of the body and the face. Then dinner and, at 9 p.m., bed time.

At least twice a month, the older students, who have been at the school for more than four years, give a performance together with their teachers to which the local population is invited. The younger students help their older colleagues by grinding and blending the colours of the make-up and arranging the various parts of the costume, thus becoming familiar with the dressing preparation. These performances usually take place on Saturday and last through the night. The next day, Sunday, the students rest. Performances are given to commemorate the birth or death of great gurus or for religious anniversaries. On such occasions, the costumes, the ornaments, the make-up paints are exposed in a room transformed into a sacred space where oil lamps are burning under the image of a guru or a god. This tradition is rooted in mimetic magic practices: the greatness and the power of the god or guru are transferred to the actor's costume.

We can distinguish two phases in the training of a kathakali actor. One consists in the mnemonic-physical assimilation of the mudras, of the facial expressions and all the postures and movements related to a role. We could call this the ideographic map of each character of a play. The other phase is preparatory to the assimilating period and involves a series of exercises aiming to develop the physical skill to execute the scores of the different characters with ease and precision. These exercises help in achieving an absolute control of each face muscle, of the smallest eye movement, of the agility of the legs and the entire body. This gymnastic-acrobatic training fosters a physical condition that easily enables the effort demanded by a whole night's performance.

It is worth noting that there are no exercises to develop the fingers' suppleness and expressiveness. These parts of the body, which through the mudras have a preponderant role in the narrative of the play, undergo no special training. Their expressive liveliness is reached through a continuous repetition of the same mudras.

Similarly, there are no make-up courses. The students become familiar with this technique during the performances in the last four years of study.

The usefulness of the students' division in two groups is evident. In one group, a boy has already reached a certain technical level after four years. At his side, a twelve-year-old boy is just beginning his training. Thus, the youngest are continuously confronted with the older ones and motivated to do their best. On the other hand, the teachers watch to see that all the students give their maximum.

A particular aspect of the actor's training is the *chavitti uzhicchil*, massage by the feet. The students go through this process during the monsoon season which, in Kerala, lasts from May to August. The body is rubbed with a mixture of sesame oil, coconut oil, and ghee (clarified butter). The student lies down, his face and chest touching the ground. His thighs are spread outward and the knees rest on pieces of wood about fifteen centimetres high. The lower part of both legs is bent inward, the feet touching each other. In this position, the upper and the lower part of the body touch the ground while the lumbar region is lifted by the pieces of wood under the knees.

Supporting himself by a horizontal bar at the height of his shoulders, the guru begins gently to massage the student's body with his right foot and toes. While massaging, he presses downward on the lumbar region until it touches the ground while the knees are still raised by the two pieces of wood. They are the only parts of the body which do not touch the ground, and this causes a deformation of the kneecaps. The purpose of the massage is to change the position of the kneecaps so that the basic position and stage gait can be performed easily. The massage lasts about half an hour and is rather painful, especially in the beginning.

Through this physical pain, the young actor achieves organically the basic position for the performance: feet parallel half a metre apart and resting on their outer edge, toes bent inwards, knees opened at an angle of ninety degrees, the trunk straight, the chin pressed in against the neck, arms stretched out sideways parallel to the ground with the hands hanging down. Let's analyse this position from a muscular point of view.

Because of the bent knees, the muscles of the calf are strained, as are the toes, which are bent inwards. The back muscles work to keep an upright posture, while the neck muscles force the chin in against the chest. The arms are stretched out to the side, the wrists and hands relaxed. This is the actor's new muscular tonus in his basic position.

This deformed stance would cause discomfort and rapid exhaustion in the uninitiated, reducing dynamic efficiency and plastic expressiveness. But, thanks to his training, the kathakali actor has achieved a control over all the muscles of his body, engaging only those which are strictly necessary even in situations of hard physical performance.

This rigorous and painful discipline turns the body into a suitable vehicle for thoughts, ideas, and emotions. The control and awareness of the anatomical structure, together with the required mental concentration, make us think of both hatha and raja yoga.

An example of similar rigour is the exercise practised by the Chakyars, a Kerala group appreciated for the excellence of its actors. It is called *nilavirikkuka*, which means, literally, to be seated in the moonlight. When the crescent moon first appears, the student sits down to train his eyes, which have been rubbed with butter, and rotates them around the moon until it disappears. The exercise lasts for about an hour on the first night. The next night, the student performs the same exercise for a longer period, corresponding to the time between the rising and the setting of the moon. He does the same on the third day, and so on, until the fifteenth night, when there is a full moon. The exercise lasts for several hours, from sunset to dawn, during which the student continually moves his eyes around, up and down, and sideways.

Another exercise enhances the eyes' expressiveness. The eyes are wide open, and the head turns around as if led by the iris. Suddenly the head stops, and the iris stares at an object which is not the chosen target. The head remains immobile while the iris moves slowly or rapidly towards the target and reaches it. Then and only then, the head turns towards the target, and, when facing it, the face reacts with a specific expression: hatred, joy, or contempt.

Two more qualities are indispensable to the kathakali actor. The first is *bhangi* – grace – corresponding to the *hana*, 'the marvellous flower' described by Zeami in his treatises on noh. It is the actor's accomplishment to render his traditional gestures and movements spontaneous, thus transforming them from

► Students training a basic stance.
►► The basic position of the feet: with knees bent and the toes curled inwards while the body's weight is on the outer edge of the feet.

a purely physical expression into intellectual and aesthetic values. He achieves this when he masters all his expressive means and uses them with virtuosity.

The second quality is *manodharma*, or imaginative ability, which enables the actor to convert the text into spontaneous and improvised action. Accompanied by the drums, he improvises in certain scenes, enacting adjectives and metaphors which are his creative contribution to the performance. Descriptions of landscapes, assemblies of gods, the beauty of the beloved or the ugliness of demons gush forth from his imagination and verve.

An example of this is a scene from *Kalyana Saugandhika*. Bhima, the Indian Hercules, is convinced by his beloved to look for a rare flower in the forest. The description of his opening of a path in this forest is a proof of his mastery as well as of his poetic and burlesque imagination. Without moving from the spot, the actor makes us see the trail which becomes narrower and narrower, the vegetation hindering and suffocating him, the difficulty of the terrain. He enacts the animals he sees, jumps like a monkey, slides like a snake and, like a terrified antelope, takes flight. Evoking their shapes, he makes us admire the huge baobabs and the slender wild palms. Beside a stream he comes upon a few women. He imitates their gait: the bent old woman and the young girl who skips self-assuredly. He shows their work: his body becomes a washerwoman, the clothes she washes, and the ripples of the stream; a carpet beater; a tuner of musical instruments with the amazing vividness of an arm that vibrates while playing a string instrument. From a vigorous masculine demeanour he slips into feminine grace, the states of mind and moods of a woman. This superb solo of acting and improvisation lasts for over an hour and is the proof of an actor's *manodharma*.

The kathakali training is a refining process of the body's expressive possibilities. Its various parts are reshaped in order to communicate what words cannot. Eyes opening wide and half closing to depict the bursting of a lotus bud into full bloom; rotating and darting irises at the sight of a swarm of bellicose enemies; trembling eyelashes following the flight of a bee; contracted nostrils, quivering chin, cheekbones and lips reflecting secret delicate feelings: this is the magic of the facial language. Psychic processes, psychological intentions, and the complex motivations for each action are revealed through physical reactions which are striking in their intuitive precision.

Here is the evil Puthana, approaching Krishna to murder him. She advances furtively sideways, feet wide apart at an angle of 180 degrees, gliding and never leaving the floor – a snake slithering towards its prey. Her gait exposes her criminal purpose. The face contracted into an apparently innocent smile reveals her hypocrisy when compared to the intentions expressed by the lower part of her body.

The kathakali actor offers his body to the gods like the juggler of Notre-Dame who retired to a monastery and offered the best of himself to the Virgin Mary: the art of juggling a few balls in the air. Just as the Virgin Mary responded to the juggler's homage by stepping down from the altar and wiping the brow of her humble worshipper, similarly for the true believer the dance is a form of yoga, a process to eliminate the ego in order to attain final identification with the Cosmic dance of Shiva Nataraja.

A comparison with the European actor would be out of place here. Let us remember a remark by the great Polish actor Stefan Jaracz, who used to say that the actor of ancient theatre sprang from the Dionysus mysteries and religious ceremonies while the modern actor was born in the brothels of the Renaissance.

Eye exercises

The aim of these exercises is to control every least movement of the eyes. Opening the eyelids with the thumb and first finger greatly increases the size of the eyes and activates the muscles around them. The students train about one hour a day for eight years. By this time their eyes have reached a vast expressive range and capacity for unusual dilation. If these exercises are to produce results, they must be accompanied by an intense pain of the eyes, tears, and a painful stiffening of the neck muscles since the irises must be pushed far into the corners of the eyes and upwards and downwards. The student sits with crossed legs, straight trunk, head immobile, and elbows parallel with the ground.

1. The first finger lifts the upper eyelid while the thumbnail presses downwards on the lower lid opening the eyelids as much as possible. The irises are rotated around the edge of the ocular cavity.
2. The same exercise is repeated without using the fingers, opening the eyes as wide as possible without lifting the eyebrows.
3. Opening the eyelids as in Exercise 1. Movement of the iris from one corner to another, first in the lower part of the ocular cavity, then in the upper part.
4. The same exercise is repeated without using the fingers.

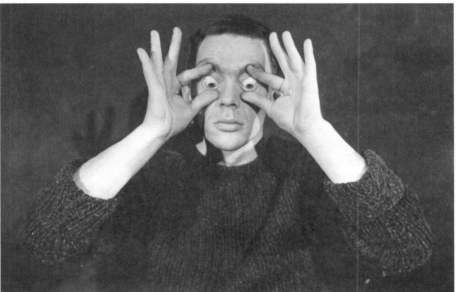

► Eye exercises.
►► Opole, January 1964. Back from India, Barba showed the above photos of kathakali eye training to Grotowski and his actors in Poland, who introduced them in their training. Here, Ryszard Cieślak.

5. Opening of the eyelids as in Exercise 1. The iris moves very slowly from one corner of the eye to the other in a horizontal line. This passage lasts about fifteen seconds. The exercise is then repeated faster.
6. The same exercise is repeated without using the fingers.
7. Opening of the eyelids as in Exercise 1. The iris moves very slowly from the centre to the left corner of the eye and back to the centre. This movement is repeated many times. Then from the centre to the right corner and back to the centre, many times and always very slowly.
8. The same exercise is repeated without using the fingers.
9. Opening of the eyelids as in Exercise 1. The iris moves diagonally from the lower left corner to the upper right corner of the eye and back again. Then the same movement from the lower right to the upper left corner and back. This is first done slowly, then very rapidly.
10. The same exercise is repeated without using the fingers.
11. Opening of the eyelids as in Exercise 1. The iris, in the centre of the eye, moves vertically upwards and downwards, first slowly, then rapidly.
12. The same exercise is repeated without using the fingers.
13. Opening of the eyelids as in Exercise 1. Starting from the left lower corner, the iris moves upwards in tiny zigzag movements of just a few millimetres, than descends to the right lower corner with the same tiny zigzag movements.
14. The same exercise is repeated without using the fingers.
15. Eyes wide open, the irises in the centre look down. The head turns slowly to left and right and back again, the irises always in the centre.
16. Eyes wide open. The head is displaced from left to right and back again with several tiny circular jerky movements. The irises precede the head movements by a fraction of second.
17. Eyes wide open focusing on an imaginary object in a predetermined spot while the head moves in different directions. The focus doesn't change during the head movements.

Exercises involving the facial muscles

These exercises serve to control every muscle of the face as a means of avoiding stereotyped expressions. It is important to engage simultaneously and with different rhythms the various facial muscles whose movements are not normally synchronised. For example, the eyelids vibrate rapidly while the cheeks tremble slowly. Or else: the left side of the face reacts rapidly while the right side reacts slowly.

1. Raising of the lower lids without moving the upper lids.
2. Raising of one eyebrow only.
3. Vibration of the eyebrows while the eyes remain open normally.
4. Vibration of the eyebrows while the eyes remain wide open.
5. Vibration of the eyebrows while the lower lids are raised.
6. Vibration of the eyebrows accompanied by head movements.
7. Vibration of the eyebrows combined with different feelings (disgust, hate, joy).
8. Vibration of the eyebrows while the face expresses a feeling and the head moves.
9. Vibration of the eyebrows accompanied by the vibration of the shoulders (these two vibrations must not be synchronised).
10. Vibration of the eyebrows while the iris moves horizontally from left to right and vice versa (the movement of the iris is slow at first, then becomes rapid; avoid the synchronization of the eyebrows' vibration with the movements of the iris).
11. Vibration of the eyebrows with the vertical displacement of the iris up and down and vice versa; avoid synchronization.
12. Vibration of the cheek muscles without moving the eyes or the mouth.
13. Vibration of the muscles at the corners of the mouth with increasing speed.
14. Vibration of the chin muscles without moving the corners of the mouth, clenching the teeth or engaging the muscles at the front of the neck.
15. Vibrations of the nostrils.
16. Vibration of the eyelashes.

Make-up

Three or four hours before the performance, which begins at dusk, the actors gather to do their make-up. Absolute silence reigns. Large oil lamps create pools of light where they sit. Their sons or young students grind into powder yellow, red and green stones, blend the colours, and prepare the *chutti*, a white paste made of rice powder and lime juice. The operation is supervised by make-up specialists.

The first phase is carried out by the actor himself. Seated cross-legged and body erect, he draws on his face a network of coloured lines which are equidistant from the nose, the eyes, and the mouth. He doesn't use brushes but small reeds. Then, a make-up specialist takes over. Completely relaxed, now the actor lies on the ground, breathing deeply and rhythmically. In this position he concentrates on the part he is going to play. Induced by the heat of the afternoon, the actor falls into a torpor during which he transforms himself into a god or a demon. At the end of this phase, the make-up specialist wakens the actor, whose gait and gestures are clearly changed.

The make-up man keeps working on the actor's face. He applies several layers of *chutti*, going from one ear to the other and passing through the chin, making a white line a little over three centimetres thick, delineating the oval of the face. Beards made of white paper are inserted in the *chutti*, which hardens in a few minutes. This operation lasts about an hour and a half.

The third and final phase is again carried out by the actor himself. He widens his eyes all the way to his ears with a white or black paste, according to his character. The rest of the face is painted homogeneously in one colour: green for gods and heroes, red for violent and ambitious characters, yellow for mortals, black for demons. The lips are painted in red with a red circle on each side of the mouth. Each character has distinctive details: demons have red nostrils; combative characters have two small white balls, one on the tip of the nose, the other on the forehead.

This colour symbolism follows the established typology in traditional Indian theatre and goes back to the *Natyashastra*, a classical text about the many aspects of stagecraft compiled between 200 BC and AD 400. But the local tantric and agricultural rituals, with their terrifying masks, the tradition of facial tattoos of the Malabar tribes and the close commercial ties, which this part of India has retained for centuries with China, have added traits to the kathakali make-up that depart from the *Natyashastra* precepts.

A distinctive trait for certain characters (women and gods) is the reddening of the white of the eyes with the seeds of *cunda poov* (*Solanum pubescens*). The result is haunting: crimson eyes stand out from the black frame that extends them to the ears.

The make-up of female characters – always interpreted by men – is closer to reality. The face is softened by a mixture of yellow and red pigments, resulting in a more natural complexion. Similarly, certain characters may have both realistic make-up and costume; for example, a Brahmin will have a long beard and the traditional red dot on the forehead.

Before he starts to put on his make-up, the actor massages his face with oil. The perspiration during the night-long performance does not undo his make-up; on the contrary, it gives it an added glow. The actor's care for his make-up is discernible in the desire to compose his face according to impeccable patterns. With unfaltering patience, he may remove his make-up and start all over again until he is satisfied with the results.

In kathakali, the make-up depicts a fixed character and not an individual personality. The actor's features disappear under the layers of colours and patterns in a performance charged with a supernatural atmosphere. The aim is dual: to startle the audience and to dehumanise the actor. The stories bring on stage divine and mythological beings. The repertory consists of religious plays, true mysteries: situations and characters that do not belong to our reality.

Originally, kathakali used masks. Later, these were rejected, and the actor's face was changed into a mask. The advantage of this is evident: the make-up has a suggestive and poignant effect, and the actor's face, retaining its natural mobility, can convey an almost endless gamut of emotions. This expressive facial versatility has become one of the main peculiarities of kathakali acting.

Psychic technique

In Oriental theatres, two forms of psychic preparation of the actor are to be found. One is purely religious, as in the Balinese tjalonarang and Barong in which the actor falls into a trance and goes through astonishing psycho-somatic reactions. The second type of psychic preparation is to be found in the Peking Opera, khon from Thailand, Japanese noh as well as in kathakali: concentration on the tasks of the role to be performed, accompanied by a series of preliminary ceremonial procedures linked to magic and religion, and aiming at arousing the actor's awareness and sensibility. I will consider a few factors that induce a particular psychic state, helping him in his acting.

One becomes a kathakali actor not by choice but by vocation. The child submits to this discipline from an early age when he enters a theatre universe which is contiguous to the religious dimension. His mind and senses are receptive to the stimuli of the new environment. He is taught absolute respect for his guru, who initiates him in a work whose secrets he is not allowed to reveal: one cannot embody a divinity unless one believes in it. Religious faith is the very basis of this theatre. The child is shaped by this sacred atmosphere, being constantly immersed in the *tremendum et fascinans* mystery of religion.

Acting is not just a craft; it is a mission, a form of priesthood. The sincerity of his vocation is tested by eight years of strict training, almost beyond endurance.

This long initiation marks him psychically and technically for the rest of his life, endowing him with a sensibility different from that of the layman.

As we have seen, the actors gather about four hours before the performance to begin their laborious make-up process, which demands deep concentration. They take off their footwear when entering the hall, which is illuminated by oil lamps similar to those on the stage, suggesting a solemn atmosphere. The silence is absolute, and any necessary communication takes place by whispering. The actor sits cross-legged, trunk erect. When a make-up specialist takes over, he lies relaxed on the floor, breathing slowly and deeply, inspiration lasting longer than expiration.

When the make-up is finished, the actor's face is no longer human like the character of Hamlet or Phaedra but has the appearance of a god, a demon, a mythical hero. Beneath these supernatural features there is no longer a mortal. Looking in the mirror, the actor would not recognise himself. Similarly, his fellow actors see the recognisable features of their colleague erased under the enthralling divine mask.

As anthropologists teach us, the mask in any ritual identifies the human with the gods. At the same time, the mask has the effect of releasing the control of consciousness and discharging repressed impulses from the subconscious. This knowledge was utilised for theatrical purposes by Charles Dullin, who made his actors act and improvise with their face covered by a rather simple mask: a sock, long hair over the face or a paper mask.

By transforming his face into a divine and supernatural one, the kathakali actor is elevated to a new dignity that frees him from his personality, thus raising him to the level of an exceptional being both subjectively and objectively.

It is worth remembering the all-pervasive role of religious feeling which is grafted onto artistic sensibility. A kathakali play is always the representation of a sacred text: myths, legends, epiphany of divinities confronting the emissaries of evil in order to subjugate them and provide an edifying example and a reason for hope for mortals. The imagination and the sensibility of the actor as well as of the spectator are still receptive to religious images and values. Before the performance, as already mentioned, two actors perform a dance of purely religious character to invoke the blessing of the divinity. Often, before beginning the make-up, the actor's guru reassures him about the forthcoming task. Each of us is sensitive to images and symbols distilled by the century-long tradition of one's own civilisation, which have the power to unbridle our imagination and awaken the most secret unconscious layers.

Theatre, in India, is a reproduction, a mimesis of the cosmic process embodied in Shiva's dance of creation and destruction. The roots of such a theatre are nourished by a religiousness whose esoteric and mythological meanings escape the understanding of us Europeans. From the very beginning, kathakali was like a form of yoga and still retains such characteristics. The pupil, *chela*, is initiated by a teacher, guru, through a long and harsh apprenticeship. He who comes close to the divinity must detach himself from what is human. The technique becomes a means to reach metaphysics. It is an offering and a consecration, a ritual procedure similar to karma yoga. For the kathakali actor, performing is an act with a value in itself and with its own reward. It is a form of prayer, a spiritual path, a true process of psychic transmutation.

Is all this mysticism? We Europeans should avoid judging with our categories a form of art that only a hasty approximation allows us to compare to our theatre.

Once upon a time, some butterflies heard about fire. They went to see what it was like. The first butterfly came near to the flame. The second skimmed it with its wing. The third flew over it. The fourth threw itself into it and burned. The others watched its body transfigured as it became one with the flame. The fourth butterfly had known what fire is but could no longer talk of it. This Sufi tale should make us reflect upon Oriental theatre and its secret tradition. In Japan, China, Indonesia, and India, no guru, no actor will tell you of the core of his art, his secrets. Is this diffidence, contempt, intolerance or impossibility to communicate through words?

It is as absurd to compare a kathakali actor to a European one as it is to compare Beethoven with a popular song writer. The actor dedicates himself to his art from childhood. After eight years, if he is considered worthy, he becomes an actor. He has no fixed salary or a theatre to which he is attached. He performs three or four times monthly, and mostly in temples for free. Unlike his European colleagues, he doesn't live by his craft. A few become teachers and open schools or have pupils at their home. Others gain a meagre living as helpers in a temple. Most of them live in poverty.

A particular atmosphere distinguishes the dressing ceremony, fuelling the actor's emotional and unconscious sphere. Similar to a high priest, the actor – his face transfigured by the make-up and with open arms as in invocation – is dressed by two assistants. Each garment of the costume is presented to him; he holds it in his hands for a few seconds, touches it lightly with his forehead and passes it back to the assistants. Each phase of this ceremony is accompanied by mantras, religious formulas murmured by the actor.

The most solemn moment is when the actor puts on his majestic head-gear. He takes it in his hands, asking his guru to assist him. After a last supplication to the gods, he places it with a resolute gesture on his head and binds it tight round his neck. Now he is ready. He advances towards the stage with bent knees and head held straight, his gown swaying at each step and accompanied by the sound of his ankle bells.

The *tiranokku* ceremony begins. On the stage, the actor is hidden behind a colourful curtain held by two students. He stamps on the spot in a dance whose rhythm becomes faster and faster, frenzied, obsessive, appearing to shake his nervous system and awaken instincts deep within him. He shouts and yells apparently meaningless sounds, or do they perhaps have a purpose which we don't grasp? If you are a believer in magic, the rhythm and vibration of an exorcising formula or a curse possess the power to bind the beings and things of the upper and underworlds to the will of the person who pronounces them, according to the conditions of the ritual. Also in theatre, it is well known that the quality of the voice as sheer vibration has an impact on the nervous system of the actor as well as of the spectator.

It is useless to ask the kathakali actor whether he is aware of his transformation. I have received only elusive answers. Are they not conscious of it, or do they simply not want to share their knowledge with an outsider? They just told me the story of Rama and Khara.

In the village of Tiru Vilva Mala, in Malabar, no kathakali performance is presented any longer. In the recent past, a tragic event took place. On the stage, the demon Khara was provoking the great god Rama. Mocking, insulting, ridiculing him. Boasting of his power, in his fury and wrath, Khara was ready to destroy everything. He was no longer an actor enacting a role, he was the demon himself. Suddenly, in a flash of lightning, Rama sprang out from the holy oil lamp on the stage. The spectators were blinded, and then their frightened eyes saw the burned corpse of the actor on the floor. The god himself had been gripped by the demon's deep-felt anger and provocation.

Have we ever witnessed on the stages of Europe a Don Juan whose sacrilegious blasphemy was struck by the lightning of the divinity and who did not get up to receive the audience's applause?

The influence of kathakali
on Grotowski and me

In February 1999, Kermit Dunkelberg, director and manager of the Pilgrim Theatre in Massachussets, USA, addressed a few questions to Eugenio Barba about the relationship between kathakali and Jerzy Grotowski's training. Dunkelberg, who had visited Odin Teatret a few times during the 1980s, was preparing a lecture entitled 'Globality and the 60s Avant-Garde: Kathakali–Barba–Grotowski–Sircar' for an international symposium in Aberystwyth, Wales, in April of the same year.

Barba's answers to Dunkelberg's questions clarify the unsubstantiated influence of kathakali and other Asian theatres on the originality of Grotowski's ideas and practice. At the same time, they are a reflection on the lasting and fecund influence of the experience Barba lived in Kerala in 1963.

The text was first published in 2004 in the second Italian edition of Land of Ashes and Diamonds: My Apprenticeship in Poland, followed by 26 Letters of Jerzy Grotowski to Eugenio Barba *(Barba 2004: 173–77). It was subsequently included in the Portuguese edition of the book.*

Holstebro, 8 February 1999

Dear Kermit,
Here you have my answers to your questions. I am glad of this opportunity since it allows me to dissipate many misunderstandings and nebulous conjectures concerning the problematics you are dealing with.

Question: What effect, specifically, did your exposure to kathakali in 1963 have on the training of the Grotowski Laboratory? What specific new exercises were introduced? Were other exercises modified? How?

I spent three weeks at the kathakali school Kerala Kalamandalam in Cheruthuruthy in September 1963. At that time, in the early sixties, no one had seen classical Asian theatre forms in Europe. Only a handful of people were interested in these, and books about them were almost non-existent. Moreover, kathakali was totally ignored, and no theatre people had ever referred to it as was the case with Balinese theatre (Artaud, José Miguel

Covarrubias), Japanese noh (Claudel, Fenollosa/Pound), kabuki (Claudel, Meyerhold, Eisenstein) or the Peking Opera (Chaplin, Brecht, Eisenstein).

When I was suddenly faced with kathakali, I received a double shock: astonishment because it was completely unexpected, and intoxication on seeing it in its own context. It was a profoundly sensorial, aesthetic, and professional experience, different from when one sees an Asian performance on tour on a Western stage. I received simultaneously a multitude of striking impressions: the open-air performances with hundreds of spectators; the profound ties with the religious sensibility and the mythological and epic themes of their tradition; the dedication of the young ten- to twelve-year-old pupils whose way of learning took place through patient imitation and repetition of dynamic patterns, scores, rhythmic sequences; the process of the slow incorporation of a knowledge which was passed on by masters without the use of words, conceptual explanations or theoretical justifications.

All this was absent from the practice of European theatre, with the exception of classical ballet and Decroux's solitary work in Paris. Nevertheless, I detected a parallel between kathakali and the anomalous situation which Grotowski's small theatre constituted in the European landscape.

At that time, Grotowski had already established a training programme which was autonomous from the work on a production. This training began in his theatre in the spring of 1962 in connection with the rehearsals for *Akropolis*. As I have explained at length in my book *Land of Ashes and Diamonds: My Apprenticeship in Poland, followed by 26 Letters from Jerzy Grotowski to Eugenio Barba* (in the 1999 edition) this training consisted of exercises which came from different sources: some were taught in theatre schools in Poland, some derived from gymnastics and acrobatics, some from pantomime and yoga.

When I went back to Grotowski in Opole in December 1963, my description of the kathakali showed that there existed a way of learning and developing the actor's skill and commitment through a technique rooted in a set of values and a vision of the theatre and the world. Grotowski had by that time already expressed his set of values and his vision evolving a corresponding technique which had been applied in several of his productions. In collaboration with his literary adviser, Ludwik Flaszen, he had fully developed his theory about the archetypical layer in a classical text, his belief that theatre should be theatrical, for example, autonomous from literature and that, by embodying a psychic and physical act, actors should have an impact on the psyche of the spectators.

On the technical level, no kathakali exercises were introduced in the Laboratory Theatre of the 13 Rows with the exception of a few eye exercises.

After a few months, these were eliminated. Personally, I think that kathakali had very little, if any, effect on Grotowski.

Question: What underlying principles related to training, presence, use of the body, rhythm of the work day, clothing worn during training, etc. did you and Grotowski adapt from kathakali?

I cannot think of any direct or indirect adaptation, especially in the case of Grotowski. As for me, my senses and my memory retained the radiance of kathakali, and no doubt it was a nourishing inspiration in my work with the actors of Odin Teatret. It was an illumination, just as was *The Mother* by Bertolt Brecht, which I saw at the Berliner Ensemble in 1961. I feel today that such illuminations helped me to find the path that belongs only to me.

Question: Would it be fair to say that kathakali served to justify the conception of a 'holy theatre', for example, to furnish a living example? You have written often of the effect on you of seeing the dawn training of the boys in Kerala. Did that experience inspire any changes in methodology or ethics at the Lab?

It must be clear by now that I was the one who was struck by the kathakali thunderbolt. It made me ask certain questions which have followed me ever since: 'How could it be possible that I, as a spectator, was interested, sometimes captivated and even moved watching actors whose conventions were unknown to me, of whom I didn't understand the language, where I was only partially able to follow the story they were telling and whose plot was not particularly meaningful for me?' These questions constituted the real impact of kathakali on me, and I came face to face with them when directing Odin Teatret, a group with actors of different nationalities and languages, performing regularly throughout Europe and Latin America for spectators with whom they had no common language. Later, I formulated these questions differently: do principles of a performative technique exist that work on a sensorial-affective level on the perception and mind of any spectator?

This was not Grotowski's concern, however. He had already expressed his conception of 'holy theatre' in 1962–63, both in Polish publications as well as during our conversations, which I published under the title 'The Theatre's New Testament' (Grotowski 1968: 27–53). The 'holy theatre' has nothing to do with a religious theatre, nor can it be associated at all with kathakali. I sincerely believe that kathakali, like other Asian theatre forms, never had any particular influence on Grotowski. He knew very well what sort of theatre he wanted to do. The roots of this theatre, from the point of view of the craft, stem from Stanislavski and the Russian experiences of the first two decades of the twentieth century.

Question: Zarrilli claims that the Cat Exercise derives from kathakali, yet it is described in Towards a Poor Theatre *in the exercises from 1959 to 1962. Is there any relationship between kathakali and the Cat? Or does the Cat derive from hatha yoga, primarily?*

The exercise called 'the Cat' existed in the training of Grotowski's actors from the very beginning of the training. As far as I remember, it was Ryszard Cieślak who had adapted it from a gymnastic exercise he knew. At that period, the 'Cat' was never associated with an exercise coming from yoga. Only much later I discovered that a similar exercise exists in martial arts. But I am sure that the Cat, as it was performed at the Laboratory Theatre, did not originate in the martial arts.

One has to remember that in the period 1962–64 not only was there no possibility of seeing martial arts or Asian theatre performances, but even books on such subjects were extremely rare and impossible to obtain, especially in socialist Poland.

Question: Did the guru–pupil relationship at the Kalamandalam influence Grotowski's more direct involvement in training after 1962 (as described in Towards a Poor Theatre)? *Did it influence your or Grotowski's approach to training at all?*

Grotowski never experienced the relationship guru–pupil in the Kalamandalam. His actors were adults who had completed theatre school or who had many years of experience in student theatre. All of them behaved among themselves as was normal in traditional theatre. The fact that Grotowski slowly implemented an artistic search, breaking the rules of what was accepted by the aesthetic and ideological criteria of socialist Poland created a special bond between him and those actors who remained at his side during the adventure of the Laboratory Theatre.

Finally I want to make a more general reflection on the subject you are dealing with in your paper. American scholars and theatre artists have been prominent in exposing themselves to Asian performative traditions, studying

► During a theatre congress in Warsaw in June 1963, Barba met Judy Jones, who worked as a secretary at the International Theatre Institute (UNESCO) in Paris. They decided to drive to India, where Barba wished to study theatre. They bought a ten-year-old Land Rover in London and left at the end of June with Judy at the wheel since Barba could not drive. Their 'passage to India' went through Yugoslavia, Bulgaria, Turkey, Iran [1] (the Land Rover in the Great Salt Desert, Dasht-e Kavir), and Pakistan [2] and ended in Kerala in the south of India. There they stopped for three weeks in Cheruthuruthy at the Kathakali Kalamandalam. On the way back, the car broke down, and they were stranded in Bombay. They could not repair the car since spare parts were not available. Nor could they leave or sell it since it was prohibited to import foreign cars into India and they had previously signed a document at the Indian Embassy in London agreeing to take the car out of the country. With hardly any money, they lived and slept in the streets. Every day they walked to the harbour to ask the captains of the newly arrived boats if they could take them and their broken-down car to Europe. After seven weeks, a German boat accepted to take them to Kuwait, where they managed to repair the car. At the border with Iraq, they were informed that a military coup had taken place. Army officers had burst into the Ba'ath Congress in Baghdad, seized the leaders of the left nationalist faction at gunpoint and had flown them abroad. In spite of the Kuwait border officers' advice, Barba and Judy crossed over and reached Baghdad, where the Ba'ath revolution was at its peak [3]. They managed to drive through the Iraqi–Syrian desert to Aleppo and from there through Turkey, Greece, Yugoslavia, Austria, Germany, and Belgium, arriving back in London in mid-December 1963. [4] Judy with a pilot at the American air base of Zahedan in Iran, where she and Barba were given welcome hospitality. After the journey to India, Judy and Barba were married. In 1964 Judy helped Barba to start Odin Teatret in Oslo and in 1967 she translated into English the texts of *Towards a Poor Theatre*, which presented for the first time Grotowski's vision and practice in book form as an issue of Odin Teatret's journal *Teatrets Teori og Teknikk*.

and spreading them, giving the possibility to the international theatre milieu to know their richness, variety, and quality. However, when American scholars analyse European artists, as in the case of Grotowski, they have a tendency to forget that on our continent the main stimulation and influence stem from a handful of theatre reformers who provoked a mutation in the way of thinking and practising theatre. These are, among others, Stanislavski, Craig, Copeau, Meyerhold, Osterwa, and Vakhtangov.

Whoever wants to understand Grotowski from a theatrical point of view has first to take into consideration three factors: Poland's tradition in the nineteenth century (Mickiewicz, Słowacki) as well as in the twentieth century with its unique experiments like those of Juliusz Osterwa, Iwo Gall, Szymon and Helena Syrkus, Andrzej and Zbigniew Pronaszko, Leon Schiller, Witkacy; second, the theatrical anomalous experiences – often called studios or laboratories – of the Russians or of art theatres like the one of Copeau; and third, the political context of socialist Poland in the 1950s and 1960s where censorship and compulsory political correctness were omnipresent forces with which artists clashed, obliging them to strive for freedom through a risky artistic practice and terminology that opposed the grey homogeneity of Marxist lore.

Wishing you all the best in your work. Friendly greetings.

Eugenio Barba

TTT TEATRETS TEORI OG TEKNIK

NORDISK TEATERTIDSSKRIFT NR. 15 - 1

Udgivet af ODIN TEATRETS FORLAG

II

Inspiration:
A theatrical Arcadia

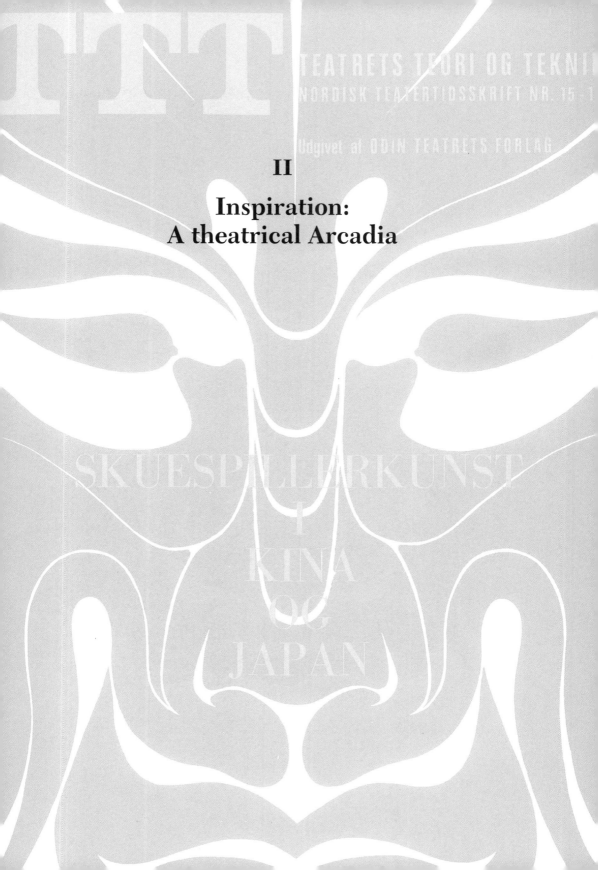

TTT

TEATRETS TEORI OG TEKNIKK

NORDISK TEATERTIDSSKRIFT NR. 15 - 1971

Udgivet af ODIN TEATRETS FORLAG

SKUESPILLERKUNST

I

KINA

OG

JAPAN

▶ 1971. Cover of *Teatrets Teori og Teknikk*, no. 15, a journal which was published by Odin Teatret three times a year. The whole issue was devoted to the actor's art in China and Japan.

The most disparate metals

During the growth of Odin Teatret's professional identity, Asian theatres are a primary factor that Barba mingles with the influence from Grotowski and with the experiences from the main directors of the Great Reform. Barba's inspiration stems from the technical excellence of the Asian actors, and he tries to attain this both in his actors' training and in the suggestive impact of their performances. In this early stage, Barba believes it possible to transplant the exercises and the formal composition of the Asian performers. He calls this 'the myth of technique'. But this text clearly shows a radical change in Barba's viewpoint and marks a turn in his approach to Asian theatres.

This is a fragment from 'Words or Presence', an article which was first published in 1972 (The Drama Review, 16 (1), pp. 47–54), and had a wide dissemination.

In spite of my experience in Asian theatre, especially kathakali, I haven't drawn directly from it. I tried to make my actors imagine this theatre of colours and exoticism, acrobatics and religiosity, by appealing to their subjectivity and imagination.

Kathakali, like all Asian theatre, cannot be copied or transplanted. It can only serve as a stimulus, a point of departure. The actors in traditional Asian theatre are immersed in a tradition that they must wholly respect. They are executing a role whose minutest detail has, as in a musical score, been developed by some master in a more or less distant past. As with a pianist or a ballet dancer, their evolution cannot be separated from virtuosity. In Western theatre, however, actors are, or should be, creators. Their clash with the text, through their own sensibility and historical experience, opens up a unique and personal universe to their spectators.

This essential difference also determines one's approach to the profession, the preparation, that which is usually called training. Even today, kathakali or kabuki actors begin their training at the same age as European children who wish to devote themselves to ballet. The psychological and physiological consequences are evident. It is meaningless to go to Japan or India and take exercises from kabuki or kathakali in order to adapt them passively to the European pedagogical tradition, hoping that our actors might become virtuosic like their Asian colleagues. Let me repeat, it is not the exercises in themselves that are decisive but one's personal attitude, that inner necessity that incites and motivates the choice of one's profession, justifying it on an emotional level and with a logic that will not allow itself to be trapped by words.

This attitude determines the creation of norms that become almost an artistic or ethical superego in the actor. Similar norms are also to be found in theatre forms based on a purely technical apprenticeship. Here the historical circumstances and the environmental conditions in which the theatre work evolves influence the development of these norms which are reflected in the technique. For example, the entire training of a young kabuki actor takes place in a rarefied atmosphere, without the possibility of contact with actors from other forms, such as noh or modern theatre, in a strictly professional hierarchy petrified in family dynasties whose mentality contrasts with the efficient industrial vocation of contemporary Japan.

The same applies to kathakali. While the kabuki actor is owned by a large impresario firm that places him in various theatres, the kathakali actor works on religious ground (the temple courtyard), dedicates his work and his performance to divinities, lives in a very modest way without the prospect of ever becoming a star like his Japanese colleague. These socio-historical circumstances, together with a particular professional tradition that still has great value and prestige for the young would-be actor, are decisive factors in the conception and elaboration of that expressiveness which is codified and so transformed into technique.

In the beginning of our activity, we too believed in the 'myth of technique', something that it was possible to acquire, to possess and that would have allowed the actors to master their own body and to become conscious of it. So, at this stage, we practised exercises to develop the dilation of the eyes in order to increase their expressiveness. They were exercises which I had seen in India while studying the training of kathakali actors. The expressiveness of the eyes is essential in kathakali, and the control of their musculature demands hours of training daily for many years. The different nuances each have a precise significance. The way of frowning, the direction of a glance, the degree of opening or closing the lids are codified by tradition and are in fact concepts and images which are immediately comprehensible to the 'expert' spectator. Such control in a European actor would only restrain the organic reactions of the face and transform it into a lifeless mask.

So, at the outset, as in a melting pot in which the most disparate metals fuse, I tried to blend together the most diverse influences, the impressions which for me had been the most fertile: Asian theatre, the experiments of the

► Bonn, 1980. Working demonstration by Peking Opera performers Tsao Chun-lin and Lin Chun-hui at the first ISTA session. It was images like these, which Barba had seen in books, that inspired his training with the Odin actors from the very beginning. In the Odin terminology, these exercises were called 'fights' and were improvisations based on an immediate action–reaction. Here are three types of 'fight': [1] with bare hands (Else Marie Laukvik and Torgeir Wethal, 1967); [2] with sticks (Torgeir Wethal and Iben Nagel Rasmussen, 1967); and [3] with props (Toni Cots and Silvia Ricciardelli, 1978).

Great Reform in European theatre, personal experience from my studies in Poland, and my collaboration with Grotowski. I wanted to adapt all this to my ideal of technical perfection even in the part of the artistic work which we called 'composition', a word that had arrived in our theatre through the Russian and French terminology and Grotowski's interpretation of it. I believed that composition was the capacity of the actor to create signs, to consciously mould the body into a deformation rich in suggestiveness and power of association: the body of the actor as a Rosetta stone and the spectator in the role of Champollion. The aim was to attain wittingly, by cold calculation, that which is warm and which obliges us to believe with all our senses. But I often felt this composition to be imposed, something external that functioned on a theatrical level but lacked the drilling force that could perforate the crust of all too obvious meanings. The composition might be rich, striking, throwing the actor into relief, yet it was like a veil that hid from me something which I felt inside myself but didn't have the courage to face, to reveal to myself or others.

In the first period of our theatre, all the actors did the same exercises together in a common collective rhythm. Then we realised that the rhythm varied for each individual – some have a faster vital rhythm, others a slower one – and we became aware of an organic rhythm. Its perpetual variation, however minute, revealed a wave of organic reactions that engaged the entire body. Training could only be individual.

Mei Lanfang

It is interesting to note Barba's strong interest in spreading information on the various Asian theatres, which, with the exception of kathakali, he knew only through the few available books at that time. This text is an example of his divulgative vocation. It was first published in Norwegian, in 1971, in Odin Teatret's journal ('Mei Lan-Fan', Teatrets Teori og Teknikk, 15, pp. 44). The whole issue was devoted to the art of the actor in China and Japan.

Mei Lanfang, 1864–1961, was born to an actors' family, who, for five generations, had specialised in female impersonators (*dan*). He lost his father as a child, a tragedy since it was the father who should have introduced his son to the craft. He began to train at the age of seven. Every morning, at five, he went to the walls of the town, using them as a resonating surface to strengthen his voice. Back in school he trained in acrobatic combat movements, manipulation of stage weapons and the *qiao* gait that reproduced on stage the particular way of walking of China's aristocratic women with their tightly bandaged feet. The rest of the day was spent in singing, singing, and singing, and learning by heart scores of roles.

At fifteen, Mei Lanfang was engaged by a troupe that performed in theatres, tea houses, wealthy people's homes, and merchants' clubs. Within a few years, his name was on the lips of every theatre fan. A tour to Shanghai in 1913 made his name known outside Peking.

The disbanding of the imperial family and Japan's expansionist politics threatening to annex huge parts of China had provoked a nationalistic upsurge among Chinese intellectuals. The Republic was proclaimed in 1912, but it soon degenerated into a military dictatorship fuelling discontent and active resistance aimed at radical change. The student movement from 1919 was the seed of China's historical development: the struggle against Japan, the civil war, and the Communist takeover.

Theatre reflected clearly these historical circumstances. The first Western performance – *Uncle Tom's Cabin*, an adaptation of Harriet Beecher Stowe's 1852 bestseller – was staged in 1907. After 1915, Henrik Ibsen and George Bernard Shaw were the most popular playwrights. Chinese artists and

► Holstebro, 1986. Mei Baojiu, son of Mei Lan-fang, enjoying the company of Barba's cat at his home.

►► The well-known actress Pei Yan-ling from Hebei Opera while she watches Judy Barba at her spinning wheel.

► Holstebro, 1986. Mei Lanfang in Peter Bysted's poster of the ISTA session on 'the female role'.

intellectuals who had been living abroad attacked the traditional Chinese theatre form, the Peking Opera, and were demanding plays with a 'message'.

Mei Lanfang was receptive to these new ideas and adapted them to his traditional stage form. He made radical stylistic modifications, changing the structure and the plots. This was accepted by his audience thanks to his artistic clout. Already in 1920 he dared to show a new opera in which a young girl refused to marry the man chosen for her by her parents, letting her emotional needs win over tradition.

Mei Lanfang was among the first to train female pupils and to let them perform in his company. Since 1916, he gathered a group of writers and composers who produced new plays while doing research into the various regional opera types. Mei Lanfang selected many elements from their results and adapted them to his own style, that of Peking Opera. Also in this undertaking he convinced the conservative audience to approve his innovations. Only by knowing the context of Chinese theatre of that period is it possible to acknowledge the significance of his process of renewal.

In 1919, Mei Lanfang toured in Japan where in Tokyo he met Utaemon V, the most known *onnagata* in kabuki. The latter's ten-year-old son saw Mei

Lanfang's performances. In 1956, during a new tour to Japan, Mei Lanfang met the child again, but as Utaemon VI, the greatest female impersonator following his father's death.

In 1930, the USA became acquainted with Mei Lanfang's outstanding acting. The honorary committee that welcomed him numbered, among others, Charlie Chaplin, Cecil B. DeMille, Douglas Fairbanks, and John Dewey. The tour lasted five months and visited New York, Chicago, San Francisco, and Los Angeles. Two universities bestowed on him an honorary doctorate.

In 1935, during a tour to the Soviet Union, Mei Lanfang met Stanislavski, Eisenstein, Meyerhold, Tairov, Tretyakov, and Brecht. It was said that Stanislavski and Meyerhold attended all his performances in Moscow.

Then came the war. In indignation over the Japanese occupation, Mei Lanfang retired from acting and grew a moustache: a sign of sorrow or protest for a *dan* actor. In spite of tempting offers from the Japanese, he refused to perform, and, during the whole war, he lived in penury. Only a few days after the liberation, however, he was back on the stage. The spectators could again admire the Great Sorcerer, as Eisenstein had called him. In spite of his fifty-one years and the long interruption, he fulfilled expectations.

In 1949, Nanking fell into the hands of the Communist Red Army. Mei Lanfang refused to flee to Taiwan. He said he had no reason to escape from his compatriots. The new regime began at once to implement a new cultural policy. In 1951, the China Dramatic Research Institute was opened, with Mei Lanfang as its leader. Most of his performances were recorded. His noble authoritative voice was heard when laying out a new pedagogy.

Three texts sum up his accomplishments: Adolphe C. Scott's book, *Mei Lan-fang: Leader of the Pear Garden 1959: 295–308*, and two articles, one by Stark Young, 'Mei Lan-fang' (1930), and the other by Sergei Eisenstein, 'Til Pærehavens troldmand' (The Sorcerer from the Pear Garden) (1971: 52–57), the last of which can be found in the same 1971 issue of *Teatrets Teori og Teknikk* (15, pp. 52–57).

Priem ostrannenija, Verfremdung, hana
Estranging devices according to
the Russian formalists, Brecht, and Zeami

In 1970, Barba gave a course on Asian theatres at the Institute of Dramaturgy at the University of Aarhus. This text is a short excerpt from it. Barba compares the procedure of priem ostrannenija *by the Russian formalists, Brecht's ideas on Verfremdung and Zeami's concept of* hana. *The correspondences that he finds between these three apparently different views concern the perception of the spectator. But these correspondences may be considered an archaeological trace of the principle of equivalence which Barba formulates a few years later in his Theatre Anthropology. The reader can follow this trace relating this text to the one entitled 'Ikebana', from 1992, included in this book (in Part III). In 'Ikebana', Barba brings his discourse on estrangement to a material technical level: that of the scenic body built as an equivalent of the daily body.*

The text was first published in 1971 in Norwegian in Odin Teatret's journal (Teatrets Teori og Teknikk, 15, pp. 46–47). A few years later, in 1980, it was published in Italian (Sipario, 406, pp. 68–70). It is one of Barba's lesser known texts.

During a visit by Mei Lanfang to Moscow in 1935, Bertolt Brecht attended a demonstration which the great Chinese actor, with no costumes or make-up, gave in his hotel room. This occurrence left an indelible imprint on Brecht and was the direct inspiration for his article 'Alienation Effects in Chinese Acting', written in 1936 (1964: 91–99). Here for the first time Brecht used the term *Verfremdung* (estrangement, alienation, distancing) which subsequently occupied a central place in his theoretical reflections.

In art, the idea and practice of using expedients and ploys that made the familiar strange has had a long life. In Europe, this estrangement process has been subject to examination and discussion especially in relation to poetry. The German Romantics spoke of breaking the illusion, resulting in a fresh perception and rediscovery of a known and immediately recognisable phenomenon. Shelley had affirmed that poetry enabled well-known things to appear as unknown. Schopenhauer thought that the purpose of art was to show objects familiar to our experience in a light which was at the same time clear and unusual.

It was the Russian formalist school that systematically analysed these problematics in the period 1918–25. The school, which was made up of young linguists and critics who later became famous – Roman Jakobson, Osip Brik, Boris Eikhenbaum, Victor Shklovski, Vladimir Propp, Yuri Tynyanov – had coined the expression *priem ostrannenija* – 'device for estranging'. By this expression, they designated the formal means and stratagems that an artist, wittingly or not, applied to infuse greater power into his work. Through the formal construction of the artistic opus, a result was reached that, estranging the content, produced the impression of being new and alien. This emphasis on the formal practices in the artistic process gave its name to the group: formalism.

As John Willett writes in his book *The Theatre of Bertolt Brecht: A Study from Eight Aspects* (1967) and in his edition of Brecht's writings (Brecht 1964), it was no coincidence that the *Verfremdung* concept, previously never employed by Brecht, entered into his terminology after his visit to Moscow. All innovative Russian artists in theatre, film, and literature – among others Meyerhold, Tairov, Eisenstein, Tretyakov, Mayakovski, and Pasternak – had drawn valuable inspiration from the formalists' research. During Stalinism, the formalist theories were condemned, and formalism was a frequent dangerous accusation to stain all those who did not follow the orthodoxy of socialist realism. Brecht and Piscator, as well as German agitprop theatres, were aware of Meyerhold's and Tairov's experiences with which they became acquainted during their tours to Berlin in the 1920s.

In his constructivist period, Meyerhold had created a training, the Biomechanics, which estranged the actors' gestures and movements through extreme theatricality. Referring to the stylised Oriental actors, Meyerhold sustained that the spectators should never forget they are in the theatre. Meyerhold's predilection for the German Romantics, especially Hoffman and Kleist, motivated a use of Romantic irony with its 'breakdown of the illusion' (*Durchbruch der Illusion*). In 1922, in *Le Cocu magnifique* by Fernand Crommelynck, Meyerhold abolished the curtain and the backdrops and destroyed the illusion-evoking stage frame, turning it into a functional acting machine by means of constructivist structures.

In 1925, in *The Forest* by Ostrovski, he made use of 'songs' that disrupted the action's continuity, while in *D.E.* by Ehrenburg, from the same year, he projected a text on several screens simultaneously commenting on the stage action.

It is probable that conversing with his friend, playwright Sergei Tretyakov and other 'formalist' colleagues in Moscow, Brecht became increasingly aware of the scope of the *priem ostrannenija*, whose direct translation in German is *Verfremdung*. This way of thinking and its application in theatre became even more evident after Mei Lanfang's demonstration. In this way, Brecht described the latter's way of acting:

> The Chinese performer is not in a trance. He can be interrupted at any moment. He won't have to 'come round'. After an interruption he will go on with his exposition from that point. We are not disturbing him at the 'mystic moment of creation'; when he steps onto the stage before us the process of creation is already over. He does not mind if the setting is changed around him as he plays. Busy hands quite openly pass him what he needs for his performance. When Mei Lan-fang was playing a death scene a spectator sitting next to me exclaimed with astonishment at one of his gestures. One or two people sitting in front of us turned round indignantly and sshhh'd. They behaved as if they were present at the real death of a real girl. Possibly their attitude would have been all right for a European production, but for Chinese it was unspeakably ridiculous. In their case the A-effect had misfired.
>
> (Brecht 1964: 95)

In the same article, Brecht gives this definition of *Verfremdung*, 'To play in such a way that the audience was hindered from simply identifying itself with the characters in the play. Acceptance or rejection of their actions and utterances was meant to take place on a conscious plane, instead of, as hitherto, in the audience's subconscious' (1964: 91).

Brecht warns us that the Chinese actors' *Verfremdung* is a primitive state of science taken from rituals of magic. Their depiction of human passions is schematic, and their vision of society static and faulty. These elements must be rejected in a realistic revolutionary theatre. It is beneficial to study them and subsequently utilise their estranging devices for social purposes.

We must not forget, however, that the process of estranging the actor's art had been dealt with and codified at the beginning of the fourteenth century. This happened in Japan, where Zeami, in his writings on noh theatre, had analysed in depth the concept of *hana*, the actor's 'flower'.

Hana is that set of abilities and technical skills which are not natural in an actor but are acquired through years of rigorous training. A clever deployment of *hana* cannot avoid striking the spectators since the enacted actions, even if recognisable, will appear unfamiliar. This is one of Zeami's several definitions of *hana*: 'It is merely the unusual as perceived by the spectator' (Zeami 1960: 109; my translation).

But the spectator's reaction to the actor's atypical gesture or movement must not be caused by an eccentric behaviour. It must have a logic of its own and be anchored in the tradition. Zeami gives the example of the old man's character when played by actors without *hana*: they bend their knees and drag their feet while their hands tremble.

> But an elderly man wants to hide his age and his movements strive to be young and vital. The actor must be aware of this and represent an old man by revealing age and weakened reflexes through a slightly delayed action in relation to the beat of the drums accompanying his movements.
>
> (Zeami 1960: 106; my translation)

This is *hana*: that which makes an action unfamiliar and peculiar, enabling the actor to maintain his attraction's power over the spectators.

It is interesting to note that Zeami emphasises this estranging process resulting from a dialectical analysis of human behaviour with the aim of achieving an emotional impact on the spectator. On the contrary, Brecht wanted to use the same procedure in order to let the spectator rationally appraise the actors' actions.

The Book of Dances

This short text, written in 1974, introduces Odin Teatret's performance The Book of Dances. *Working with his actors, Barba realised that singing and dance-like movements have an emotional impact on the spectators of any social class and culture. In their training, Odin actors have achieved a physical and vocal skill that summons up the vibrance of dance and the musicality of singing. It is through this technique that their performances have imposed themselves internationally. The dramaturgy of* The Book of Dances *is unusual for the period. It doesn't tell a story but interlaces dynamic sequences selected from the training exercises with impromptu songs and music played by the actors themselves. Barba gives a historical justification for his actors' way of working, recalling the example of the 'total' Asian actors: they know how to sing, dance, and interpret a text. He coins the term 'actor who dances' that will become a leitmotif in his writings.*

This text was first published in The Floating Islands *(Barba 1979: 195) and also in the French (1982), Greek (1982), Spanish (1983) and Catalan (1983) versions. Later translations of the book don't include it.*

Dance has always characterised the actor's expression within the Western tradition and that of other cultures.

In Japanese noh and kabuki, in the many types of Balinese performance, in Thai khon, and in Indian kathakali, the actor is above all a dancer. In Europe, until the Renaissance in the sixteenth century, when text became pre-eminent, dance was the actor's main expression. Buffoons, jesters, fools, mountebanks, jugglers, commedia dell'arte performers – all communicated through patterns of movement whose tension, composition, and energy belonged to the world of dance.

Dance – the body's emotional expression – is the fundamental element in popular culture which does not manifest itself with written words but through a relationship based on physical presence: the dancer, the singer, the storyteller. Dance unites the community, through it the bodies acquire life and turn into a 'book' that conjures up history and norms.

The Book of Dances is a performance about the elementary dramas that distinguish the emotional universe of human beings: struggle and violence –

both of man and nature – hopefulness and anguish, irony and a plunge into the sphere of dreams and personal fantasies.

Aware of this historical legacy, Odin Teatret has attempted to rediscover the actor who dances, shaped by the conditions of our time.

A dreamed and reinvented Arcadia

In this text, Barba sums up the significance Asian theatres had for him from the foundation of Odin Teatret (1964) until the creation of ISTA, the International School of Theatre Anthropology (1979).

In a first phase, up to 1972, this 'theatrical Arcadia', imagined above all through books, was a strong stimulus to build Odin Teatret's professional know-how and identity. This stimulus didn't spring from a religious, cultural or mythical background. It was the emulation of the Asian actors' technical excellence and the allure of their performances that nourished the difference of the Odin. At that time, the Asian theatres didn't form part of the cartography of any European theatre. They were present only in the books of a few scholars.

After 1972, Barba had a direct knowledge of Asian theatres through the seminars he organised in Holstebro on Japanese theatre (1972), Balinese and Javanese theatre (1974), and Indian theatre (1977). These seminars represented an anomaly in the panorama of European theatre and emphasised the difference of the Odin. However, they represented a significant means for increasing Barba's technical competence.

This text stems from an interview with Ian Watson (Barba and Watson 2002: 234–62). Later, Barba turned his answers into an article, 'The Conquest of Difference', from which we publish here an excerpt. The article was first published in 2005 in Italian ('La conquista della differenza', Teatro e storia, 26, pp. 271–90).

We can always make use of a multicultural perspective to observe theatrical facts, but the relevance of such a perspective must be demonstrated.

Of course one can say that Odin Teatret is intercultural or multicultural. It was created in Oslo by Norwegian would-be actors whose Italian-born director had received his professional imprint in Poland. On emigrating to Denmark, Odin Teatret called itself Scandinavian Theatre Laboratory and, in addition to its original Norwegian members, took in Danes, Swedes, and Finns who did not always understand each other's language. Later on Italians, French, English, Spaniards, Germans, North and South Americans, Japanese, and Sri Lankans joined too. We travel and stay for long periods in many countries and have established a tight network of initiatives and collaboration with performers and scholars from many nations. Our venues in Holstebro are a caravanserai that host individuals and groups from all over the world.

I did not search for all these people, cultures, traditions, for the images I saw and the performances I attended in order to enrich my personality. My reason was another: they should help me to escape. From where? From my culture of origin, from the theatre tradition I had grown up in, from the small tradition and results I myself had created.

As a cognitive instrument or an analysing tool, the word 'intercultural' does not help to throw any light on, interpret or explain the specific professional identity of the Odin Teatret and its people, the convictions that imbue their work or the inner dynamics that enabled the same core of people to remain together artistically active for decades. Odin Teatret's history and commitment, which makes it unique, unrepeatable, and at the same time capable to withstand new trends and generation changes, have to do only with our working ethos. This is what makes us a micro-culture, a small world apart. It has nothing to do with an accidental coming together of a 'foreign legion' of actors, a gathering of artistic temperaments with different passports.

Artistically speaking, the intercultural factors are not determining. More important are the rigour of the chosen performative genre, the director's aesthetic vision and specific personality, and the 'superstitions' or emotional forces that drive the single artists. In a theatre company, the biographical-historical background of the performers – usually called cultural identity – can be very different, even poles apart. The agglutinating factor is the reciprocal agreement to submit to a set of technical principles and to the aesthetical, political or other values that impregnate these principles. Japanese can be brilliant ballet dancers, and North Americans can become valued noh or kyogen performers. Nobody would call the Danish Royal Ballet intercultural, in spite of its French Bournonville technique and the many foreign dancers who are part of it. Danish or Argentinean actors in Tadashi Suzuki's or Bob Wilson's productions are highly creative in accordance with the personal artistic universe of these outstanding directors.

I often say that my roots are in the sky. It sounds like a rhetorical image. Yet it conceals the reality of a turbulent life and the choice of an interminable mutation which is not an end in itself but the determined attempt to refuse the tendency to set root. Perhaps my theatre's most significant relationships, encounters, and decisions could be re-recounted in the light of this restless spirit of adventure.

When somebody looks at our past, or when we ourselves let our memories flow, we seem to forget our many zigzags, deviations, and senseless detours. These were not conscious 'searches' for anything in particular, merely symptoms of uneasiness, disquiet, desire for undertaking blended with an irresistible presentiment that luck was waiting for me elsewhere. Many of my sudden apparently thoughtless decisions were the result of a fortuitous meeting with a woman, of sympathy or antipathy towards a man. Today I know that it was not just a wish to learn, to risk, to face unexpected situations and outstanding personalities. A burning red thread has guided me in my condition of emigrant – of perpetual foreigner – in this meandering filled with confrontations, escapes, and longings: the need to protect my dignity and my chosen condition of not-belonging. Looking back now, I clearly discern the ultimate goal: theatre as an island of difference which has to be conquered.

In my withdrawal from my Italian culture, for many years I immersed myself in books about Hinduism and Buddhism. My Asia consisted of a few geographical names inhabited by hermits, philosophers, and wandering ascetics: the populous Bengali outskirts of Dakshineswar and Ramakrishna's temple and home, the highlands of northern India where Nagarjuna lived, the Tibetan plateau where Marpa and Milarepa dispelled their magic powers, the route through China followed by Bodhidharma, the steppe of the Mongolian shamans. This Asia became a region of my Country of Speed.

In the history of Odin Teatret, our first years as autodidacts were an essential factor together with the need to justify our choice of doing theatre and the search for sources of learning in a milieu which was indifferent towards us. More than ideas or theories, constraints led towards unsuspected solutions.

One such constraint – fundamental in the shaping of the Odin's technical and emotional identity – was the emigration from Norway to Denmark. Odin's Norwegian actors had difficulty in making themselves understood by Danish spectators at our new home in Holstebro. For us it was a question of life and death to create performances where the dramaturgy was not based mainly on the interpretation of a text and the understanding of its words, but on proximity and intimacy, on sensual, sensorial, vocal, and dynamic ensnaring, perceptible actions or 'attractions' as Eisenstein would have said.

The term 'intercultural' was unheard of in the late 1950s when my interest in theatre was aroused. Almost nobody cared about a meeting between the European and the Asian theatre cultures. There was no first-hand knowledge of performances from other continents. The striking productions of Bertolt Brecht's Berliner Ensemble, Marcel Marceau's pantomimes, which amazed huge audiences with their textless, physical exploits, and avant-garde texts by such writers as Ionesco, Beckett, Adamov, and Mrożek were the cause of considerable ferment in Europe.

Yet books recorded the interest of Meyerhold, Eisenstein, Dullin, Artaud or Brecht in traditional Asian forms. But with the exception of Paul Claudel, who had lived in China and Japan, the above mentioned artists had not seen Asian performers on their home ground, only on tour within the framework of European stages and audiences.

As an autodidact I was obsessed with the acquisition of professional efficacy. In spite of my lack of experience, I had to teach my would-be actors. I began with the core of exercises which I had seen Grotowski's actors doing during my stay in Opole. Some of my young actors had followed – as amateurs – courses in pantomime or ballet, so they became 'instructors' in these fields, although they were just beginners. Rather than a mixed or syncretic theatre culture, it looked more like a mish-mash. How could we extricate a genuine knowledge out of this mish-mash?

I relied on books which could give concrete examples and advice. Texts by Stanislavski, Dullin, and Vakhtangov were extremely useful. We studied the photos from the European Reformers' pedagogical work and productions and tried to reconstruct their actors' postures as exercises. I did the same with pictures from kabuki and the Peking Opera. Out of a static image, the Odin actors and I built up a dynamic structure, an 'exercise' which we integrated in our training. This reconstruction had very little to do with real Japanese and Chinese acting technique, yet this operation had a profoundly stimulating and creative impact on all of us. This applied also to records by different singers, from Italian opera to Louis Armstrong, from Gregorian chants to the Peruvian Yma Súmac, from Indian raga improvisations to the hunting songs of the Pygmies, from bunraku *joruri* recitation to Sicilian puppet storytellers. We repeated these intonations, vocal asperities, and modulations, in an effort to uncover and revitalise the multiple possibilities and nuances of the human voice which we possess at birth and then lose when growing up in a specific language and culture. Thus we discovered our voice.

During my first years, the theatres of Asia had for me the power of a mirage, and I ran after them to break out of my confines. They were a sort of dreamed Arcadia, a half-rediscovered, half-reinvented example, a dynamic idea that encouraged me to emancipate myself from the restraint of autodidactism. I imagined mighty heroines and graceful warriors, wild fantasy animals, trembling boats on still blue waters, silent mountain peaks … all embodied by the art of the same actor. Excellence of craftsmanship was the model which I wanted my actors to emulate. I was not looking for 'authenticity' in a mythical Orient. Theatre for me was commitment towards the polis, the possibility to take a stand and follow the way of refusal. Traditional Asian theatres are not the most evident models of social and political engagement.

In 1972, eight years after Odin Teatret's beginning, we experienced Japanese theatre, not only through performances of its different styles but also through the working demonstrations of such artists as Sojuro Sawamura, Mannojo Nomura, Hisao and Hideo Kanze. The invaluable help of the American professor Frank Hoff allowed us to organise a seminar in Holstebro which seemed impossible at that time, bringing together under the same roof noh, kyogen, kabuki, and Shuji Terayama's contemporary actors.

A couple of years later, Odin Teatret organised a seminar on Javanese and Balinese theatre and dance. Here I met I Made Pasek Tempo, the Balinese master, who, in 1980, was among the founders of ISTA and collaborated with me until his death in 1991. Finally, in 1976, during another Odin seminar on Indian dance and theatre, I met a young odissi dancer, Sanjukta Panigrahi, and her husband Raghunath. It was a reunion with a sister: clever, beautiful, strong and sensitive, courageous and generous. I admired and loved her deeply. I recall the many questions we asked each other, the long conversations at night when everybody else was asleep, her detailed yet suggestive demonstrations and very personal explanations. Sanjukta was not only one of the founders of ISTA, she was its undeniable queen. For me, the immense effort and the painstaking perseverance and struggle to collect funds for an ISTA session were compensated by the expectation of meeting again Pasek Tempo, Katsuko Azuma, Kanichi Hanayagi, Raghunath. But most of all Sanjukta. I have never been able to accept the injustice of her early death.

India, Japan, Bali, China – their culture and traditions belong to faraway countries. But the people who, with the years, have become my working companions belong to my same country. They have brought their knowledge and their demands, stirred my curiosity, shared my questions, helped us from the Odin to shatter the delicate and precious patterns we had built.

I am aware that the Odin Teatret's history may appear from the outside as a project to bring together various theatre cultures, to set them one over the other, to compare them, to harvest the fruits of their complementarities. But when I recall Sanjukta and other artists, I feel a bond of deep respect, admiration, even love because of their knowledge, rigour, and loyalty towards an artistic discipline which is a profession of ethos. They mingle together with other members from my professional family – European, North and South American, as well as my actors.

Today, thinking back on my youthful dreams about Asia, I know why they were essential to me. The suggestive universe of its theatres was like a rope that made me climb out of the obvious Western professional world – to which I didn't want to adhere – as well as out of the rules which I had invented and was too apprehensive to set aside. Odin Teatret started unwillingly as 'different' because we were young, inexperienced, and born at the margins of the main theatre tradition. Then we chose to be 'different' by vocation.

This is the reason why, for me, theatre cannot be limited just to the performance. It must always find new ways to nurture its subversion. The craft provides the possibility for a particular rebellion that hinders inherited ideas and habits, as well as our personal convictions, from solidifying into a prison.

From the very first days of my activity as a teacher and director, I asked myself two questions. First, why did Stanislavski and Meyerhold invent the exercises to prepare an actor? My experience showed that an actor could be excellent in the exercises without reaching the same quality during the rehearsals and the performance. There was no automatic connection between the results in the training and the creative results. Why then do the exercises?

The second question came about after I saw kathakali in India in 1963. I knew nothing of this theatre form since there were no books or information about it. I did not understand the language, nor was I familiar with its code of acting. I knew little of the enacted stories and was confused by the audience's laid-back behaviour. However, in certain parts of the performance, one particular actor was capable of captivating my attention, bewitching my senses and binding me to each of his actions. How did he achieve this? What forces or factors were active in our interaction, based only on sensorial stimulation? Was it a matter of talent, of divine grace or individual temperature? Or had technical skill something to do with it? And in which way?

These two questions, or enigmas, became obsessions that still haunt me. They have determined the two poles of interest in my professional life: on one hand the transmission of experience, of the learning process of tacit knowledge and of the work on oneself; on the other, Theatre Anthropology, which investigates the performers' technical principles at the basis of an efficient relationship with the spectator. These two questions have influenced most of my decisions. They are at the origin of ISTA, the International School of Theatre Anthropology, of the choice of people with whom I want to work, and of my search and research.

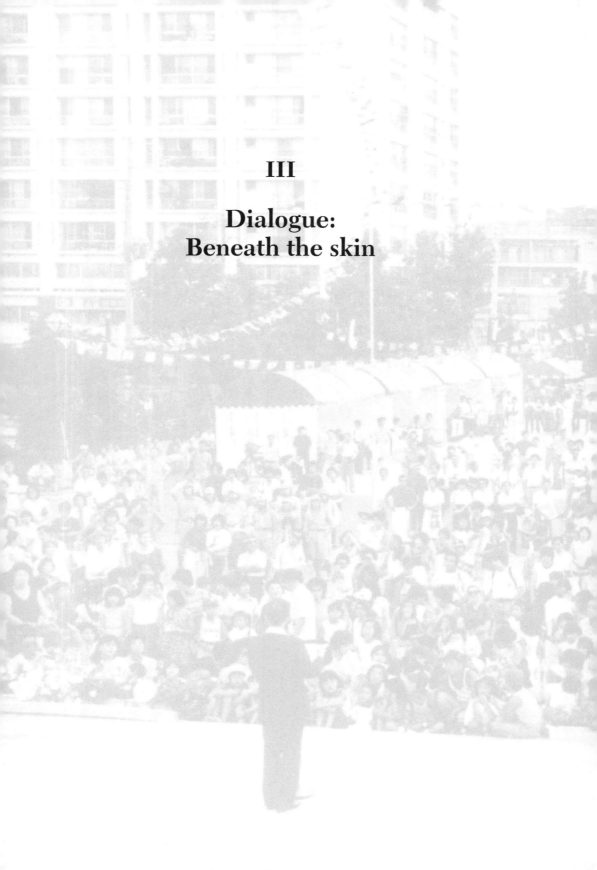

III

Dialogue:
Beneath the skin

► Nagoya (Japan), 1980. Eugenio Barba addressing the spectators before an Odin Teatret performance.

The museum of the theatre

This text marks a development in Barba's way of relating to the various Asian theatre forms. He explains for the first time that the Asian actors' scenic presence is the consequence of a transition from their daily body culture to the other body culture of the stage. Later, Barba will call it 'extra-daily behaviour'. The Asian theatres are no longer a distant reality with which to measure oneself and gain inspiration. They are a material reality which may be studied separately from their original context. Thus, they can be compared to other acting styles and genres in order to detect the laws underlying the transition to the body culture of the stage. Barba speaks of two of these laws (which he will later define as 'principles'): alteration of balance and opposition. 'The museum of the theatre' has a historical value in so far as it is the first text in which Barba applies the perspective that will steer his future research in the field of Theatre Anthropology.

The text was written in September 1979 to introduce Odin Teatret's The Museum of the Theatre. *This included three work demonstrations: one by Toni Cots on Balinese theatre, another by Tom Fjordefalk on kathakali, and the third by Iben Nagel Rasmussen on her Odin training entitled* Moon and Darkness. *In his introduction, Barba presented each of these demonstrations. The text is published here for the first time. It doesn't, however, contain the section on* Moon and Darkness *since it does not fall within the subject of Asian theatre. Part of the introduction to Tom Fjordefalk's work demonstration on kathakali stems from Barba's text 'Another Culture of the Body', written in 1978 and published by Nicola Savarese in his book* Il teatro aldilà del mare *(The Theatre Beyond the Sea) (1980: 27–30). The rest of the text is published here for the first time.*

A museum induces respect and a sort of reverence, but it can also guide us towards a new knowledge.

A museum always implies the detachment of an artefact from its environment, severing it from the functions it originally fulfilled. A crucifix hanging in a certain church, for example, becomes a masterpiece representative of the Siena school of painting; a glass is no longer a recipient for holding liquids for daily or ritual purposes but is labelled as a specimen of Minoan culture or Chinese Tang Dynasty art; masks of animals and divinities are no longer expressions of a community's obsessions for its physical or spiritual survival but turn into sculptures appreciated according to aesthetic categories.

In our time, a museum is a setting in which the objects exhibited become artistic fetishes. From this perspective, theatre is always a museum.

The fact of removing an object from its context can result in a fetishistic effect, but it may also trigger a distancing process and one of acquiring a new perception and insight.

The theatre museum which you are going to watch implies a distancing attitude: here the actor presents scenes from different cultures' performances with the perspective of unearthing how physiological processes are transformed into communicative stage presence. The display of a scenic technique, which is a particular way of using the body, discloses how this technique is related to the body culture characterising a specific society. This theatre museum lays bare the ways different cultures have developed theatre and dance techniques starting out from their own body culture and submitting it to a few laws that make the actor/dancer's body achieve a stage presence.

The rooms of this theatre museum don't exhibit artistic specimens but expose the living process of the actor/dancer at work. You are confronted not with the art of theatre but with its biology.

The Balinese Room: Puputan
(a work demonstration by Toni Cots)

Among the more than 4000 islands of the Indonesian archipelago, Bali is an exception. Its 2 million inhabitants have preserved the Hindu religion while, since the fifteenth century, all the other islands have absorbed the belief of their Muslim invaders.

Still today it is amazing to watch in Bali the deep bond between daily life and its numerous ceremonies and performances. It is as if the concept of Art, understood in the West as the unusual result of a creative personality, is absent in this culture. From an early age, children are taught to carve wood, to perform traditional dances or to play in the gamelan, the Balinese percussion orchestra.

This culture, although fearing the divinities' excesses, is not afraid of human action, even at its most extreme. Trance, an alteration of consciousness, is accepted and regulated by religious and cultural norms within the community's psychic balance.

Spectacular situations bring together the community to confirm the mutual bonds between individuals as well as between humans and divinities, arousing in us a fascination and thoughts of a paradise lost for ever: a theatre with a deeper meaning. But we are aware that to extract a performance from its

► 1979. Two situations from *Puputan*, a work demonstration by Toni Cots without and with costume.

local context and to present it to foreign spectators is like studying an organ amputated from the organism that keeps it alive and that it keeps alive.

In 1905, the Dutch occupied Bali. The Rajas from the southern part of the island refused to surrender. Surrounded by their wives and courtiers, lavishly dressed in their most magnificent clothes and royal ornaments, accompanied by their guards with silver spears and daggers embossed with precious stones, the Rajas advanced with dancing steps towards the Dutch soldiers. In front of these grotesque opponents, so full of dignity, the Dutch soldiers hesitated to shoot. The officers, pointing their guns at their own soldiers, convinced them. So the first row of Balinese aristocrats and warriors fell, together with their Rajas. The following row moved forward over the corpses with the same dancing steps, to the rhythm of cymbals and drums. The battle ended when the last member of the courts was killed. In the annals of Balinese history, this episode is known as *puputan* ('fight to the last man').

When today in Bali we attend a performance of Barong or *Ramayana* in a luxury tourist hotel or in a *banjar* – the village meeting place – we wonder whether we are witnessing a new *puputan*, a culture that slowly moves away from the ground in which it flourished towards the clicks of the cameras that petrify it in exotic images.

In this room of our theatre museum, the Western actor performing the Balinese dances seems to participate in the *puputan* of cultures. But it could also be said that this actor tries to graft onto his own organism the external forms of a foreign wisdom and of the life of another body, as if he wanted to preserve them while fighting to discover their inner secrets.

The scenes of this demonstration stem from baris, a warrior dance, and from topeng, the mask performance characterised by improvisation and dialogue with the spectators, mixing both the daily Balinese language and the ancient religious Kawi which today is incomprehensible.

The Kathakali Room: The Liberation of Puthana
(a work demonstration by Tom Fjordefalk)

Kabuki, noh, kathakali, tjalonarang, Peking Opera, etc., should be defined as dance. Nothing, however, forbids us for our convenience to call them theatre. Thanks to this double value, the Oriental theatre-dance has constituted an important point of reference both for the development of modern dance (Vaslav Nijinski, Ted Shawn, Ruth Saint-Denis, Glen Tetley, Frederick Ashton, Maurice Béjart) and for the mutation of Western theatre (Stanislavski, Meyerhold, Copeau, Artaud, Brecht, Grotowski).

The understanding of a theatre from another culture derives not only from the identification of its conventions and aesthetic criteria. From an acting point of view, it is fundamental to become aware of the type of logic underlying the actors' body culture on stage, their way of moving in space, their transformation of weight into energy and into a particular physical presence. This premise is necessary when we approach kathakali.

Kathakali, which literally means 'story play', started to develop about 300 years ago in Kerala, in the south of India. It recounts episodes from the two great Indian epics, the *Mahabharata* and the *Ramayana*. All roles, both male and female, are performed by men.

The kathakali actor enacts mythical stories of war, love, malevolent and divine exploits through a varied and complex range of movements established by tradition. This somatic language has its own vocabulary, grammar and syntax, precise facial expressions, leg and feet positions, and hand gestures (mudras) whose equivalent, in the Western culture, would be the deaf-mute language.

Two drummers accompany two vocalists who sing the story, which is not understood by the spectators since it is in Sanskrit. The actor enacts the plot with the totality of his physical presence, in a structured dynamic language of energy and vigour, and at the same time with a sort of distance to the sung story that accompanies him.

Even if most spectators don't know the actor's gesture language and are unable to understand the word corresponding to the movement, they are moved at a sensorial level by his power of expression. A logic is irradiated by the assimilated stage body culture, and it follows clear-cut rules. For example, the actor's basic stance with his weight on the outer edge of the feet. In order to preserve balance, he opens the knees wide while holding the spine erect. Even in stillness, this position provokes a series of organic tensions so that the whole body's energy is ready to shape physical actions-words.

Another characteristic is the actor's tendency to make wide circular movements with the hands and the torso, constantly modelling the energy into a physical language.

It is not just a question of technique or aesthetic conventions. In kathakali, like in all other traditional Oriental theatres, we can detect a knowledge about and a respect for biological laws, for the complementarity of 'life' itself, where any manifestation is rooted in opposition: on the one hand, gravity pulls our weight towards the ground; on the other, our spine keeps us erect, turning our weight into energy perceivable on the outside.

Watching kathakali is not only an opportunity to appreciate and become acquainted with an acting technique. It allows us to compare our Western stage body culture with one from another tradition. This comparative process lets us discover our limits and, above all, the inability to be present on stage with all our energy, especially while immobile, which is also a sign of life.

Beneath the skin

In this key text from 1992, Barba clarifies the radical change in his approach to Asian theatre. The author evokes the decisive situations that put him on the track of the pre-expressive level and the principles of Theatre Anthropology.

This is an excerpt from Chapter 1 of The Paper Canoe: A Guide to Theatre Anthropology *(Barba 1995: 5–7). The book was published for the first time in Spanish in 1992.*

After the founding of Odin Teatret in 1964, my work frequently took me in the 1970s to Asia, especially to Bali, Taiwan, and Japan. I witnessed much theatre and dance. For a spectator from the West, there is nothing more suggestive than a traditional Asian performance seen in its context, often in the open tropical air, with a large and reactive audience, with a constant musical accompaniment that captivates the nervous system, with sumptuous costumes that delight the eye, and with performers who embody the unity of actor–dancer–singer–storyteller.

At the same time, there is nothing more monotonous, lacking action and development, than the seemingly interminable recitations of text, which the performers speak or sing in their (to us) unknown languages, melodiously yet implacably repetitive.

In these monotonous moments, my attention developed a tactic to avoid giving up on the performance. I attempted to concentrate tenaciously on and follow just one detail of a performer: the fingers of one hand, a foot, a shoulder, an eye. This tactic against monotony made me aware of a strange coincidence: Asian performers performed with their knees bent, exactly like the Odin Teatret actors.

In fact, at Odin Teatret, after some years of training, the actors tend to assume a position in which the knees, very slightly bent, contain the *sats*, the impulse towards an action which is as yet unknown and which can go in any direction: to jump or crouch, step back or to one side, to lift a weight. The *sats* is the basic posture found in sports – in tennis, badminton, boxing, fencing – when you need to be ready to react.

► The bent knees of Iben Nagel Rasmussen (1972) and Roberta Carreri (1974) during their training.

►► Iben Nagel Rasmussen and Toni Cots learning baris from Tutur in Ubud, Bali (1978).

My familiarity with my actors' *sats*, a characteristic common to their individual techniques, helped me see beyond the opulence of the Asian performers' costumes and seductive stylisation and to notice the bent knees. This was how one of the first principles of Theatre Anthropology, the change of balance, was revealed to me.

Just as the Odin Teatret actors' *sats* made me see the bent knees of the Asian performers, their stubbornness provided the opportunity for new conjecture and speculation, this time far from Asia.

In 1978, I asked my actors to leave the theatre for three months. The purpose was to let them search for new stimuli that might help them shatter the crystallisation of behaviour that tends to happen in every individual or group. They dispersed in all directions: to Bali, India, Brazil, Haiti, and Struer, a small town about fifteen kilometres from Holstebro. The pair who had gone to Struer to a school of ballroom dancing learned the tango, Viennese waltz, foxtrot, and quickstep. Those who had gone to Bali studied baris and legong; the one who had been in India, kathakali; the two who had visited Brazil, capoeira and the dances of the Orixás from Candomblé. They had all stubbornly insisted on doing what, in my view, ought absolutely to be avoided: they had learned codified styles – that is, the results of other cultures' and people's techniques.

Bewildered and sceptical, I watched during our daily training these flashes of exotic skills, hurriedly acquired. I began to notice that when my actors did a Balinese dance, they put on another skeleton/skin that conditioned their way of standing, moving, and becoming expressive. Then they would step out of it and return to the skeleton/skin of the Odin actor. And yet, in the passage from one skeleton/skin to another, which completely transformed them, they applied similar principles. The application of these same principles resulted in the same actor assuming totally different body postures and dynamics.

What was later to develop into Theatre Anthropology was gradually defining itself before my eyes and in my mind as I observed my actors' ability to assume a particular skeleton/skin – that is, a particular scenic behaviour, a particular use of the body, a specific technique – and then to remove it. This 'putting on' and 'taking off', this change from a daily body technique to an extra-daily body technique and from a personal technique to a formalised Asian, Latin American or European technique, forced me to ask myself a series of questions that led me into new territory.

In order to know more, to deepen and verify the practicability of these common principles, I had to study stage traditions far removed from my own.

Classical ballet and mime, the two Western scenic forms which I could have analysed, were too close to me and would not have helped me establish the transcultural aspects of recurring principles.

In 1979, I founded ISTA, the International School of Theatre Anthropology. Its first session was held in Bonn and lasted a month. The teachers were performers from Bali, China, Japan, and India together with their musicians. The work and the research confirmed the existence of principles that, on the pre-expressive level, determine scenic presence, the body-in-life able to make perceptible that which is invisible: the intention. I realised that the artificiality of the forms of theatre and dance in which one passes from the 'spontaneity' of everyday behaviour to 'stylisation' is the prerequisite for a new surge of energy in the actor, resulting from the collision of an effort with a resistance. In the Bonn session of ISTA in 1980, I found the same principles among Asian performers that I had seen at work in Odin Teatret actors.

It is sometimes said that I am an expert on Asian theatre, that I am influenced by it, that I have adapted its techniques and procedures to my practice. Behind these assertions lies the opposite. It has been through knowledge of the work of Western performers – the Odin Teatret actors – that I have been able to see transcultural principles beyond the technical and the stylistic results of specific traditions.

Knowing with the mind
and understanding with the body

This description of the research Barba was conducting in the early 1980s shows his new approach to Asian theatres. Their performers have played an important role in formulating the first two principles in his Theatre Anthropology: the principle of opposition and that of alteration of balance. Moreover, the text furnishes interesting information on Barba's way of proceeding in his field work with Asian actors.

The text is the transcription of a lecture in Palermo in May 1980 during the international symposium 'Theatre Research and Cultural Diversity'. Barba gave this lecture again with variations in Warsaw in the same month of May 1980. He reworked the text of this second lecture and published it in Polish, in 1981, with the title 'Antropologia teatru: pierwsze hipotezy' (Theatre Anthropology: First Hypotheses) (Dialog, 1, pp. 94–100). It became a well-known text within Barba's bibliography with this definitive title and was published in the various translations of his book Beyond the Floating Islands *(1986: 114–22). The original lecture held in Palermo was published in Italian, in 1983, with the title 'Sapere e comprendere' (Knowing and Understanding) in* Quaderni del laboratorio teatrale universitario, *edited by B. Mazzone (Palermo: Palermo University Press, 1983, pp. 24–34).*

The text of the original Palermo lecture and that of the definitive article based on the Warsaw one are different not so much in their content as in their style, tone, and detail. I have omitted the Warsaw text and have chosen the Palermo one since the latter clearly shows Barba's particular way of interacting with Asian actors.

It is difficult for me today to express my reactions on listening yesterday to Ludwik Flaszen.[8] I could say it was emotion. I heard again, in this room, the voice of one of my masters. Together with Jerzy Grotowski, Ludwik Flaszen was the person who helped me to find my own way of seeing when I was fumbling blindly. With a self-ironic frustration I listened to the questions which were addressed to him: the same questions I had asked when I was in Poland. He spoke as a poet, and poetry does not change the world, I thought. I came from my political activism in Norway and had a robust 'spirit of geometry'. To know doesn't mean to understand: for me, at the time, the important thing was to possess knowledge, pure erudition. I skipped the essential part of this

---

[8] Editor's note: Barba refers to a previous intervention by Ludwik Flaszen at the Palermo symposium.

process: the competence to steer the mechanisms below the surface, the understanding with the body.

Sons and daughters don't exist in theatre, but filiations exist. Even unknowingly, one artist inspires another with a kernel of energy that becomes the seed from which one's own plant grows. The plants are not all equal, each one is different from the other even when they make up a single environment such as a forest. It was in Opole that I used the word 'anthropology' in an attempt to explain to those who had never seen Grotowski's and Flaszen's performances how they should imagine what was happening in their Theatre of the 13 Rows, which was just half the size of the room in which we are sitting now. I came upon the formula 'Anthropological Theatre'. I envisaged theatre like an anthropological expedition penetrating into unknown territory and confronting different individuals, societies, and histories. At that time, I thought that Anthropological Theatre was just a suggestive image to illuminate this new way of seeing, practising, living the theatre and linking it to the life of other people.

I left Poland, returned to Norway and founded Odin Teatret with a few young people rejected by the State Theatre School in Oslo. The problems of surviving didn't leave much time for theoretical questions and suggestive images. I had to live up to the unfamiliar task of turning into a teacher, of inventing a training and a discipline that stimulated the different individuals in our group. I felt compelled to provide practical solutions so each of us could be assured our daily bread. I had to check that the repetition of exercises – something totally new at that time – didn't lose its sense for each of us and become merely gymnastics. I had to make sure that the smallest things we did generated a shared feeling of something essential that bound us together.

My worries and obligations were associated with a feeling of inferiority over being autodidactic. I had never completed theatre school. In Opole I just sat for nearly three years watching Grotowski work with his actors. I had never done any practical theatre work. Back in Norway, I suffered from a complex: that of not knowing enough. Reading compensated for my insecurity. Books furnished me with an intellectual armour and much erudition. However, I believed in something, I had seen this something in Opole. It had become a kind of ideal for me: the actors on stage had to be able to perform actions which were not achievable in daily life. I firmly believed that theatre opened up to other conditions than those of daily life when it came to mental and physical time and space. I looked for other proofs of what I had experienced at Grotowski's theatre, other models and points of reference. Oriental theatre and its actors became for me a mine of information and inspiration.

When in 1963 I saw the first example of Oriental theatre, I didn't understand it. In the kathakali performances in Kerala I had difficulty in following the story. Although I had studied history of religions, their mythology left me emotionally cold. Instead, what struck me was the performers' way of being on stage. I could not detach my gaze from them. It was as if they were revealing a secret and I was caught in the web of their actions. I didn't doubt that their technique could help my actors to reach this degree of virtuosity and force of persuasion, this power to sharpen the spectators' receptiveness, to make them understand, not only rationally but above all through the deeper layers of their bodies.

We have only two ways to absorb knowledge: one through an analytical rational process, the other through experience. They are two equally important ways to come into contact, to assimilate, to transform, and to distil both into conceptual knowledge and bodily understanding that which we experience and feel. But they are two complementary ways, and the one cannot be translated into the language of the other.

For me, theatre is experience, it is not intellectual knowledge. It is simultaneity, dialectical coexistence of many contrasting elements in space and time. Simultaneity makes theatre different from the other artistic expressions, which must be linear, like writing or singing: one cannot say or write two things at the same time. I began to study Oriental actors and their technique in the few books available. It has taken me fifteen years to get rid of the European interpretation of Oriental theatre, to free myself from the 'imprint' I had received from books and 'experts' and to which I had myself contributed with my conjectures.

I thought of Oriental theatre as a repertory of various techniques, styles, and conventions, just as those who had written about it before me. But three years ago, something happened that shook my 'imprint' and all the misunderstandings it had produced. Some of my actors had spent a few months in different Asian countries and, back in Holstebro, they showed me what they had been doing. It was like a kind of technical journal that they presented in a practical form as is customary in our theatre. I was taken aback by what I saw: two of my actors began to perform Balinese dances and a longer kathakali episode. I was stupefied for two reasons: first, because in our theatre we had a deep mistrust of the value of learning mechanically and reproducing other theatrical forms; second, because I could not understand, at a creative level, how this could be useful to an actor in contemporary theatre. If you learn kathakali, you can show it once. 'Good!' people say, 'You have learned kathakali. Do you want to be a kathakali actor?' But if you don't intend to become a professional kathakali performer, repeating and personalising this codified style, what you have learned is superficial, like an ornament. You must find the way to extract something from it for your personal development in your individual training within a theatre group that works in specific cultural and historical conditions. Otherwise, what you have learned is not much use.

While watching the training of my actors, however, new questions arose. I noticed that they used their bodies in a different way. It was as if, through kathakali and the Balinese dances, they had uncovered, in their personal training, other patterns of movement which they were unaware of before. This simple observation – a different way of using the body – put me on the track of what has become the starting point for my research: Theatre Anthropology.

What does Theatre Anthropology mean? The word 'anthropology', as defined at the beginning of this century, is the study of human behaviour both at a biological and a socio-cultural level. Theatre Anthropology is the study of man in a performing situation on a biological and socio-cultural level. Is such a science possible? In order to accomplish any research, a departure point, a clear-cut field and selective criteria are needed. In daily life, we use our body according to an established technique, e.g. specific procedures. This daily technique derives both from biological conditioning (I cannot fly, I cannot take a step of more than a certain number of centimetres, and so on) and from socio-cultural imprints from the society in which we live.

But another technique exists – I call it extra-daily – and it is the way of using the body in performing situations. When we see an Oriental actor or a Western ballet dancer come on stage and use a technique – that is, a particular use of the body – most of us accept it at once. Those who see them for the first time may smile, because the performers behave strangely, almost extravagantly. We are accustomed, for example, to walk placing the whole foot on the ground; but in classical ballet we see people who stubbornly displace themselves on the tip of their toes. It is the opposite of our spontaneous functionality, of our organic way of standing and walking. In noh theatre, the actor slides his feet along the floor, never lifting them; in kathakali, the actors bend their knees and support the weight of their whole body on the outer edge of the feet. This posture radically modifies their balance. The same is true in kabuki or in Balinese dances where the toes are kept raised, resulting in a limitation of the body's supporting base and in a precarious balance. What strikes us, when we are confronted with an extra-daily body technique, is that it tends towards a modification, a deformation of the customary daily technique. This happens not only in theatre and dance but also in martial arts, the tea ceremony or meditation postures, which are also extra-daily techniques.

Hence, a statement similar to a truism or to Columbus's egg: in all codified theatre forms a deformation of the daily way of standing, moving, gesticulating or assuming a position can be registered.

In reality, as Craig and Brecht never tired of repeating, the art of the actor is absent in the West. The art of the actor cannot be reformed, sighed Brecht, because something which does not exist cannot be changed; actors do as they want, no norm is treasured, only styles, fashions, and conventions thrive, no nervous system can be found, no skeleton to support and on which an individual art can develop.

It is no accident that the codified ballet is the only performance genre in the West where a new beginner succeeds in assimilating the technical experience of countless generations. A child, in the course of eight years, can learn what numerous choreographers and ballet teachers have discovered and practised for over 300 years. But for a youngster who steps into a drama school, there is no technical experience ready to be assimilated. The student will be introduced to distorted interpretations of the methods and systems of distant totems such as Stanislavski, Brecht, Grotowski, and so on, or he must comply with the taste and personal inventiveness of his teachers. It is impossible to assimilate the experience of the past in a theatre school. The art of the European actor is an individual magma, while in all codified performances one generation after another can verify the technical legacy of the past, look for constant features and measure itself against them. But which constant features will they encounter and focus on?

What struck me first was the change in balance of my actors when practising Balinese dances and kathakali. I detected this quite easily because this also happens after about a year's training at Odin Teatret. The repetition of exercises and their variation in rhythm results in a slight bending of the knees. But only then – when they were practising the Oriental styles – did I become aware to what extent this knee bending modified the balance and had a repercussion on the spine transforming weight into energy. I discovered that balance could be measured thanks to one particular indicator: the pressure of the feet on the ground.

Let's make an experiment. Could you all please get up and just stand immobile looking straight ahead. After a few seconds you will notice some tiny movements, a minute swinging back and forth. In order to keep your balance, you must press downwards on your feet. A standing body is never immobile, even if its movements are invisible to our eyes. The position you have taken while standing is functional, not requiring much energy, almost inert, supported by your weight. Now try to press your weight slightly downwards. This causes your knees to bend a little and you feel your position is a bit unstable. Be aware of how your balance functions while fixing your new posture. You are still standing, although in a less secure position, your balance adjusting to oppose instability. You are now in a position of readiness, when all your energies are on the verge of being released: you can sit, leap or move at once in whatever direction you want. In this stance of readiness there is a mobilisation of all your energies which are prepared to be projected and materialised into an action.

Observing how this law of the alteration of balance works, I became aware of a second law, that of opposition. This is the necessary condition for being in life. According to the law of gravity, I ought to fall down because of my weight, but my spine holds me up. This is the first opposition. When, yesterday, Odin Teatret's actor Tom Fjordefalk was demonstrating the basic kathakali stance, you could perceive how oppositions are multiplied.[9] The more oppositions exist, the more poles of life are engendered in the body. There was the fundamental opposition between weight and spine, the torso lowered and the arms raised, the knees bending and pointing outwards to the side in opposition to the usual daily way of standing, while the feet were parallel and well planted on their outer edges on the floor with the big toe tensed upwards. Tom emphasised the tendency to circular movements in kathakali. We were thus reminded of the importance of circular movements in extra-daily technique, which enhances the dynamic of the actor's movements, charging them with energy: the pre-expressive condition. We will later see why these circular movements are so important. All this still has nothing to do with art or expressivity. It simply concerns the ability of the individual to understand how to use his own energies, awaken them, project them with awareness while shaping them into actions.

When speaking of energy, we generally commit the error of thinking only of movements and muscular activity. In theatre, we still don't have an understanding of the various types of energy at the different levels of

[9] Editor's note: Barba refers to a work demonstration by Tom Fjordefalk held the previous day at the Palermo symposium.

organisation in our organism. Mental energy, for example, manifests itself through physical signs that show an ongoing process, a way of being active, though this activity doesn't develop through movements in space. How can the actor be in life, how can he let his whole body radiate? When I speak of body I don't mean flesh, blood, and bones, I think of our psychic, mental or spiritual energies, the intangible aspect that makes each of us unique. How can an actor awaken all his energies, retain them, and then discharge them in each action he does?

The law of opposition pushed me to study books on a topic which had never been among my preferred: biology. Thanks to them, my knowledge about Oriental theatre became broader. Let me tell you an anecdote. Grotowski had travelled to China in 1962 for a couple of weeks and observed several technical features in Chinese Opera. One was extremely puzzling, and when he came back to Opole, we called it 'the Chinese principle'. Every time a Chinese actor has to do a movement, he starts it from the opposite direction. If I want to look at Flaszen, I don't turn my head to the left to stare directly at him. I begin by turning my head to the right, then I make a semicircular movement towards the left, stopping to focus on Flaszen. I thought it was a functional device: the actor amplifies his movement, making the spectator perceive more clearly the trajectory of his action. It was only many years later that I understood how 'the Chinese principle' enabled the actor to emphasise biological laws.

Let's focus for a moment on the term 'energy' and how Oriental actors see it. They use words which, when I heard them for the first time, sounded strange. When, in Tokyo, I asked a kabuki actor if there existed in his theatre a term for the actor's energy – his presence, his way of 'being alive' – he answered yes, such a word did exist: *koshi*. I wrote in my notebook: *koshi* means energy in kabuki. A few days later, I met René Sieffert, the French nch specialist, and asked him the same question. He answered the same: *koshi*, and explained that this word doesn't mean 'energy' but 'hips'. When I spoke again with the kabuki actor, I could not refrain from saying, 'But *koshi* doesn't mean energy, but hips.'

'You are right, hips', he answered and proceeded to show me the relationship between hips and energy. When walking, kabuki actors move the body along diagonal lines, and, by bending slightly at the knees, they block the hips so that these do not automatically follow the leg movements. This creates an opposition, which has an effect on the spine and the balance, thus transforming weight into energy. To have 'hips' for a kabuki actor means to generate energy, to be alive, present.

When we study the hips from a biological point of view, we learn that they are the critical part of the body in man's evolution. When man raised himself up from walking on all fours and became *Homo erectus*, it was in the hips that the maximum muscular development took place. The strongest muscles developed in the buttocks. The mechanics that keep man erect and allow him to move function through the legs, whose femurs, the two upper bones, are attached to the coccyx, which supports the spine. Kabuki actors discovered empirically the relationship between the hips, the spine and walking. By modifying the behaviour of the hips, they modified this relationship.

I asked Hideo Kanze, the well-known noh actor, 'Do you use the word *koshi* in your work?'

'Not normally, but my father did', he answered.

'Did he say "you have *koshi*"?'

'No, he did like this, look.' He asked me to walk like a noh actor. I started to walk, sliding my feet in a ridiculously awkward way. He seized my hips from behind and held me back inciting me to continue walking. When held back, I had to engage and push the whole body to go forward. 'You see', Kanze concluded, 'my father meant this: *koshi* implies that you want to walk, but someone holds your hips back preventing you from moving forward.' What an extraordinary demonstration of the law of opposition. If you want to walk, and someone holds you back by your hips, you will automatically press and slide the soles of the feet along the ground: precisely as a noh actor.

Let me give another example of the way Oriental actors think of 'energy'. In noh, there exists a psycho-technical device which I call the law of three-tenths. I was told that an actor should execute three-tenths of his action in space and seven-tenths in time. He wants, for example, to pick this lighter up from the table and place it beside the tape-recorder on my left. To do this, he uses only three-tenths of the energy in the movement and keeps seven-tenths of it within himself. This means that he is engaging much more energy than necessary to do the task. Keeping the action within himself (doing it in time) implies that he has simultaneously to create an opposing action with respect to the movement.

What seems to be pure philosophy becomes clear through our anatomy. Our muscles can both stretch and contract. In daily life, when I stretch my arm, the contracting muscles remain unengaged. But the Japanese actor stretches and contracts his arm at the same time. His action says simultaneously yes and no, and he achieves this by engaging simultaneously both the stretching and contracting muscles. The consequence is a 'waste' of energy, the prerequisite of scenic presence. Note that a similar device is applied regularly in Western pantomime.

Another rule struck me while watching the Oriental actors, which was connected to space. They had a tendency to move in circular trajectories. 'The Chinese principle' remarked by Grotowski is a clear application of this circular rule. The Odin actor who yesterday demonstrated the basic kathakali technique reiterated several times the importance of this circular feature. What can the reason be?

The muscles in our body activate the joints. The joints account for our movements, it is their function to realise the intention of the muscles. In daily life, to save energy, we move through straight lines, and engage as few joints as possible. The Oriental actor, with his circular movements, sets in motion more joints in a movement which in fact requires fewer. Yet another case of 'wasted' energy. This 'waste' both estranges and enhances the movement because of the excess of energy. Moreover, moving in round orbits displaces the weight, thus upsetting the balance and obliging the actor to use the hips, *koshi*, in a different way.

The study of biology and codified techniques can help to define new perspectives in teaching would-be actors in modern theatre. Pedagogy must become a practical process – like the exercises in the training – in order to enable an understanding with the body. This is what should characterise a pedagogical process: a learning which is corporeal understanding and that generates a professional knowledge and intuition as well as a pragmatic vision of the inner mechanisms: that which flows alive beneath the skin.

We could begin by picking out a few elementary biological laws which are unwittingly applied both in the codified Oriental and in Western theatre techniques. The first law to investigate should be the weight–balance relationship as a source of scenic energy.

It is often said: the Oriental actor dances. No, the Oriental actor doesn't dance as we Europeans believe, because when we Europeans dance, we do it with the legs. The Oriental actor doesn't dance like this. In kathakali or in Balinese dances, the movements of the legs are limited. The actor dances with his hands, arms, spine, eyes. Yesterday, watching the Odin actress Iben Nagel Rasmussen, I was aware that what makes her presence alive was her 'dance' with the upper part of the body, her fingers, neck, torso, and not just the legs. It is not a question of turning the Western actor into an Oriental one but of training him according to rules that can trigger his energy, set it in motion as we can clearly perceive beneath the Asian codifications.

I speak the whole time of energy and actions and not of expressiveness because I'm referring to the stage of the actor's work where his presence is built: the pre-expressive level. Here the law of the change of balance and that of opposition will enable him to enhance his stage presence, which, in a later phase, will become representation – performance which the spectators will judge for its expressiveness or lack of the same. We are expressive in spite of ourselves. The actor who wants to be expressive steps into the quicksand of exaggeration and pathos. When focusing on an action, moulding it out of his personal need, ideological belief, and artistic vision, he has a chance to become expressive in spite of himself in the eyes of the spectators.

The relationship between science and theatre is not one that appeals to theatre people. Yet this relationship has nowadays become the field of research which I conduct together with a few scientists within the International School of Theatre Anthropology (ISTA). They are biologists, psycholinguists, and neuro-psychologists. Here with us today we have one of them, Peter Elsass, who researches changes of consciousness at the University of Copenhagen.[10] They all share an interest in theatre, and in ISTA they will have the opportunity to study scientifically the laws or maybe the hypotheses which I have exposed to you.

They will observe the working process of about twenty-five Oriental performers with their musicians who will train fifty experienced actors and directors from all over the world. Since a school should give its pupils the possibility to understand with the body, I had to find the best teachers to do this, but ones who could never be imitated. My choice of Oriental actors relies on the conviction that it would be senseless to teach Oriental theatre techniques to Western actors for only a couple of months. What would they do with this? A mocking and superficial repetition?

The Oriental actor induces his pupils into a bodily understanding. The pupils must not be blinded by the conventions, the stylistic properties or the suggestive language but must be able to grasp the laws that drive their teacher's presence and to apply these laws to their Western bodies. Thus, a new teaching path opens up to a personal understanding of the anatomical processes leading to presence, to a scenic body.

Briefly, this is the journey I have undertaken since I began with Grotowski's and Flaszen's Poor Theatre, arriving at what today I call Theatre Anthropology.

---

[10] Editor's note: At the time, Peter Elsass, a Danish psychologist and anthropologist, was one of Eugenio Barba's close collaborators. Elsass participated in the Palermo symposium and gave a speech.

For the time being, Theatre Anthropology can be introduced only through this arid language, a bastard scientific-theatrical terminology. But in two or three years, after much experiment and experience, I believe that many things will change in my way of speaking and in your way of receiving.

The pedagogical paradox

During his investigation into the pre-expressive level in the actor's work, Barba realises the didactic potentialities of such research. This text from 1980 shows how, within the context of ISTA (the International School of Theatre Anthropology), Barba tries an alternative way of teaching that eludes the criteria of the time. The Asian actors become the protagonists of this new pedagogy. Their radical diversity is an effective detour because it hinders any real imitation since the pupil must focus not on the external forms but on the pre-expressive principles that underlie them. Barba will later speak about 'learning to learn': the ability to become aware of the principles that trigger scenic presence by observing or executing Asian and other acting patterns.

The text resumes two conversations with Franco Ruffini after the first ISTA session (Bonn 1980) and was published by Ruffini in his La scuola degli attori *(The School of Actors) (1980: 25–28). It is one of Barba's lesser known texts although it was translated into French (1981) and Serbian (1981).*

The impasse of customary theatre pedagogy is that it prepares conformists or misfits: actors who identify themselves with a theatre which is generally acknowledged or actors who, rejecting this attitude, are unable to adapt to the existing situation.

This is what we witness when we examine schools preparing actors for traditional or avant-garde text-orientated theatres. I have called them the First and the Second Theatre. But a Third Theatre exists, a heterogeneous galaxy where the actor's training does not consist in preserving or revolutionising the existing dramaturgical structures but in conceiving the craft as a continuous confrontation with the unforeseeable. The whole tradition of the past must be observed with fresh eyes and interpreted anew, not absorbed without question as is the case in theatre schools. We face the almost insuperable obstacle of designing a pedagogical practice that has no models. Hence the appeal of individual artists or theatre groups who in our time invented a practice of their own. Here lies the paradox. To acquire professional experience, a young actor should look for points of reference with alien technical experiences and results – i.e. totally different theatre visions, traditions, and forms – allowing him to grasp the technical laws that govern these particular styles and genres without adopting them as models.

Here lies the core of a pedagogical process: how to absorb a technique, a know-how, that makes the actor independent of a specific style, or, rather, able to escape the danger of specialisation. A personal technique enables an actor to face any creative situation without falling into automatisms and set solutions. This knowledge is steeped in a continuously renewed relationship with oneself, one's tradition and the circumstances of the time, with a text, a particular space and with the spectators.

The circumstances that forced me to invent my own theatre also helped me discover the hidden rules beneath the skin of the Oriental theatre's conventions. I had often wondered why, during training and rehearsals, my Odin actors assumed certain stances and postures. Musing about Western actors' work helped me to formulate similar speculations when I saw Oriental actors and to look at them with different eyes. I started to realise that, in spite of the variety of their formal languages and styles, these actors followed principles similar to those of the Odin. The hands, for example, were never inactive or relaxed, usually above the belt and animated by minute tensions, with each finger assuming a particular position and direction. This was clearly noticeable in the Odin actors as well as in the Oriental ones. How could this be possible? Trying to explain this bizarre coincidence to myself, I became aware that identical rules were at work, and these were evident once one focused one's attention on them. These rules are clearly discernible in their physical manifestations and are recurrent in any context when an actor performs in front of a spectator.

Until today, my teaching has always happened in collaboration with my actors. In ISTA, the advantage of collaborating with Oriental masters is that they can teach in a physical, technical way without explanations, unlike theatre schools in Europe. For instance, when a young actress sees the Odin's Iben Nagel Rasmussen, she may be struck by her expressive power and take her as a model: a peak to be reached at the end of the road. But the young actress is in a hurry, impatient and unwilling to follow the long road. She believes that she can express the same intensity and reach this peak immediately. Here, in this desire to express, lies a danger. For this reason, ISTA focuses on the pre-expressive stage in the actor's working process.

If I decide to grab your hand, the body assumes a particular readiness at the moment in which the thought turns into an impulse: this is the pre-expressive moment.[11] Then the action of grabbing your hand takes place, and it always acquires an expressive quality in the eyes of an observer: an intention, a meaning, a feeling, a certain relationship. In everyday life, without knowing or willing it, we always manifest a certain degree of expressiveness in the eyes of others when we are occupied with something and don't think about how to express what we do. The problem of expressivity is a central one in our craft and is connected to the actor's peculiarity: the desire to be expressive. He does not realise that he only achieves an effect of vividness for the observer by renouncing this desire and simply focusing his awareness on a concrete task or thought, and reacting to them. When the actor wants to be expressive, he self-imposes a command with regard to his doing on the stage, while in everyday life expressivity is the result of not being aware of what we are doing. There is an essential difference.

Pre-expressivity has to do with a change in the muscular tone; it depends on a variety of tensions that displace the body's centre of gravity and hence change its balance. I am standing in front of a wall, ready to jump over it: an immediate change takes places in my muscular tone. It is as if I am already performing the jump although standing still on the spot: this is pre-expressivity.

At ISTA, because of the lack of time, a Western actor working with Oriental teachers is unable to reproduce their artistic form; he learns their basic body postures and how to make their first steps in space. They undeniably reproduce unfamiliar movements and gestures, but this process is at a pre-expressive level and characterises any development towards artistic autonomy. You always have a reference at the beginning: your parents, an older brother or sister, a teacher or a friend. Only when you have absorbed the patterns of this reference can you appropriate it and make it your own.

Already on the first day of work with an Oriental teacher, the Western actor experiences the passage from his usual daily body technique to an extra-daily one. This transition follows precise norms and criteria: a particular

---

[11] Editor's note: At this early stage of his research, Barba was exploring the concept of pre-expressivity, trying to appraise its consequences. Here he identifies pre-expressivity with the impulse, the phase that precedes the action. Later on he defines pre-expressivity more broadly as the level of stage presence. In other words, pre-expressivity is the performer's work on his body-mind in order to achieve an expressive result for the spectators. Therefore, pre-expressivity is a working dimension that belongs to the process and not to the results. It is also worth noting that in the texts of this early period, Barba speaks indiscriminately of 'rules', 'principles', 'norms' and 'laws'. Later, he clarifies his terminology, distinguishing between 'rules' and 'principles'. The rules belong to a specific technique, while the principles are a recurring technical premise linking the rules of the different techniques. He no longer uses the word 'law' to avoid misunderstandings between scientific and pragmatic laws. Grotowski wrote a lucid text on this topic, 'Pragmatic Laws' (Barba and Savarese 2005: 268–69).

basic stance in stillness, ways of transferring the weight and thus the balance, a new use of eyes and looking. It is not a short-cut to artistic expressivity: it is a rigorous and disruptive phase that prepares for it. This transition provides a physical knowledge, an understanding with one's own body that what counts is not the formal aspect of an acting style but the norms underlying this style. These norms involve a certain way of thinking in order to reshape and revitalise the physical presence, altering and engaging it in a way suitable for theatrical purposes.

The fact of alternating the work with different Oriental teachers is a means to dislocate the Western actor, to deprive him of his spontaneity and usual body control, while preventing him from absorbing his teacher's style. He undergoes again the experience of being a beginner. In everyday life, we have assimilated a whole range of movements and gestures that have automatically become our dynamic mother language. In theatre, exploiting this language, it is inevitable that its automatisms influence the creative process. It is necessary to discover mental and physical procedures that produce changes in this language. This can only happen if we find a different way of using our physical and mental presence.

The real danger is specialisation. Let's take pantomime as an example. Its extra-daily technique differs from the daily one. But, once acquired, you have become a specialist, which can either be a source of creative freedom or a stylistic prison from which you cannot escape. The Oriental actors are super-specialised. In the Peking Opera, the actress who has specialised in the role of a warrior is unable to make the simplest movements as a courtier.

At ISTA, these super-specialised experts teach actors how to avoid specialisation. They demonstrate how the beginning of a bodily specialisation depends on a reshaping that seems like a deformation. The shortness of the pedagogical process prevents the Western pupil from absorbing the style he is learning. The purpose is to make the experience of how one's own normal way of using the body can be altered without absorbing that of a different theatre style. The alternation of teachers helps to become aware of the connection between the various Western and Oriental acting techniques. The first days of any actor's apprenticeship help him to recognise the rules which he is following in his extra-daily stage behaviour and which are common to all acting styles. However, this knowledge cannot be purely intellectual. It is necessary to know how to apply the rules to one's own body by first learning an unfamiliar form and later introducing those rules to one's own training and creative work.

Of course, a Western actor is also able to build a personal extra-daily technique. When we observe and analyse the stage behaviour of Dario Fo, the same laws applied by Oriental actors can be detected in his acting. The danger is that Dario Fo's results – his personal style – becomes a model and is involuntarily imitated. When you learn the first elements of an Oriental actor's genre, then style and convention are not evident; you are absorbing only basic patterns of movement, which could be considered as exercises. These are distant abstract models, yet concrete from a physical point of view. That which seems the easiest and most 'natural' thing for a Japanese actor presents a degree of difficulty which is almost insurmountable for a Western actor's body. This comparative confrontation develops a physical intelligence, an awareness of the tensions that decide the body's scenic 'life'. 'Life' is perhaps a generic and ambiguous term. One could speak of an elementary dramatic effect irradiated by the actor's body.

Western actors unconsciously use their bodies on stage according to the laws of pre-expressivity. Through empirical and pragmatic solutions they have succeeded in mastering a particular use of their bodies, a personal style that produces an effect on the spectators. If they teach, however, what appears to be important to their students is the external manifestation of this style. Oriental actors are striking because of their alien scenic behaviour, although they are difficult and inappropriate models to follow. Here we are witnessing a highly refined dialectic: only by experiencing an alien technique can an actor succeed in overcoming his mannerisms and be able to step into another level of physical awareness. This alien scenic behaviour has nothing to do with decontextualisation, as some scholars maintained during the Symposium on Theatre Anthropology here in Bonn.

If I see an Indian dance and I am acquainted neither with its historical, religious, and social background nor with the representation of its symbols, images, and positions, or if I ignore the story the dancer is enacting, it is evident that the possible meanings of this dance will escape me although I may have an aesthetical or rhythmic experience. But at ISTA we don't focus on meanings, on the results of the individual artistic expressivity directed at the spectators but on the pre-expressive stage, the actor's work process preceding the final meaning. We concentrate on the phase in which an actor builds up his technical knowledge through which he will later articulate ideas, stories, associative and emotional signals. Scholars arguing about the context raise a false problem.

Awareness and denial

In this text from 1982, Barba underlines the usefulness of perceiving any actor in such a way that we are able to distinguish between the actor's scenic behaviour – or stage presence – and the cultural and religious values, symbols, and meanings that this presence conveys.

This procedure facilitates the perception of the fundamental premise of Theatre Anthropology: a stage behaviour that alters the actor's 'natural' spontaneity and which is the consequence of self-imposed limitations and resistances. This is a principle to be found in all types of pre-set performances, and Barba calls it 'coherent incoherence'. At the end of the text, Barba applies this principle to the pedagogical practice of twentieth-century European theatre reformers. The exercises in their training elicit the same logic which is found in the formalised patterns of Asian performers. The Western exercises impose resistances on the actors in order to break down the conditioned reflexes of their daily behaviour, without, however, enclosing them in a codified form. This process generates a kind of energy which is at the root of an actor's scenic presence. Thus, it is through the exercises that Western actors may learn to be scenically present.

From a historical point of view, the value of this text consists in showing how Asian performers made Barba grasp both the principle of 'coherent incoherence' as well as the inner logic and purpose of the exercises in different Western training forms. The text stems from a lecture by Barba in Rovereto, Italy, in 1982 during the East–West Festival. It is published here for the first time.

Let's start with the correlation between awareness and denial, the latter envisioned as a creative act. The process of denying doesn't imply a static attitude but one that generates a transformation.

Béla Balàzs, before becoming a known film theorist, had directed an agitprop theatre group in Germany. In one of his writings he asks himself some questions. Why do people go to the theatre? Why do men and women who experience the thousand nuances of life, who interact with the vibrant turmoil of the streets, enjoy the feeling of shelter in their homes, fulfil the most interesting tasks and challenges in schools, offices, and factories, who love, travel, and daydream – why do these people feel the need to shut themselves in a building and watch other men and women pretending to think, feel, and act? What need drives them to immerse themselves in a reality that is just a substitute for what they are and live? Balàzs explains it with the longing to be in the present (1980: 38–40). We are incapable of remaining at length in the present with all our senses and mental faculties, of consciously registering what our eyes see, or of listening, as if for the first time, to the sounds perceived by our ears. In theatre, the spectators suspend the two dimensions of past and future and focus closely on the present moment experiencing what happens before their eyes.

This is denial that becomes awareness. This sentence, which sounds like philosophy or metaphysics, acquires another meaning if we follow Balàsz's reasoning. As soon as I deny the surrounding reality and concentrate my attention on an object, an image, a sound, or even on the artificial way of behaving and speaking of an actor, I sharpen my awareness of being in the present.

There are many systems of psycho-physical techniques that attempt to 'deny', i.e. to resist the individual's psychological and mental automatisms. Under the label of meditation, exercises or work on oneself, they have thrived within religious, esoteric, and even secular circles. All over the world, in all cultures, the aim is one of inner growth. A recurrent practice is to disrupt the flow of the mind and anchor the attention on the reality of what is seen, heard or imagined *hic et nunc*, the here and now. These practices try to keep our permanent mental bustle from leaping incessantly from one thought to another, from the past to the future and vice versa. The suspension of our brain's normal activity increases our awareness and helps us to be and act in the present. Such knowledge has been used in modern Western theatre; it is not an accident that Sergei Eisenstein remarked how much the Stanislavski system owed to the spiritual exercises of Ignatius of Loyola.

Let's look at a Chinese or Japanese painting inspired by Taoism or Buddhism. It represents a landscape, often barely sketched and plunged in a dimension of void: most of the canvas is white, unpainted. A figure sits under a tree, not far from a stream or a waterfall. The artist has portrayed a monk or a hermit in meditation, fixing his attention on the sound of the flowing water.

In everyday life we have to make an effort to keep our attention on something. Already after a short while other thoughts invade our brain and we have difficulty in maintaining the same focus. Mentally we begin to slip somewhere else. We constantly experience this situation: we are doing something, yet, at the same time, we are not there since our thoughts are elsewhere. We walk, take off our shoes, cook, dress, even read a newspaper, but the unity between our mental I and our bodily I is interrupted. The body moves, acts, and reacts in an adequate but automatic way, while our mind flutters away from it.

This is a central problem in theatre practice since the actor, on stage, must be present in his totality. He cannot be divided. His mind cannot anticipate or delay what the body has to accomplish. Hence the necessity for the actor to master the knowledge of how to achieve the unity of thought and action during the entire performance and – according to Balàsz – let the spectator live the rare and difficult experience of being in the present.

Don't lose sight of reality: be concrete

An anecdote can give us stuff for reflection. In the mysterious Orient, which so much inflames our imagination, a teacher known for his wisdom has attracted many disciples. He has a habit of answering questions with silence, just slowly lifting skywards the index finger of the right hand. The disciples ask about religious themes, metaphysical matters, family problems, what is the best diet, why death and what is the purpose of life. The teacher keeps answering with the same gesture, until the day of his death. When, on his deathbed, surrounded by his mourning disciples, one of them implores him, 'Teacher, what did your lifted finger mean? Some of us understood: listen to the silence in yourself; others: that reality cannot be split in two, everything is One; yet others: address yourselves to whoever is on high, pray, faith is salvation. How can we agree on your gesture?' The teacher raises his index finger with difficulty. 'What is this?'

'A finger.'

'Don't lose sight of reality. Be concrete', smiles the teacher.

When we approach the East and the actors of its traditional theatres, we are like the disciples questioning the teacher and forgetting to take into account the anatomic fact of the lifted finger. The actor's presence is so pregnant that we attribute values, meanings, symbols, and motivations which undoubtedly exist at a determined level but which don't belong to the level of stage energy: the concreteness of his presence.

We often use the word 'energy', but what are we talking about? In an Indian text, Patanjali's *Yoga Sutras* (1962), energy is defined as the union of man and woman: the word is the man, and the breath is the woman. Ideas reside in the words, while beast-passions live in the breath; the beast-passions transport the ideas in the words, dancing freely in the rhythm. Once more this sounds like philosophy and mysticism. But let's not lose sight of reality, of what is concrete.

The flow of our breathing follows the emotional waves that dominate us at a given moment. These fluctuations can be long, short, disconnected, violent, may slow down or accelerate. Breathing informs about what is happening within us. Yet its free movement is denied when it meets resistance: the words. The verbal patterns of the words and their articulation are tied to breathing. The words are the channel through which the beast-passions express themselves.

With a suggestive image, Patanjali describes the beast-passions awakening in our body: the snake uncoils at the base of the spine, the lion stretches itself in the breast, the elephant knocks at the wall of the forehead. He depicts the tumult of all the animals striving to escape through the body's orifices and limbs: our legs start trembling, our arms open and close in agitation, our gaping mouth screams, sings, cries.

When the breathing of the beast-passions traverses the entire body, then the whole body means. And the dance of being happens. But if the beast-passions are directed only through the channel of the words-ideas while the rest of the body is not involved, only words and ideas come out.

Bharata Muni's *Natyashastra* (between 200 BC and AD 400) is the most ancient text about Hindu dramatic art. René Daumal, who translated it into French, commented that in our European culture we have sowed in the mouth the wheat of the dance of being that lives within us; and this wheat is barely able to stir the words (Daumal 1970: 61–62). The main difference between Western theatre and the traditional one of the East lies in this dance, which the Indian texts speak about and their actors express through their entire body. It is as if, in the West, we have let this dance spin on the stage only through words.

The first time I watched Oriental theatre at any length in its context was in India in 1963. I was not able to see the concreteness of the particular tension in the lifted finger. I was seduced by the demon of rational interpretation, so typical of my culture. I explained the Kathakali actor and performances through references to religion, tradition, veneration to the guru, the actor's apparent yoga attitude, without forgetting historical and economic circumstances. But at the same time I experienced this dance of being. I must have perceived it, although in a confused way, as a personal shock which I could not explain in intellectual terms. I wrote that Shiva's cosmic dance was the model for the kathakali actors. Yet, at the same time, I described in detail for pages and pages their exercises and physical training as the concrete road to this dance.

A presentiment pushed me to see in their long apprenticeship the foundation of a somatic knowledge, the pillars of their undivided stage presence.

Now, fifteen years later, when I watch a kathakali actor, I have a double vision: on the one hand, the superlative richness of his expressivity, on the other, stretching tendons, flexing muscles, vertebrae and joints, contractions and relaxations. I see the mystery of the dance of being and a scenic anatomy following precise laws.

When today I experience Oriental theatres in this way, it is because I learned over fifteen years to observe the training of my actors for several hours a day. I am now aware of the rhythm of learning through the body. I am acquainted with the resistances and the paradoxes through which an actor assimilates a particular way of thinking, joined with a particular physical intelligence and know-how. This long schooling has taught me to look at Oriental theatres with other eyes. I can see underneath their alluring forms and recognise the technical principles which the actors apply to give them life. Via a completely different road, the Odin actors too in their years-long apprenticeship with exercises and repetition of individual scores have come upon and applied the same principles. One of these is the correlation between denial and awareness. In order to be creative and to reach a dimension of inner and outer freedom, the actor denies his spontaneity – the way he is accustomed to use his body in everyday life. He submits to procedures and obstacles that estrange his body's shape and intensify his presence.

Dancing through obstacles

We forget that the Oriental actor starts his apprenticeship as a child: at eight or nine years old, sometimes earlier. The spirituality which for us Europeans appears to imbue some of these theatres, is experienced by the child not as a religious practice but as a physical technique. In kathakali, bowing to greet a religious image or a photo of a guru when starting work will remind him that his craft is tied to an ancient tradition and to particular values. The same concerns the greeting to the earth. Touching the ground in a sign of respect for the place in which one will develop one's craft is a custom we meet in the East, not only in theatre but also in martial arts. But let's not lose sight of reality, of what is concrete. What the child faces from the very first day of his apprenticeship is a physical discipline, a way of using his body to deny what he has known and done up to that moment.

New rules of behaviour limit his freedom of movement and gesture. The point of departure is a gradual process of reshaping his bodily posture and dynamics, absorbing an artificial way of standing, moving and displacing himself in space. A similar process is found in one traditional Western genre, classical ballet. Here, a coherent yet peremptory discipline twists the functional habits absorbed during the first years of personal and social life. This discipline involves keeping the legs and feet in painfully difficult positions that reduce the balance, making them move in a bizarre way, stand in eccentric postures, turn around in a pirouette on one leg.

Why does this discipline try to change radically the student's behavioural identity which has taken years to develop? Why does this artistic technique deny what is spontaneous and normal?

Many actors in Japan, Bali, India, and Taiwan told me that as children they didn't understand what they were doing. Their teacher never bothered to give them an explanation. They simply repeated what the teacher showed. This repetition leads to the emergence of a second body that has nothing mystical about it. It is a body whose anatomy, through estranging devices, enhances the actor's stage presence. It is a reshaped alter ego of the everyday body. But according to which principles is this body modified?

Any human movement has two dynamic possibilities: to slow down or to accelerate its speed. It is worth noticing that in all traditional theatre forms actors move quicker or slower than in everyday life. This results in a transformation of their energy with a subsequent effect on the spectator's perception. If I want to take the sheet of paper which is on the table and I restrict the speed, I act under a double impulse: one moving forward and another holding back. I extend the arm, and, at the same time, I deny this action. I cannot achieve this result mechanically. I have to be present in what I am doing.

Some acting traditions and the empirical practice of the individual actor link the delaying or speeding up of their physical behaviour to their breathing. They even introduce on purpose tiny pauses to break the automatism of everyday behaviour. Breathing in and breathing out is synchronised to the speed of a movement or to a pause, this being a refined strategy to fight automatisms and mannerisms.

In traditional Oriental theatres, as in the Western ones until the nineteenth century, the music that usually accompanies the whole performance imposes on the actor another pace – slower or quicker. He must always take into account this relationship with the music, exploiting the possibility of negating the rhythmic expectation or stressing it. In classical ballet, this is called 'phrasing' and is a skill that distinguishes a dancer's excellence. In Meyerhold's performances, live music accompanied the actors who moved according to its particular rhythms. All Odin Teatret's performances have a soundtrack created by the actors who also comply with it: a theatre that dances. In Japan, a rule doesn't allow the synchronization between music and the actor's acting. Music, instead of helping the swiftness of movement, becomes an obstacle, a sparring partner that deceives and must be deceived, demanding total awareness in the actor. These self-imposed rules – paradoxical ways of thinking and behaving – have nothing spiritual about them but are useful stratagems in preventing mechanical habits. They help to build a fictive scenic body, a reshaped organism which is not the consequence of a psychological process but of a principle: the denial of our usual freedom of which we are unaware in our individual behaviour.

The difference between Western theatres and the traditional ones from the East hides a loss: the demise of the dance of being described by Patanjali, and which on our Western stages is reduced to a movement of words and ideas. This movement can produce interesting and even extraordinary performances. Yet the sense of loss persists.

At times, I watch television and turn down the sound. On the screen, someone speaks, but I don't hear the words. It is fascinating to follow his dance: the shaking of the head, the torso that twists and sways back and forth, the sudden motionlessness, the striking gesticulation with hands and fingers stressing certain words and intonations. Every sentence spoken by even the most self-controlled people – a prime minister, a general or a priest – is accompanied by a physical echo. Or, rather, the body follows the oral music of the words. It is a ceaseless dance, even while seated.

Every individual possesses this capacity to engage the whole organism. How is it possible that this dance disappears when the would-be actor climbs on the stage and we perceive his heaviness, his embarrassment over his corporality, the panic of the hands that don't know what to do or where to go. He seems unable to respect the dynamics of speech. He breathes according to the punctuation of the written text he has learnt. The spectator is disturbed by a convention that belongs to writing: at every full stop or comma the actor breathes in or makes a pause. This solidifies the breath's pace and anarchic modulation. The actor meets an obstacle: the words, the articulation, the diction. But he is unable to exploit it, transforming it into a denial that generates unexpected intensity.

Only by mastering the process of negating can the actor succeed in being expressive in spite of himself.

Not movements but actions

There is a difference between movement and action. When I gesticulate, I make many movements with my hands, yet the rest of my body is not engaged at a muscular level. This happens only when tensions in the torso modify the body's total muscular tone, with repercussions on the balance. On stage, any action is a reaction that produces a change within our body's tonic state and, consequently, in the onlooker's perception.

In everyday life, when we are mentally and physically involved, the snake, the lion, the elephant begin dancing in the whole of our body. Why do we lose this dance on stage? We can reproduce it through artifices of the mind, stratagems of the imagination and psychology. We apply Stanislavski's 'magic if': 'Ah, if I was Hamlet, how would I behave in this situation?' Or think in the third person, as Brecht suggested: 'He, Hamlet, what is he doing at this moment?' These ways of thinking colour the behaviour, infuse nuances and variations, rhythmic modulations and transitions, micro-tensions and immobility – a set of expressive signs that estrange and enliven the actor's private way of being.

Watching a Japanese or a Balinese actor, an unavoidable question arises: will the effect produced by his technique remain or even become greater after repeating the same performance for several years? Or will his technique ossify and confine him in a prison of stereotypes? This question concerns an actor's creative renewal and can be answered only individually. However, the question emphasises a problem: the actor must know how to work if repetition is to become the path to artistic and personal growth. This knowing how to work allows an actor in the East to achieve excellence after having played the same performance all his life.

In Europe, when an actor tells us he has been playing Hamlet for three years, we often think, 'Poor guy, three years of Hamlet!' Yet we are impressed when an Oriental actor tells us: 'I have played this performance for forty years.' Why these different ways of judging?

We should perhaps ask, why is an Oriental actor considered a master only after having played the same performance for thirty or forty years? Is it possible that repetition contains a germ of artistic growth and individualisation?

► ISTA Salento 1987. Katsuko Azuma's gaze while performing *Yashima*.

What does repetition hide? Is repetition a miasma that suffocates the dance of being, rendering it automatic? Or is repetition a germ that enhances and intensifies this dance?

Repetition, which seemingly reproduces the same result and effect, forces the actor to invent an individual knowledge. We could say that both in his apprenticeship and later in his career the essential attitude is learning to learn in order not to be blinded and imprisoned by the external form of the artistic results. This attitude decides whether repetition becomes a fatal trap or a process that renews the experience of being present in what the actor is doing in spite of how many times and for how long he has been doing it.

In a session of ISTA, the International School of Theatre Anthropology, Katsuko Azuma, a performer of nihon buyo, showed a short play with a scene in which a Buddhist monk crosses a field where in the past a bloody battle had taken place. Suddenly, the ghost of a fallen warrior appears. The actress

► Tokyo, 1980. From left: Eugenio Barba, Moriaki Watanabe, Tadashi Suzuki, and Richard Schechner (second from the right) at the Symposium on noh theatre at Hosei University.

alternately plays the monk, the ghost, and other characters related to the battle and to the death of the warrior. Katsuko Azuma repeated this scene three times. Could we notice what was different in each version? All of us, actors and directors from various countries and cultures, had not observed the least variation. The scenes seemed identical. The actress explained that she had improvised in each of the three scenes. The first time, the monk sees the ghost at a distance of three metres, the second at about ten metres, the third over fifty metres. Then Katsuko presented the three versions again, and I could detect the tension in the eyes and the neck depending on the distance. It is this tension – imperceptible to the spectator – that sparks the actor's presence, the first step towards the dance of being. Katsuko concluded her demonstration saying that she had performed this scene many times, yet at every performance the ghost surprised her when it materialised.

It is as if the senses of the spectators had a consciousness and a subconscious. he actor can manipulate the senses' subconscious without the spectators realising it or being able to explain why they were struck by an actor in a particular scene so that they remember it for years.

An action doesn't necessarily occur in space. Ethologists define as movements of intention the particular dynamism of an animal even when immobile: for example, a tiger lying in wait for its prey already has in its body the muscular tension of the leap although still crouching.

It is in immobility that the excellence of Oriental actors can be admired, when the maximum of intensity implodes. As spectators, we experience the presence of opposites: a dynamic stillness, which is the negation of inert immobility.

The logic of the exercises: Think paradoxically

The actor's dance of being surfaces through the concrete materiality of the body and materialises through actions. To be able to make actions which have an effect on the spectator, the actor forges another body for himself. Our behaviour in everyday life is the result of a process of inculturation, which, over a long period, is determined by our family, education, and social class. Today's would-be actor brings this inculturated naturalness to his theatrical apprenticeship since the convention of most modern theatre is based on it. In reality, this naturalness consists of mental, physical, and vocal conditioned reflexes. Spontaneity is made up of personal clichés which may function in contemporary theatre or film.

In traditional theatre forms in East and West, such as classical ballet or pantomime, the student is obliged to depart from his naturalness and learn a totally different way of standing, sitting, looking, and moving in space. It may be called stylisation, but, in effect, it is a process of acculturation that negates everyday naturalness and recreates an equivalent of our behaviour in the life of every day.

In contemporary Western theatre, the use of physical exercises in the actor's training has been common since its invention and use by Stanislavski, Meyerhold, and Copeau, and with its revival in the early 1960s by Grotowski and others, among them Odin Teatret. These exercises are fixed dynamic patterns intended to be repeated. They contain the same principle of denying what is done easily in everyday life by introducing difficulties and obstacles.

The exercises teach how to assimilate and repeat dynamic patterns by involving the whole body. It is not a conceptual learning process. They have neither a meaning nor a narrative function. They make the student aware of the flow of energy, shaping it into vigorous or softer nuances, controlling its different phases and changes. Consider the flow of energy in this very simple example: if I move my arm close to the table to pick up a sheet of paper, it has the tension necessary to lift this object with its particular shape, weight, and consistency. This tension changes at the moment when the manipulative muscles of my fingers grasp the sheet while, at the same time, other muscles in the shoulder lift the arm, bending it towards my face so that I can read what is written. But if I approach the table and am in doubt whether to take the sheet of paper or the dictionary beside it, and I decide for the latter, my tensions immediately change even if I do not carry out the action. This immobility corresponds to a movement of intention, dynamic stillness. Only if these continuous tonic adjustments exist as a kind of alternating current even in a motionless state, the spectator may perceive the logic of life within the actor's body. These are signs shaped and structured in the language of Patanjali's beast-passions and manifested through the totality of the actor's presence.

Exercises can easily become pure gymnastics. What makes them technically appropriate is the fact that they negate the naturalness or obviousness of usual behaviour. An exercise must possess a fixed structure as well as a potentiality to change itself in order to renew its function as an obstacle, thus offering an unexpected resistance to the actor. Learning through exercises implies a physical intelligence. It is not a question of one's IQ or an accumulation of theoretical knowledge but of a somatic cleverness achieved through experience.

It is undeniable that, for an actor, the acceptance of years of rigorous discipline, the denial of in-grown habits, the nurturing of a scenic anatomy and a paradoxical way of thinking result in the onset of a particular awareness. I could conclude that this is the premise for creative freedom and, with Balàzs in mind, for the experience of holding the actor and his spectator fast in the present, the here and now.

Ikebana

This text from 1992 is an example of the articulate and systematic dialogue that Barba developed with Asian theatres from the perspective of Theatre Anthropology. The text deals with the principle of equivalence and is taken from Chapter 3 of The Paper Canoe: A Guide to Theatre Anthropology *(Barba 1995: 30–32). The book was published for the first time in 1992 in Spanish.*

If we put some flowers in a vase, we do so in order to show how beautiful they are, to please our senses of sight and smell. We can also make them take on ulterior meanings: filial or religious piety, love, recognition, respect. But beautiful as they might be, flowers have a shortcoming: taken out of their own context, they continue to represent only themselves. They are like the performer described by Decroux: the man condemned to resemble a man, the body imitating a body. This may well be pleasing, but it is not sufficient to be considered art. 'For art to be', adds Decroux, 'the idea of one thing must be given by another thing' (1985: 30). Flowers in a vase are, however, irremediably flowers in a vase, sometimes subjects of works of art, but never works of art themselves.

But suppose we imagine using cut flowers to represent the struggle of the plant to grow, to rise up from the earth into which its roots sink even deeper as it reaches up to the sky. Let us imagine wanting to represent the passage of time, as the plant blossoms, grows, droops, fades and dies. If we succeed, the flowers will represent something other than flowers and will be a work of art. We will have made an ikebana.

The Japanese ideogram for ikebana means 'to make flowers live'.

The life of the flowers, precisely because it has been interrupted, can be represented. The procedure is clear: something has been wrenched from the normal conditions of its life (this is the fate of our daily flowers arranged in a vase), and those conditions have been replaced and rebuilt using other equivalent rules.

We cannot represent the flowers' blossoming and withering in temporal terms. But the passage of time can be suggested with an analogy in space.

One can bring together – compare – one flower in bud with another already in full bloom. With two branches, one thrusting upwards and the other pointing downwards, one can draw attention to the directions in which the plant is developing, to the force that binds it to the earth and to the force that pushes it away. A third branch, extending along an oblique line, can show the combined force that results from the other opposing tensions. This composition seems to derive from refined stylisation but is, however, the consequence of the analysis and dissection of a phenomenon, that is, the transposition of energy acting in time into a composition of lines that, with a principle of equivalence, extend in space.

This equivalent transposition opens the composition to new meanings, different from the original ones. The branch which is reaching upwards becomes associated with Heaven, the branch extending downwards with the Earth, and the branch in the centre with the intermediary between these two opposing entities: the human being. The result of a schematic analysis of reality and the transposition of this reality following principles that represent it without reproducing it becomes an object for philosophical contemplation.

'The mind has difficulty maintaining the concept of the bud because the thing thus designated is prey to an impetuous development and shows – in spite of our thought – a strong impulse not to be a bud but a flower.' These are words which Bertolt Brecht attributes to Hu-jeh, who adds, 'Thus, for the thinker, the concept of the flower bud is already the concept of something which aspires to be other than what it is' (Brecht 1967: 493; my translation). This 'difficult' thought is exactly what ikebana proposes to be: an indication of the past and a suggestion of the future, a representation through immobility of the continuous motion that turns the positive into the negative and vice versa.

Abstract meanings derive from ikebana through the precise work of analysis and transposition of a physical phenomenon. If one began with these abstract meanings, one would never reach the concreteness and precision of ikebana, whereas by starting from precision and concreteness one does attain these abstract meanings. Performers often try to proceed from the abstract to the concrete. They believe that the point of departure can be what one wants to express, which then implies the use of a technique suitable for this expression.

Ikebana shows how certain forces that develop in time can have an equivalence in spatial terms. Decroux insists on this use of equivalence, which is a recurring principle. His mime is based on the rigorous substitution of extra-daily tensions equivalent to those necessary for the body's daily techniques. Decroux, during his seminar at Odin Teatret, in 1968, explained and demonstrated how an action from daily life can be believably represented by acting in exactly the opposite way. The action of pushing something is shown not by projecting the chest forward and pressing down with the back foot – as one does in the daily action – but by arching the spine concavely, as if instead of pushing it was being pushed, and bending the arms towards the chest and pressing downwards with the front leg and foot. This consistent and radical inversion of the forces characteristic of the daily action produces the work involved in the daily action. It is a fundamental principle in theatre: on stage, the action must be real, but it is not important that it be realistic.

Everything takes place as if the performer's body were taken apart and then recomposed according to successive and antagonist movements. The performer does not relive the action; he recreates the life of the action. At the end of this work of decomposition and recomposition, the body no longer resembles itself. Like the flowers in our vase or like Japanese ikebana, the performer is cut from the 'natural' context in which daily techniques dominate. Like the flower and branches in ikebana, performers, in order to be scenically alive, cannot present what they are. They must represent what they want to show by means of forces and procedures which have the same value and the same effectiveness. In other words, they must give up their own 'spontaneity', that is, their own automatisms.

The various codifications of the performer's art are, above all, methods to break the automatic responses of daily life and to create equivalents to them.

Naturally, this rupture of automatisms is not expression. But without this rupture, there is no expression.

An Odin actor, Tage Larsen, speaking to his director, explains his own criteria for acting: 'I speak in the third person and name someone, but I wait for a moment before indicating him or turning towards him. Or, I describe a fact. When I want to underline the text with physical actions, I delay them. First I speak and then I describe physically' (Barba 1981: 109; my translation).

'Kill the breathing. Kill the rhythm', Katsuko Azuma's master repeated to her. To kill breathing and to kill rhythm means to be aware of the tendency automatically to link gesture to the rhythm of breathing, speaking, and music, and to break this link. The opposite of linking automatically is consciously to create a new connection.

The precepts that demand the killing of rhythm and breathing, as expressed by Katsuko Azuma's master, show how the search for oppositions can result in the rupture of the automatisms of the body's daily techniques. Killing the rhythm in fact implies creating a resistance, a series of tensions to prevent the flow of words from coinciding with the actions that accompany them and to prevent the movements of the dance from synchronising automatically with the cadences of the music. Killing the breathing means slowing down or withholding the exhalation, which is a moment of relaxation, by means of a contrary force.

All these principles are not aesthetic ways of suggesting how to add beauty to the performer's body nor how to stylise it. They are means to remove what is obviously the body's daily aspect, in order to avoid it being only a human body condemned to resemble itself, to present and represent only itself.

Working on energy

This text, also from The Paper Canoe: A Guide to Theatre Anthropology *(Barba 1995: 63–72), indicates the multiple possibilities of dialogue with Asian theatres provided by Theatre Anthropology. Barba takes up the concept of 'energy' and describes how it is practically possible to shape it and render it perceptible for the spectator.*

During apprenticeship, individual differentiation passes through the negation of the differentiation of the sexes. The field of complementarity dilates. This is noticeable when the work on the pre-expressive level takes no account of what is masculine and what is feminine (as in modern dance or the training of many theatre groups) or when a performer explores masculine and feminine roles indiscriminately (as in traditional Asian theatre). The double-edged nature of the performer's particular energy becomes tangibly evident. The balance between the two poles, animus energy and anima energy, is preserved.

Also in Indian tradition, performers work within the polarity of the energy and not according to the correspondence between the character and the performer's gender. The styles of Indian dance are divided into two categories, *lasya* (delicate) and *tandava* (vigorous), depending on the way the movements are executed and not on the gender of the performer.

The world of Indian dance develops between these two sides of a single unity; not only the styles but also each element of a single style (movement, rhythm, costume, music) is defined as *tandava* if it is strong, vigorous, exuberant, while, if it is light, delicate, gentle, it is defined as *lasya*.

For the Balinese, *bayu* ('wind', 'breath') normally indicates the performer's energy, and the expression *pengunda bayu* refers to a well-distributed energy. The Balinese *bayu* is a literal interpretation of the increase and decrease of a force that lifts the whole body and whose complementary aspects (*keras*/ vigorous and *manis*/soft) reconstruct the variations and nuances of life.

In the terminology of Theatre Anthropology, animus and anima refer to a discordant concord, an interaction between opposites that brings to mind the poles of a magnetic field, or the tension between body and shadow. It would be arbitrary to give them gender connotations.

Keras and *manis*, *tandava* and *lasya*, animus and anima do not refer to concepts which are completely equivalent. What is similar, however, in different cultures, is the necessity to specify, by means of an opposition, the extreme poles of the range in which the performer mentally and practically breaks down the energy of his natural *bios* modulating it into scenic *bios*, that enlivens, from the inside, his technique. These terms do not refer to women or men or to feminine or masculine qualities but to softness and vigour as flavours of the energy. The Indian warrior god, Rama, for example, is often represented in the lasya, 'soft', way. The alternation of anima energy and animus energy is clearly perceptible in Indian, Balinese, and Japanese performers who tell and dance the stories of several characters; or in Western performers who, from the beginning, have been formed by a training that does not take gender differences into consideration.

One form of essential research, common both to Theatre Anthropology and to our craft's empiricism, is research into the constant polarities hidden beneath the variety and fluctuation of styles, traditions, genres, and different work practices. To give a name to the flavours, to the performer's experiences, to the spectator's perceptions, even the most subtle of them, seems a futile abstraction. But it is a premise for leaping from a situation in which we are immersed and that dominates us, to a real experience, that is, something which we are able to analyse, to develop consciously and to transmit.

It is the leap from experiencing to having experience.

Before being thought of as a purely spiritual entity – platonic or Christian – the word 'soul' (Latin *anima*) meant a wind, a continuous flow that animated the motion and life of animals and human beings. In many cultures, the body is compared to a percussion instrument: its soul is the beat, the vibration, the rhythm.

This wind which is vibration and rhythm can change face, while remaining itself, by means of a subtle mutation of its inner tension. Summarising a millennarian culture, Dante believed that when anima – the living inner wind – is drawn towards something external, it turns into animus.

In the course of his career, the performer comes to realise that the most insidious obstacle is not difficulty in learning but that having learned so much he has become invulnerable. He senses that his technical shell awakes interest, commands respect and dazzles. He becomes, for the observer, a deforming and revealing mirror.

But because he is invulnerable, his shadow has withdrawn into his shell.

The shadow can emerge only from a fracture, when the performer is able to open a vent in the armour of his technique, exposing himself, undefended, like the warrior who fights with bare hands. Vulnerability becomes strength.

This takes us back to the performer's origin, to the first day of apprenticeship, when the gamut of unrealised and invisible potentialities collided with the tangible work of selection and crystallisation. Here, energy, the wind that blows through the shell of technique and that animates it from inside, risks becoming tamed by the dominant models of scenic behaviour and performance. The dynamic relationship between the animus and anima potentialities, their consonance and dissonance, tend, with time, to become stabilised in a consolidated technique.

But the fracture through which the shadow can filter is determined by the simultaneous presence of animus and anima, by the performer's ability to explore the range between one pole and the other, to show the dominant profile of his or her energy and to reveal its double nature – vigour and tenderness, vehemence and grace, ice and snow, sun and flame.

And thus the spectator discovers the invisible life that animates the theatre and experiences an experience.

The double profile of the wind in the armour, the dual tension that characterises energy on the theatre's cellular level, is the material source of this spiritual experience.

Zeami: Piling up snow in a silver bowl

In a short, obscure treatise written around 1420, when he was almost sixty years old, Zeami laid out a scale of nine steps corresponding to the nine degrees of perfection in the performer's art (*Kyui*, 'The Nine Steps'). For each of the nine steps he chose a poetic image drawn from the literature of Zen monks. Here are the first three images:

> In Silla, in the dead of night,
> the sun shines brightly.
> Snow covers a thousand mountains;
> why is there one peak that is not white?
> Piling up snow
> in a silver bowl.
>> (Zeami 1984: 120–21)

Reading these lines one after another as if they were a poem, I am struck by the difference between the first two images and the third. I will not try to interpret them but to comment on them freely within the context of our argument, not Zeami's.

In the first and second image, the complementarity or correspondence between the opposites is obvious, while in the third one it is veiled by a fundamentally monochromatic image brought alive by the nuances between the brilliant whiteness of the snow and the dazzling yet warm luminosity of the silver. I emphasise 'warm'; in a subsequent verse another gleam of metal appears in which a cold quality is explicitly referred to ('The shadow of the metal hammer moving; the cold gleam of the sacred sword', Zeami 1984: 122). The image of the snow in the silver bowl, however, transforms the natural notion of cold into serene, clear light. One could say that the impression created is one of spring in the heart of winter. Here as well, then, there is a complementarity, but now it is dissimulated by the absolute absence of dissonance.

Zeami goes on to use the image of the snow and the silver to discuss the imperturbable presence of the performer who achieves the unusual without any visible dramatic effect. We will use it, however, to conclude these reflections on the various temperatures of energy.

One of the most insidious pitfalls that lie in wait in books dedicated to the procedures of art derives from the radical difference between the tactics that guide conceptual comprehension and those which, on the other hand, guide practical comprehension through experience of action.

In order to understand rationally the existence of a gamut of different possibilities, it is helpful to emphasise extreme points, as we have just done with animus and anima. But we must remember that the purpose of this insistence on extremes is the clarity of the discussion and not practical effectiveness. In a work situation, if one concentrates on extreme poles, what one attains is only technique gone mad. In order to understand the criteria that can lead us towards a conscious modelling of energy, it is important to insist on polarities such as *keras* and *manis*, animus and anima, sun and midnight, *lasya* and *tandava*, black and white, fire and ice. But in order to translate those criteria into artistic practice, one must work not on the extremes but on the gamut of nuances that lie between them. If this does not happen, instead of artificially composing the energy in order to reconstruct the organicity of a body-in-life, one produces only the image of artificiality.

The couplet 'Piling up snow / in a silver bowl' can represent, in our context, an antidote to the tendency towards extremes. It reminds us that making the *bios* visible depends on the imperceptible nuances of rhythm, of single waves, each one different from the other, that make up the living current.

► Zeami's recommendation to play an old man with vigour was embodied by the young kyogen performer Kosuke Nomura at the ISTA session in Blois/Malakoff, France (1985).

But we must not forget that the softness of the snow and the hardness of the silver in which it is contained are also themselves two extremes that condense, in an oxymoron, the simultaneous action of two divergent forces. For Zeami, the secret of the unusual, the performer's 'flower', his scenic *bios*, lies in this ability to give life to an opposition.

In the treatise, *Fushikaden* (Dictates on the Style and the Flower), we read:

> When performing nō, there are endless matters that must be kept in mind. For example, when an actor plans to express the emotion of anger, he must not fail to retain a tender heart. Such is his only means to prevent his acting from developing roughness, no matter what sort of anger is expressed. To appear angry while possessing a tender heart gives rise to the principle of novelty. On the other hand, in a performance requiring grace, an actor must not forget to remain strong. Thus all aspects of his performance – dance, movement, role playing – will be genuine and lifelike.
>
> Then, too, there are various concerns in connection with using the actor's body on stage. When he moves himself about in a powerful way, he must slide his foot in a gentle way. And when he stamps his feet strongly, he must hold the upper part of his body quiet. This matter is difficult to describe in words. It is better to learn this directly from a teacher.
>
> (Zeami 1984: 58)

Another treatise by Zeami, *Shikado* (The True Path for the Flower), introduces us to the nuances found between extremes. This text should be read in conjunction with another treatise: *Nikyoku Santai Ezu* (Two Arts and Three Illustrated Types).

Zeami draws the performer's attention to the importance of three figures: the Woman, the Warrior, and the Old Man. Three apparently different roles. In Shikado he writes:

> An actor who is beginning his training must not overlook the Two Arts (*Nikyoku*) and Three Types (*Santai*). By the Two Arts, I mean dancing and chanting. By the Three Types, I refer to the human forms that constitute the basis of role impersonation: an old person (*rotai*), a woman (*nyotai*), a warrior (*guntai*).
>
> (Zeami 1984: 64)

The three basic types of which Zeami is speaking are not, however, roles. They are not actual 'types', as they are usually understood to be, but *tai*, that is, bodies guided by a particular quality of energy that has to do neither with gender nor with age. Zeami's three basic *tai* are distinct ways of carrying the same body, giving it a different scenic life by means of specific qualities of energy. One of the other meanings of *tai* is, in fact, semblance.

It is particularly important to look not at the extremes – the woman and the warrior – but at the body, the tai, of the old person such as it is described and drawn in the treatise *Nikyoku Santai Ezu*.

Zeami defines the three types as follows: 'Old Man Type: serenity of spirit, distant gaze' (1960: 155; my translation); 'Woman Type: her substance is the spirit. She has no violence' (1960: 156; my translation); 'Warrior Type: his substance is violence. The spirit is applied to detail (delicacy in force)' (1960: 156; my translation).

Alongside these definitions, Zeami places the drawings of the three tai: three naked figures in whose bodies the architecture of the three semblances is clearly recognisable.

In the sketch of the Old Man, who is leaning on a cane, Zeami has drawn a line to indicate the direction of the Old Man's gaze, upwards, which contrasts with the bent posture of an individual who is so weak that he must support himself with a cane. A tension is created between the nape of the neck and the upper part of the spinal column.

This drawing reveals the secret of the three bodies; through the body of an old man, the performer consciously manipulates the two faces of the energy – animus/anima – that coexist within him. In this way, the performer makes the authentic *hana*, the flower, blossom, that, according to Zeami, characterises the great actor. In *Fushikaden* he writes:

> Playing the role of an old man represents the very pinnacle of our art. These roles are crucial, since the spectators who watch can gauge immediately the real skills of the actor [...].
>
> In terms of stage deportment, most actors, thinking to appear old, bend their loins and hips, shrink their bodies, lose their Flower, and give a withered, uninteresting performance. It is particularly important that the actor refrain from performing in a limp or weak manner, but bears himself with grace and dignity. Most crucial of all is the dancing posture chosen for the *tai* of an old man. One must study assiduously the precept: portrayal of an old man while still possessing the Flower. The results should resemble an old tree that puts forth flowers.
>
> (Zeami 1984: 11–12)

Thought in action: The paths of energy

Let us consider the *jo-ha-kyu*, one of the criteria – or paths of thought – which in Japan regulate the arts and therefore also the various forms of traditional theatre.

Three phases:

1. *jo*: the initial phase, when force is put in motion as if overcoming a resistance;
2. *ha*: the transition phase, rupture of the resistance, increase of the motion;
3. *kyu*: the rapid phase, an unbridled crescendo ending in the sudden stop.

Let us translate literally: resistance, rupture, acceleration.

But we have not yet even begun to understand this regulatory principle. One of the impediments to our understanding is the fact that this principle is applied to all levels of the theatre, from performing to dramaturgy, from the composition of the programme of a noh evening to the music. We will focus only on the performer's physical action.

The third moment is characterised by a sudden stop. The impression given to the spectator by the performer is that of someone who comes to an abrupt halt at the edge of a ravine. The performer's feet suddenly stop, the trunk sways slightly forward while the spine extends and the performer seems to increase in size. In fact, the moment of the stop is a transitional phase. Some performers say that in the *kyu*, they do not exhale completely and keep enough breath to start the action again without having to inhale. The movement is interrupted, but the energy is suspended. As a Peking Opera performer summarised to me in an effective remark: 'movement stop, inside no stop'. In other words, the final moment of the phase in which the performer stops is a *sats*, the point of departure for a new *jo*. The *jo-ha-kyu*, in short, is cyclical.

We have made a step forward in our understanding, but we are still a long way off.

One might think that *jo-ha-kyu* works like the 'infinite' or 'perpetual canon' of traditional Western music. This is not the case. When referred to in books, it can seem to be a metre based on three phases, each with a different speed. In fact, each of the three phases is in turn subdivided into *jo-ha-kyu*. When, after having first explained the rudiments of *jo-ha-kyu*, the traditional Japanese performer goes on to analyse the structure of his action, he begins to speak of a *jo* of the *ha*, of a *ha* of the *kyu* of a *kyu* of the *jo*, and so on. The performer can carry out an entire dance while explaining the different phases, and the sub-phases of each phase, to those who are watching.

The observer then begins to get lost. Trying to find a fixed point on which to focus, he pushes the question to the absurd: 'But does that mean that there is also a *kyu* of the *jo* of the *ha*?'

'Exactly', the performer replies. Beyond a certain limit, he also begins to get lost. We realise that *jo-ha-kyu* is not really a rhythmic structure but a pattern of thought and action. On the macroscopic level, it is a clear technical articulation, but once a certain threshold has been passed, it becomes a rhythm of thinking.

Does it then cease to be something that is relevant to practice?

The Japanese performer who is demonstrating the basic techniques of his art cannot continue to indicate to us the infinitesimal sub-phases of each action. They are no longer actual segments of a score. This does not exclude them from being accents of the thought, of the mental behaviour that enables the performer always to vary imperceptibly his way of being in an action. It is thought that etches and sculpts time, thus becoming rhythm. The action is rigorously codified in its detailed score, but there is a kind of sub-score along which the performer improvises. He does not change the form; the same design of movements is executed, while the performer invents innumerable *jo-ha-kyu* relationships, each time as if it were the irst time.

'I first heard the term *jo-ha-kyu* as an adult. When I learned the word, I already knew what it was', says kyogen actor Kosuke Nomura during a demonstration at the Blois ISTA in April 1985. Kosuke was twenty-five years old and already had twenty-three years of theatrical experience. He began to work with his grandfather at the age of two and a half, for fifteen minutes a day. He could already perform 300 of the 1000 roles that make up the repertoire of a kyogen actor. *Jo-ha-kyu* is not only an important quality of his style. It has marked his identity as a performer.

Let us visit the beginner's class at the Ballet School of the Royal Theatre of Copenhagen and observe how the luxury balance of the ballet dancer is acquired. The teacher points out one young girl from among the other students. It seems to me that her way of doing the exercises is just like that of all the other students. The teacher explains to me that it is not a question of technical ability but of the quality of her phrasing. This means that the child is following the music without abandoning herself to it. In spite of the elementary level of the exercises, she already shows an ability to withhold and model her own rhythm – her own energies – in a personal dialogue with the music. Even though her dancing is inexpert, the way in which she thinks it with her whole body is not mechanical.

We have several times repeated that the performer's energy is not impetuosity, overexcitement, violence. Neither is it, however, an abstraction or a metaphor, with which one cannot work.

In its basic, material form, energy is a muscular and nervous force. But it is not the pure and simple existence of this force, present by definition in every living being, which is of interest to us. Nor is it enough that this force undergoes change; every moment of our lives, consciously or unconsciously, we are modelling our physical energy.

What must be of interest to us is the way in which this biological process becomes thought, is remodelled and made visible to the spectator.

In order to reshape his own energy artificially, the performer must think of it in its tangible, visible, and audible forms. The performer must picture it, divide it into a scale, withhold it, suspend it in an immobility that acts, guiding it through the design of movements with varying intensities and velocities as if through a slalom course.

We note, therefore, that what we call energy is in fact leaps of energy. The principle of the absorption of the action, the *sats*, the ability to compose the transition from one temperature to another (animus and anima, *keras* and *manis* …) are all different stratagems for the production and control of the leaps of energy that enliven the performer's *bios*. These leaps are variations in a series of details that, intelligently assembled in sequence, are called 'physical actions' (Stanislavski and Grotowski), 'design of movements' (Meyerhold), 'score' (Stanislavski, Grotowski, and others), *kata* (Japanese traditional acting) in the various working languages.

It does not matter what names the performer uses, whether he resorts to scientific metaphors or poetic images, follows the dictate of a tradition or a personal way of thinking. What is important is that in the practice of the apprenticeship and in the experience of his thinking, he knows how to construct and subdivide a precise route that makes it possible for the energy to leap. This verb is used in scientific language to describe the behaviour of 'quanta' of energy. In Latin, it means to dance.

Let us again listen to Toporkov working with Stanislavski. He is now the spectator, while Konstantin Sergeyevitch Stanislavski is doing the exercise of a man at a news-stand:

> He would buy a newspaper when there is a whole hour before the departure of the train and he doesn't know how to kill the time, or when the first or second bell has rung, or when the train has already started. The actions are all the same but in completely different rhythms, and Konstantin Sergeyevitch was able to carry out these exercises in any order by increasing the rhythm, by diminishing the rhythm, by sudden change.
>
> (Toporkov 1979: 63)

The exactness with which the action is designed in space, the precision of each of its characteristics, a series of exact fixed points of departure and arrival, of impulses and counter-impulses, of changes of direction, of *sats*: these are the preliminary conditions for the dance of energy.

Natsu Nakajima, a direct heir of Tatsumi Hijikata, who founded butoh dance together with Kazuo Ohno, is explaining and demonstrating her way of working (Bologna, ISTA, July 1990). She chooses a series of images for each of which she establishes an attitude, a figure for her dance. She thus has available a series of immobile poses sculpted into her body. She now assembles the individual poses one after another, passing from one to another without interruption. She obtains a precise design of movements. She repeats the same sequence as if meeting three different types of resistance, which must be overcome with three different types of energy: it is as if she were moving in a space as solid as stone, in a liquid space and in the air. She is constructing, on the basis of a limited number of poses, a universe of images, a choreography.

Up to this point, watching her demonstration, we have seen a rigorous work of combination characterised by precision and by recognizability of every single fragment. But when Natsu goes through this combination of fragments again, without varying the order of the pattern, all of us who had previously watched the long and passionless preliminary anatomy, now have the impression that she is improvising her dance.

And Natsu is actually improvising, just as Stanislavski was improvising in his scene at the news-stand. Natsu has a completely different culture, tradition, aesthetic ideals, repertoire of images and concepts, but the basic principle which she is using (not her technique, but the technique of her technique) is no different from that used by Stanislavski.

Let us consider, for a moment, how misleading is the ghost of the word 'improvisation'. This term often crops up in professional discussions, sometimes to indicate an ideal to be achieved, sometimes to warn one about a form of decay to be avoided. When the word 'improvisation' does not mean a lack of precision, when it is used in a positive sense, it denotes a quality of the performer that derives from a refined work on the various levels of scenic *bios*. It is thought/action on a riverbed of a physical score. It does not matter if this score is created by the performer during the long and patient work of rehearsal, if it has been fixed by tradition, or if, on the other hand, the performer composes it at the same time as executing it, while carried by the 'second nature' (according to Stanislavski and Copeau) of his extra-daily body.

A message from the past

In this excerpt from The Paper Canoe *(Barba 1995: 131–34) Barba focuses on the need and longing for fixed formal patterns – a score – to trigger the actor's 'life' as well as the spectator's perception. The text concentrates on Japanese* kata, *relating it to the working languages and demands of Western theatre reformers.*

At the beginning of the twentieth century, Edward Gordon Craig fired broadsides at the concept of the 'actor's art'. He lamented the absence of physical scores that were sufficiently refined, rigorous and complete. He concluded that the word 'art' when applied to the actor was unjustifiable. Craig was the son of the famous actress Ellen Terry, the student of Henry Irving, a devoted spectator, in Italy, of Tommaso Salvini, Giovanni Grasso, Ettore Petrolini, and Eleonora Duse. He said that they were more than actors – and something less than artists:

> Acting is not an art. It is therefore incorrect to speak of the actor as an artist. For accident is an enemy of the artist. Art is the exact antithesis of pandemonium, and pandemonium is created by the tumbling together of many accidents [...].
>
> In the modern theatre, owing to the use of the bodies of men and women as their material, all that is presented there is of an accidental nature. The actions of the actor's body, the expressions of his face, the sounds of his voice, all are at the mercy of the wind of his emotions: these winds, that must blow for ever round the artist, moving without unbalancing him. But with the actor, emotion possesses him; it seizes upon his limbs, moving them whither it will [...] emotion is able to win over the mind to assist in the destruction of that which the mind would produce [...] emotion is the cause which first of all creates, and secondly destroys.
>
> (Craig 1962: 55–58)

In his first books on the theatre, Craig had strongly refuted the preoccupations and needs that had nourished Stanislavski's and Meyerhold's empirical research. Craig presented the ideal image of the Über-marionette, capable of incarnating Form. Stanislavski, Meyerhold, and all those who followed them and would follow the roads opened by them, spoke of rigour in physical actions. Copeau defined the actor as one who knew how to be a natural human being and a marionette at the same time.

With the hindsight of our perspective, these words of Étienne Decroux are almost an answer to Craig with respect to the destructive force of the emotions:

> The mastery of emotion? When the actor undertakes to express himself in lines of meticulous geometry, risking his balance and thus suffering in his flesh, he is indeed forced to hold back his emotion and behave as an artist: an artist of drawing.
>
> (Decroux 1985: 7)

From Meyerhold's working language to that of Decroux, the design of movements assumes different nuances, according to the two men's different artistic biographies, and yet remains substantially the same: a principle which is unavoidable for the performer who refuses the self-indulgence which our society confers upon the theatre. This principle is found throughout the entire twentieth-century tradition, from Stanislavski to Grotowski, and in others after him.

Meyerhold retraced this same need going back in time and quoted Voltaire, for whom the actor – as opposed to the dancer – is not an artist. 'Dance', Voltaire said, 'is art because it is bound by laws' (Meyerhold 1969: 130).

To have a score, defined in every detail and disciplined in its form, is one of the performer's primary needs. This is one of those evident truths which we usually call a 'Columbus egg'. In order to see this truth clearly, all one has to do is lift the veil of commonplaces created by theatrical self-indulgence.

The word *kata* is found throughout the tradition of Japanese theatre and dance. It could be defined as a message from the past, transmitted from one generation to another by means of small or large vocal and movement sequences. Some of these sequences of fixed details have a title or are accompanied by a suggestive comment. For example, 'the moon on the water', which is explained as follows: 'the action is not calculated, it springs forth without visible force, it is the unity of separate elements, not overshadowed by the clouds of thought'. The poetic images that describe the *kata* also serve to hide it, to protect its secret from being penetrated by competitors and adversaries.

On its own, the word *kata* has nothing mysterious or esoteric about it. Semantically, in common speech, it corresponds more or less to words like 'form', 'stamp', 'pattern' in European languages. For the performer, it can refer to a single movement or position, a structured sequence of actions or to an entire role. A *kata* can transmit the detailed version of a realistic action making us think of Stanislavski's 'physical action', or a design of symbolic movements. Our mind, which seeks out analogies, turns to Craig, who maintained that actors, in order to avoid the state of servitude in which they find themselves, must create a way of performing made up of symbolic gestures: 'To-day they impersonate and interpret; tomorrow they must represent and interpret; and the third day they must create' (Craig 1962: 61).

In some cases, the title and comment that accompany a *kata*, this sort of hieroglyph-in-action, have been lost, and the *kata* has become a kind of score without evident content. It is executed and appreciated for its dynamic, rhythmic, and aesthetic qualities – and hence our thought turns towards the choreographic work which is closest to it: to Meyerhold, to his work on rhythm, to his use of music during rehearsal in order to impose a tempo on the design of movements.

Experience teaches us that if a performer learns to execute a *kata* which is for him a precise but empty score, repeating it over and over again, then he will succeed in personalising it, discovering or renewing its meaning. An empty score does not in fact exist. Ideoplastic precision – the sensation that passes through the body of the performer who has mastered a precise pattern – makes it possible, in time, to extract a meaning from what seemed to be pure form.

Extract a meaning or discover the meaning? Whichever it may be, to learn to execute a *kata* is not an intellectual task but requires corporal effort, in which, however, mental activity is always present. This is why the *kata*, like the design of movements in Meyerhold's school, can be passed on. And it is useful if it is passed on from the person who has composed it to someone who will know how to recompose it.

James Brandon, the American specialist in Japanese theatre, affirms that the process by which performers from one generation to another learn the same *kata* is an essential part of the art of kabuki. From the point of view of the individual performer, to learn to represent a *kata* is a process which is closely connected to the search for his own personal and artistic individuality. This leads to a fertile dialectic between conservation and innovation, because the performer must create a new *kata* in order to assert his own individuality and so doing contradicts his own profound respect for the traditional *kata*. These two opposing tendencies are in contraposition in every artistic society, but when they are present in physical scores with rigorous forms they can transform the contrast into harmony:

> The two forces tend to check each other, with the result that in the actor's work neither unregulated newness, applauded by some segments of the audience, nor slavish adherence to tradition, rewarded by family elders, become dominant. They are balanced in a state of healthy tension. The balance will differ for each actor – some inclining toward new ideas and some toward established forms – and according to

circumstances, but it has always been maintained. As long as actors can continue to create within the framework of traditional kata, kabuki will remain the living theatre art that it is today.[12]

(Brandon 1978: 124)

The quote refers to the *kata* understood as the score of an entire role. It does, however, also apply to the *kata* understood as scores or segments of actions (a noh performer, for example, will never move from a seated position to a fast walk without two intermediate *kata* that elaborate the micro-action of standing up and the micro-action of beginning to walk).

The term *shu-ha-ri* defines the process of apprenticeship and development by means of the *kata*. *Shu* indicates the first phase of work: to respect the form, to learn it in all the accuracy of its details. *Ha* (one is reminded of the second phase of *jo-ha-kyu*) refers to the moment in which the performer becomes free of the technique, not because its dictates have been transgressed but because they have been respected and the performer can now move with a new 'spontaneity', as if with 'a second nature'. The *kata* has been incorporated. *Ri*, the third phase, refers to the moment in which the performer moves away from the form: he models the form that modelled him.

Following the design of the *kata*, the performer's thought seeks to find out how to avoid the fixity of the form that offers a resistance to him, how to dilate the form without exploding it. A technically elaborated and fixed behaviour becomes a means of personal discovery. Some commentators define the *kata* as 'physical *koan*'.

When referring to the performer who has discovered how to dominate the various phases of this process, one speaks of 'ability which has no ability', of 'technique which has no technique', of 'art without art'. Images which have strong echoes and relationships with those used by Craig when he spoke of the actor as the Über-marionette. He recalled an ancient axiom, one repeated ad infinitum and very difficult to understand: 'The highest art is that which conceals the craft and forgets the craftsman' (Craig 1962: 83). Intellectually, it is easy to believe that one understands what this means. But in practice, what does one do? How does one help the performer 'give himself', 'burn', go beyond himself and, at the same time, hide the artifice?

The answers to these questions, formulated at different times and in different working languages, all converge towards the procedures necessary

---

[12] Regarding the same topic, see the detailed description of the interpretations of the *kata* in *Kumagei's Battle Camp*, performed by Danjuro IX (1839–1903) and Nakamura Shikan (1830–99), in Leiter (1991).

for the construction of a real action. The pre-expressive appears to us, then, as the dynamic matter circumscribed and worked on by those principles which, in a transcultural dimension, help bring alive the precision of a design.

Thus, when the design of a movement is organically developed and brought alive, it leads to a leap of meaning. A word or phrase can change colour, and an action can reveal an unthought-of aspect of a character's behaviour or of a situation.

The many faces of the guru

This text deals with the role of the guru in Asian theatre culture. By comparing this role to the way in which European actors of the past learned their craft, Barba emphasises the importance and the value of the theatre company whose configuration and relationships acted in a way analogous to that of the guru.

This is an excerpt from the article 'Tacit Knowledge: Heritage and Waste', first published in 2000 (New Theatre Quarterly, *16 (3), pp. 263–77).*

Traditional apprenticeship in theatre has always been based, on the one hand, on the professional authoritativeness of the master, the guru, the *sensei*, or certain models, and, on the other, on the tradition (or the breaking of tradition) that they represent.

Today, guru is a common word, even outside the Indian context. Its use is often the fatuous sign of a fashion, but it also points to an unsatisfied need: an apprenticeship that establishes a pedagogical relationship which is difficult, full of risks, rigorous, demanding; that is, more profound and personal than a scholastic one.

For centuries, in theatre practice, continuity and also the seeds of change have been rooted in a situation in which apprenticeship took place in a real work situation, not separated from that of the public exercise of the profession. The process of learning was pragmatic and was integrated into the daily routine of repetition, variation, and competition within a family or a company.

In Asian traditional performance genres, the relationship between master and pupil was (and often still is) modelled on the relationship between parents and children in a culture in which the authority of the parents is absolute and, equally, their commands represent a moral imperative. In many cases, it actually is a question of biological parents and children. In others, the master 'adopts' the chosen pupil, giving the child the family name and thus creating a veritable dynasty as with kabuki, noh, and certain families of actors and dancers in Bali and India. Like kings and popes, great kabuki actors supersede one another in a long line in which the different individuals are distinguished by a number indicating the continuity of a single lineage running through the changing generations: Ichikawa Danjuro I, Ichikawa Danjuro II, Ichikawa Danjuro III up until Ichikawa Danjuro XII, spanning the period from 1660 to the present day.

Apprenticeship consists of much practical routine work, of imitation and identification with the professional norms embodied by the master. In addition to the pupil's professional duties, there are sometimes filial ones such as taking care of the day-to-day needs of the master-parent. In return, the master-parent feels responsible for the development of the pupil-son and not merely for his ability within the profession.

The process of selection is a personal one: the apprentice chooses the master and the master the apprentices. The long period of trial before making a final choice allows possible merits and weaknesses to come to light on both sides. This is the very opposite of what happens in modern theatre schools (in Asia, Europe or any other continent), where the entrance exam lasts an hour at the most and attempts to take into account the aspiring pupil's talent, maturity, age, previous studies, and predisposition towards the art.

In the traditional relationship between master and pupil, learning by doing is not limited to three or four years but takes place in a slow succession of phases allowing the pupil to absorb and take possession of the craft. This craft does not consist merely of skills but also of certain intuitive knowledge for which no rules exist. There is no didactic system or formalised method of teaching when it comes to matters such as how long to insist on certain details, how to confront an impasse during the rehearsals or how to deal with the conflicts that arise in the working relationships.

If it is true that the art of the actor cannot be taught, and yet that certain people can learn it, this means that the characteristics of the relationships within the working environment make more or less possible the assimilation of scenic knowledge.

In many traditions, in Asia as in classical ballet, emphasis is placed on the mute aspect of apprenticeship in which words are considered to be superfluous. The skills and values that the pupil gradually incorporates are not necessarily translatable into precise formulas. When an apprenticeship is successful, the pupils know far more than they think they know. Only *a posteriori*, when they themselves are ready to become masters, do they begin to question themselves about the principles that are implicit in what they have incorporated.

The master, the guru, has many faces. He is a keeper of technical knowledge as well as a spiritual guide. He is a professional and a moral authority. He is master and parent and, at the same time, head of the working ensemble or family. He is the indisputable judge of the quality of the work, thus allowing the pupil not to be kept on a tight rein by the fickle and imprecise tastes of the audience.

It cannot be emphasised enough how important it is for actors, for their independence and above all for their courage, to be able to address themselves to one spectator whom they trust completely and whose judgement is worth more than that of all the other spectators or all successes and failures.

In the environment in which transmission occurs within the relationship of master–parent and pupil–son (or daughter), the guru retains this position with all its authority for as long as he or she lives, even when the pupil has become an expert artist, perhaps even more skilled and famous than the guru, and even when the pupil is transformed into a master.

This method of guaranteeing the handing down of experience appears today to be 'archaic' and contrasts with the criteria that rule modern society. It survives with difficulty and is an exception, an exoticism. Today, those who train for the profession rarely manage to resist the need to do many things and all of them in a hurry, programming their time, the curriculum and the itinerary to follow. A way of thinking prevails in which having your own personality means doing without outside influences instead of constantly struggling with them.

Soon there will be no true gurus left, not so much because they themselves will disappear but because the conditions that make their function possible will no longer exist. Gurus are being replaced by teachers.

'How can we call them back to life?' This is not an appropriate question. The right one would be, 'How do we avoid wasting the essence of the relationships the gurus were able to establish?'

The collective guru

In the tradition of Western theatre there has never been anything comparable to the apprenticeship guaranteed by the relationship with a guru. Something similar can be found in the ballet or in the bel canto tradition, but this is a forced similarity.

It is true that often, in the history of Western theatre, experience seemed to pass from parents to children since many actors came from a family of artists. But even when actors received their training in their theatrical family, the learning process did not involve the intensity and the dangerous relationship characterising the bond between the guru and his pupil.

Nevertheless there was a guru: a collective one.

Let us see what happened when an actor was trained within a theatre company or by moving from one company to another. There was no separation between the moment of learning and that of exercising the profession. The environment, with its hierarchies, habits, and customs, with its tacit rules of behaviour, shaped the attitude of the apprentice towards the craft. It provided a vast range of artistic models, some based on routine, others on exceptional originality. They could be observed at close hand, evening after evening for months and years, opening possibilities for choices and comparisons.

In the beginning, the apprentice imitated. But he could decide on the direction to take, thereby discovering a didactic path in a context with many examples of high quality. By combining imitated elements, selecting them here and there and reorganising them, he was able to obtain original effects.

The apprentice played small roles (he was a kind of unskilled theatre worker and as such suffered financial exploitation) until faced by the challenge of a more demanding role that provided him with a foothold to advance in his career. He did not have a master who had the time and desire to dedicate himself to him. From time to time, his companions – the more experienced and skilful actors – let fall a word of advice or a piece of practical information. It was a reticent form of teaching, one drop at a time, with many voices and often abounding in contradictions mingled with shows of indifference, disapproval or appreciation from the spectators.

The young actor was moulded by the presence of two different audiences: spectators and fellow actors. The first were quick to applaud and to disapprove, and ferocious in their indifference; the second were more sceptical and cautious, familiar with the tricks of the trade, difficult to surprise or convince, clever at noticing the details and symptoms of a so-far-unexpressed potentiality, accustomed to fighting against the audience's tastes without giving in. The older actors' language, information and explanations contributed to developing the reflection-in-action of the younger inexperienced actor (a 'reflective practitioner' in today's terminology).

The rigour of the 'collective guru' was not revealed in the person of the master-parent but through a wearisome routine with little time for indulgence and beautiful words. In this situation, nobody seemed anxious to teach, and the word 'steal' seemed more suitable than 'learn' when referring to the appropriation of a technique or of a 'secret' of the craft. The numerous characters interpreted were at the same time the instruments and the proof of advancement in one's career where almost every evening one had to confront a frightening audience.

The condition that I have called the 'collective guru' seems wretched and chaotic when compared to the other which is characterised by the presence of a master-parent. It is surprising to note, however, that in spite of appearances it was an appropriate response to a process of learning in which the only fixed elements were the texts from the repertoire. Rigid relationships between master and pupil would have been counterproductive. Learning could only happen through trial and error, along the rough path of autodidactism.

Autodidactism can be defined as the capacity to have a dialogue with a master who is not there. It presupposes the ability to discern what may be of use, laboriously picking it out from among all the information, rules, encounters, misunderstandings, relationships, and clashes within the context in which one lives. It demands, above all, an attitude of hanging on doggedly to something which, at first, one is unable to grasp.

It would be easy to accentuate the negative aspects of apprenticeship with a traditional guru or with a 'collective guru' or, on the contrary, to idealise the 'archaic' systems of theatre apprenticeship, contrasting them with modern deficiencies. But the systems of the past are neither good nor bad. They are past. Our task today is to create an equivalent of their positive characteristics.

Almost everything can be eliminated from the traditional theatre apprenticeship except for the capacity to organise an environment in which learning is not the direct consequence of a teaching programme.

It was precisely the quality of this environment that the twentieth century's European theatre reformers tried to achieve. They struggled against the tendencies of our time, or rather against the ideology (or the illusion) of an industrialised society that makes people believe that an actor's learning process consists only in absorbing everything a group of teachers in a school is able to teach according to an efficient didactic method and programme.

Half human, half ghost
Techniques that are learned and a technique to elude techniques

This text expounds the particular dramaturgy created in South Korea at the end of the 1980s which, during the same performance, blended forms from the old shamanistic tradition together with acting from contemporary theatre. Barba uses this example for a more general reflection. He compares the value and function of the actor's technique between the various Asian theatres and those of the different European reformers.

This text was first published in 2013 in the programme of Ave Maria, *an Odin Teatret solo performance by Julia Varley, directed by Eugenio Barba.*

When I say 'half human, half ghost', one's attention is attracted by the word 'ghost'. In fact, we come across men and women all the time, but we don't often see ghosts. What does the image of a human being represent then, when it is also half ghost? The answer is simple: it is one of the ways to define the actor.

To clarify this thought, we have to step into a world in which ghosts are the point of departure and human beings appear changeable and ephemeral.

In the years of the so-called Cold War, immediately after the Second World War, Korea lived through a bloody war. Today, Seoul, the capital of the Republic of South Korea, is one of the world's most populated metropolises. The country is one of the planet's industrial powers, an outpost of high technology with a wealth developed since 1953 after the end of the conflict in which the Soviet Union and the USA confronted each other behind the screen of South Korea and North Korea. The feared planetary atomic apocalypse materialised in small doses in a war fought as in the old days, without the use of weapons of mass destruction. It was followed with yet greater ferocity by the Vietnam War, but always within the limits of old-fashioned massacres. But, unlike Vietnam, South Korea emerged from it bloody, certainly, but stronger and richer.

One of the consequences of opening up to the Western world and material growth was the search for its own cultural roots. The foundation of the Korean spiritual and national identity, which in the past was trampled on by Asian and Western powers, was the shamanist tradition: the practices, rituals, and beliefs that regulate the relationship between the dead and the living. This tradition, which also fed the resistance during the Japanese occupation for almost half a century, still thrived among the population.

In 1962, the Association for the Protection of Intangible Cultural Goods was founded with the aim of restraining the Westernising process. Shamanism as an effective mass antidote was identified as a valuable means to resist the imported culture and the artistic manifestations of the Western world. In 1988, the Association for the Preservation of Shamanism started a series of activities to transmit the shamanistic thinking and vision with its dances, music, songs, and rituals. The process of shaping classical models which had glorified dances and theatres in other Asian countries, in Korea was directly applied to a culture in close contact with popular beliefs and the realm of the dead. Theatres were invaded by shamanistic songs and dances.

The consequence was an interesting dramaturgical form inspired by the structure of shamanistic rituals. Performances conceived in this way took place in the open air and in closed spaces, even as agitprop during the violent students' manifestations for democracy. In 1988, on the occasion of the Olympic Games in Seoul, innumerable dance and dramatic shows presented such characteristics.

Three phases distinguish this particular dramaturgical form. At the beginning of the performance an actor sings and dances according to shamanistic rituality evoking the characters of the play (the other actors). These appear on the stage of the living, enact their story and, in the final part, are ritually dismissed by an actor who sends them back to the world of darkness from which they came.

Although many Koreans and foreigners appreciated this daring marriage between wild thought and modern rational thought, in most cases the strength of the performance was unbalanced. The performance's framework with the characters' evocation and dismissal was built according to the forms of a convention with the ritual's energetic dances and suggestive sonorities. But the central part, in which the actors interpreted the story of a contemporary or classical text, suffered from this comparison and almost always exposed a tautological weakness: stage actions of a daily nature representing daily actions. The spectators had the clear feeling that, extrapolated from the shamanistic framework, the rest was insipid and self-referring theatre. Joseph Conrad had called it 'theatre of horror' – the horror of watching human beings pretending to be human beings.

Conrad's words against the London theatre of his time emphasise a spectator's discomfort in front of a performance whose limit is just to communicate yet remaining biologically inert: the actor doesn't succeed in in-forming, in giving a living form to her relationship with the spectator. It is not enough that the object of this relationship is recognisable or verisimilar. It needs to move the spectators' senses, allowing them to orientate themselves on the performance's possible narrative and associative horizons. Delving deeper into this relationship, the spectators should be able to establish a contact with their own experiences and with those of the contemporaneity as well as with the layers of their archaic biology and the immovable time in their inner universe.

A performance becomes form-in-life through the actor's language of signs impregnated by rhythmic, narrative, and evocative energy, inducing a dialogue between the different natures of each spectator's mind. A theatrical relationship becomes alive when the signs of the actor's language, like minute points of acupuncture, radiate kinaesthetic, mnemonic, associative, instinctive, and conceptual resonances. This happens with poetry when language separates itself from everyday prose. In the case of theatre, we could ask, what are the distinctive factors that, on stage, turn human behaviour into aesthetical and artistic communication?

The South Korean theatre tried a bold graft, but its goodwill was not supported by a sufficiently effective acting technique. This judgement stems from my direct experience. During the performance's shamanistic sections I felt enthused and driven by the actors' way of acting. Their rhythm and energy conjugated in precise forms of intensified life in which I intuited a sense, but which also had an impact on me when I was unable to grasp them. When the actors began to enact the play's characters, the sails almost always sagged, I could discern the route and the tide, but the wind's unpredictable strength had vanished.

The material presence of the ghost – of the character or the dead who returns – was built with the precision of a convention distinguishable from the predictability of daily behaviour. When the actor let the ghost/character enact situations from historical reality or artistic fiction, as a spectator I didn't sense the consistency and the shadow of the world, distant yet close to me, from which it had arrived. It was no longer a ghost and not yet an actor. It irremediably ended up becoming a human being pretending to be a human being.

The perfection with which the actor observes

The South Korean performances adopting shamanistic ritual conventions disclose one of the hidden problems in the art of theatre: first comes the Ghost, then the Actor. In other words, first comes the form, the artificial/ artistic marionette, the void which is shaped and thus is ready to be haunted, inhabited: the mobile statue of a heroic or funny character. Then, in this marionette and in this statue, life is inserted: the animate power of the actor's person whom we spectators can watch as if she were one of us. In reality, the actor's person preserves her mystery, she doesn't exhibit it: she has let the character swallow it. Thus, while we recognise that the actor is similar to us spectators, we also have to acknowledge she is in no way similar to us. We ascertain the intensified life and the amplified sense of her actions. But we also see the ripples of gestures, intonations, actions, stillness, and thoughts, and it is as if these remained unknown to us.

The actor's 'as if' is a real process only if it provokes a similar 'as if' process in the spectator, one which is articulated and recognisable *a posteriori* just as that of the actor is built *a priori*.

Every time we try to define the genuine art of the actor, we resort to entangled sentences, scientific explanations or poetic formulations. The same thing happens with a good wine, which, as we all know, doesn't have an imaginary taste. It is so real that it intoxicates. But when we try to describe its taste, words become inadequate and float in the air like smoke, not because they point out something vague but because we want to define an experience that is so elementary that we do not find elementary words.

When we begin to explore the actor's inner life, we climb or sink towards her spirit. Or, as a reaction, we deny that a spiritual problem exists and assert that what matters is the design's precision and the gestures' score. Both are misunderstandings: the precision of the watch and the depth of the bathometer are equally inert elements. The actor becomes a body-in-life through mystery, technique, and spirit of observation.

Bertolt Brecht, in his speech to the Danish actor-workers, expressed it with words that could be those of Stanislavski or any experienced performer: the actor, before every other ability, must possess the art of observing. It doesn't matter how he is seen, what he has seen and shows. What he knows deserves to be seen. We observe him in order to see the perfection with which he has observed (Brecht 1975: 137).

Techniques that are learned and a technique to elude techniques

The South Korean example, under the aegis of shamanism and *p'ansori*, helps to clarify some of those aspects which always made the grafting of the Asian dance-theatres onto Western theatres problematic. The difficulty of this grafting has its roots in a contradiction: the distance between those techniques which are learned, on the one hand, and, on the other, what we could call a technique that tries to elude techniques.

A close examination of our craft's history makes it easy to ascertain that European theatres have often used mannered behaviours, characterisations, clichés, and scenic know-how. But the actors have always avoided codified body techniques such as those which we find in the field of singing, dance, acrobatic or martial arts.

It is difficult to establish the existence of a tradition without real assessable techniques. These techniques must be identical for all those who practise the same kind of theatre, with the possibility of being diversified in well-organised subgenres, thus establishing a quality standard with a scale of values to measure excellence and significance. It is arbitrary to establish a dialogue without real assessable techniques. Two different traditions can communicate with each other, may find points of contact, interlacements, and even a symbiosis. But this is impossible in a meeting between a measurable technical tradition and another one that programmatically escapes from a strict definition.

In the twentieth century, European actors and directors have often expressed this impossibility and regretted the absence of solid acting techniques comparable to those of dance, song, music, and Asian traditional theatres. They have voiced their longing for the existence of forms independent of the actors who should enliven them.

But we can envisage the absence of well-defined techniques as a fascinating adventure and not as the symptom of a lack. I believe that we would end up finding within the stage ghost – or the character – the actor's difference.

Since the end of the nineteenth century, various directors, starting with Stanislavski, realised in their practice something which had never happened in the history of European theatre. They tried to define in a detailed way the fundamental techniques of the actor's art with a view to a pedagogy with foundations similar to those of other performing arts: song, dance or pantomime. On looking more closely, however, the techniques of the European theatre reformers were completely different from the other 'techniques', which, having once established their point of arrival – the excellence of a form at which they aim – look for suitable means to reach it. The reformers' techniques were, rather, attempts to work out individual strategies and procedures. When they wrote about their technical knowledge, the question they tried to answer was 'What did I do when I did what I was doing?' and not 'What should you learn to do, and how should you do it, if you want to adhere to this or that artistic convention?'

The technique that eludes techniques looks for challenges and the adventure of the solitary artist, neglecting the nobility of Tradition in order to discover the shock of an unexpected invention and accepting to be surrounded by the craft's mediocrity. It is not an insufficiency of the Western theatre. It has become the feature of every form of contemporary theatre in any continent. And it involves an abnormal peculiarity – abnormal when observed in the context of the performing arts which have been codified by the various civilisations of our planet.

The dance between the two halves – the half-actor and the half-ghost – is a test that may generate an unpredictable result. This challenge doesn't consist in the arduous ascent to embody an artistic form to perfection. It is similar to the struggle between two momentary adversaries: the character's ghost and the actor's person. It is reminiscent of the struggle between Jacob and the Angel, one of Western culture's founding myths which the Old Testament has passed on to us. Yet in contemporary theatre the actor cannot always affirm after a performance: I challenged a ghost and was not defeated.

The ripe action

Here Barba sums up his dialogue with Asian theatres from the perspective of Theatre Anthropology. He compares his dialogue with the interest in 'Oriental' theatre shown by twentieth-century reformers. It is worth noting the discrepancy between Barba's perspective and that which often, in the present global culture, drives the exchanges, fusions, and approaches between Euro-American and Asian theatres.

The text comes from a lecture delivered by Barba at the symposium 'Theatre East and West: Revisited' in honour of Leonard Pronko, Pomona College, USA, April 2002. It was first published in 2003 (Mime Journal *special issue, ed. by Carol Davis, 2002/2003, pp. 237–50).*

Let me start with a question.

Why, in Europe today, are most actors and directors, dancers and choreographers not interested in the knowledge inherent in Asian theatre forms? There are, of course, exceptions. But the flagrant evidence of such exceptions as well as frequent Asian performances should not lead us astray. The patrimony of knowledge of the various Asian styles is ignored by theatre schools and practitioners.

In order to answer this question, I have to pose another one. Why, at the beginning of the twentieth century, were the most seminal theatre reformers in Europe attracted towards Asian performances, considering them not only an aesthetical and formal inspiration but also a mine of objective information to be applied to their very personal and specific visions and practice? I am referring to Craig, Stanislavski, Meyerhold, Eisenstein, Copeau and, one generation later, Artaud and Brecht.

When I speak about the lack of interest in the knowledge inherent in Asian classical traditions, I am referring to the attitude characterising the protagonists of the Great Theatre Reform in Europe in the early twentieth century and not to a generic interest or a generalised curiosity. In spite of profound changes in historical perspectives and aesthetic judgements, paradoxically the lack of interest remains unchanged.

Yesterday and today

Looking around, we cannot say that today there is a lack of interest in traditional Asian theatres. Many of their performances tour extensively and participate in European and North American festivals. There is an abundant bibliography on them. Chinese, Japanese, Indian, Javanese, and Balinese actors and dancers hold courses in Western theatre schools and universities. Innumerable Western actors or would-be actors travel to Asia to learn the rudiments of theatre and dance techniques. Numerous Western companies faithfully stage performances according to traditional Asian forms, reaching a professional level comparable to the original models. These are rare but significant examples of contact and assimilation. Frequently performers from traditional Asian styles are integrated in performances together with actors and dancers of Western styles. Moreover, many performances, both in the East and the West, stage European texts – from the Greek classics to Shakespeare, Beckett, and others – in accordance with traditional Asian styles.

The list could continue ad infinitum. It conjures up a vast panorama of intersections and grafts, blending and fusion, revealing a reciprocal interest and the awareness of possible encounters never before envisaged in the history of theatre. The situation is radically different with respect to the beginning of the twentieth century when Asian theatres were unknown. In the few cases in which they were taken into consideration, they were seen as 'primitive' and fascinating because of their exoticism. In World Fairs and on adventurous tours such as those of Sada Yacco and Hanako, they were presented as 'the art of barbarians who were not deprived of genius', according to the expression used by Voltaire for Shakespeare.

What distinguishes yesterday's lack of interest from today's interest? And what do they have in common? Let us say at once that we should not be blinded by ciphers. The comparison only becomes significant if we confront today's numbers with those of yesterday in an analogous context. It is evident that the present Western panorama of intersections, grafts, and fusions with Asian styles is very restricted in comparison with the whole panorama of current theatre. Today, just as yesterday, it is a question of minority zones, experimental, and exceptional outposts. Comparison shows us that in these minority zones, encounters between Western and Asian theatres are far more numerous than in the first decades of the twentieth century. At that time, such encounters were more than rare and could be counted on the fingers of one hand. Nevertheless, they turned into illuminating discoveries and a renewed awareness on the part of the few dance and theatre reformers in Europe.

Yesterday's lack of interest was, above all, determined by the awareness (or illusion) of an insuperable cultural difference. Those theatres from the regions where the sun seems to rise could easily be ignored or, at the most, admired as a fanciful diversity that could give no nourishment to the culture of European origin.

We do not need reminding once again how much our planet's cultural geography has changed and how every diversity concerns us.

Other reasons which are inherent in theatre craft stimulate interest in Asian traditions. Cinema and television have spread a uniform way of acting over the entire planet. The acting conventions of European origin adapt themselves to the standards of acting in film and television. No wonder that numerous minority theatres turn to Asian conventions as both recognisable and acknowledged formal models with the aim of distinguishing themselves. For example, *Hamlet* performed in kabuki style, before evoking classical Japan, expresses the need for a way of acting shaped by a tradition, i.e. a codified form of acting which is distant from the verisimilitude of daily behaviour. Today, a passionate theatre-goer anywhere recognises in kabuki a style and an aesthetic that belong to a common cultural patrimony, and not merely to the Japanese one. Similarly, singing bel canto or performing on an Italian stage do not mean imitating Italians, appropriating their culture or expressing nostalgia to return to the 'origins' and the Renaissance.

New conditions and new needs explain why today the situation has changed with regard to yesterday's lack of interest towards Asian theatres.

However, both yesterday's lack of interest as well as today's increased interest have a point of contact. Both of them are the result of an appreciation of the forms belonging to different traditions. Above all, the aesthetic and stylistic aspects are taken into consideration. I would call it the 'surface', if this word did not arouse negative reflexes.

Surface has nothing to do with superficiality. In an artistic product, the surface is the perceptible formal dimension which is the culmination of the creative process. It is a point of arrival that becomes a bridge for a live relationship with the spectators.

Creative processes, however, have points of departure. These are quite different from the points of arrival which are the results. The points of departure do not coincide with what our eyes perceive, or with form, style, and aesthetics.

That which the skin reveals is totally different from the blood, nerves, muscles, organs, and bones which the skin beautifies and hides.

The Asian classical theatres' traditions beautify and hide a knowledge that belongs to the anatomy of theatre and concerns the scenic life (the performer's *bios*) at a basic level, independently of formal results and aesthetic choices. This knowledge belongs to science, not to theatre aesthetics.

In the beginning, I asked myself about today's lack of interest in this science, in this anatomical perspective on Asian scenic forms. What surprises me is not the indifference or ignorance but what little effect the example of the first European theatre reformers has had. Today we rarely see the need to pursue the tradition of research and the attitude that they proposed to successive generations as a challenge to be faced and brought to fruition.

Organic effect

For European theatre artists, the need for a new way of being present on the stage as well as in society grew with the anthropological mutation which their craft underwent at the end of the nineteenth century. The first generation of reformers – Stanislavski, Appia, Craig, Meyerhold, and Copeau – felt, each in his own way, an urgency to oppose the degradation and loss of existence in their craft. The word 'existence' must be taken literally: the capacity for being and feeling alive and for transmitting this awareness to the spectators.

Their search went in two complementary directions. On the one hand, they strove for a meaningful presence for theatre in society, for a purpose that clearly delineated its social function. On the other, they concentrated on devising new ways of introducing young people into the craft, elaborating various pedagogical methods to develop a condition of expanded scenic life intended to give the actor an effective presence in relation to the spectators. Already at the end of the nineteenth century Appia had defined theatre as a 'living work of art' and Artaud, twenty-five years later, insisted that it was necessary to give life back to theatre. Between these two assertions we have Stanislavski's life-long revolutionary research on organicity, and Meyerhold's achievements in the realm of Biomechanics (bios = life, mechanics = the field of physics that studies motion).

The search for the actor's scenic life was motivated by the reformers' individual needs as well as the artistic and social aim expressed explicitly by each of them. But for them all, the objective of this very personal research was to let the actor embody 'authenticity', 'sincerity', 'cruelty' and 'to live according to the precision of a pattern'. All these different definitions imply a technically steered mental/somatic dynamic that could give life to the shaking essence of Ibsen's, Strindberg's, and Chekhov's plays as well as unleashing potential energies for those who do theatre as much as for those who watch it.

Theatre history tells us how the European reformers set out on an intra-cultural as well as an inter-cultural journey in the quest for inspiration and professional information. Greek tragedy, the Elizabethan and the Spanish Golden Century's theatres, commedia dell'arte, circus and cabaret, religious ceremonies, sport and dance were some of the performative genres which they dug up from their continent's own past and present. The same was the case with rituals and festive celebrations from other cultures which the newly established cultural anthropology made accessible. And, of course, Asian theatre forms. The reformers had no first-hand knowledge of these, and books on the subject were almost non-existent. Their intuition and experience, but first of all their personal interest, pierced the exotic surface and perceived the extraordinary core of information in such diverse acting techniques as the Japanese, Indian, Chinese or Balinese. They had seen Sada Yacco and Hanako, and these spurious examples must without doubt have strengthened their belief in the necessity for a 'composed behaviour' in order to achieve the impression of real life through fiction. The Asian artists provoked an 'organic effect' – a sensation of life – that persuaded the reformers, who, as spectators, accepted and were even moved by their highly stylised (i.e. artificial) scores.

The reformers had enough insight to be aware of a situation which any practitioner knows well. It sometimes happens that an actor experiences certain actions as organic, whereas the same is not true for the director and spectators. On the other hand, it also happens that the director and spectators perceive as organic certain actions which the actor experiences as not alive, tense and artificial.

This disparity of judgement or awareness contradicts the ingenuous belief in a direct correlation between what the actor feels and does and what the spectator experiences. In fact, there is no such correlation, but there can be an encounter. It is the efficacy of this encounter that determines the meaning and the value of the theatre.

The efficacy of a performance depends on the organic effect obtained by the actor in respect to the spectator. Organic effect means the capacity to make the spectator experience a body-in-life performing real actions, maybe not intelligible but coherent. The actor's main task is not to be organic but to appear organic to the eyes and senses of the spectator.

'Organic: of, pertaining to or derived from a living organism. Organicity: the quality of the state of being organic' (*New Shorter Oxford Dictionary*). In the theatre and dance, 'organic' is used as synonym of 'alive', 'credible'. Stanislavski introduced this term into the theatrical working language of the twentieth century. For the Russian reformer, *organichnost* (organicity) and *organicheskij* (organic) were an essential quality in the performer, the premise for the spectator to perceive fictive actions as real and alive and react with an unconditioned 'I believe'.

For the actors, the search for the organic effect is often accompanied by a feeling of unease, by a sense of the inorganic character of their own body and actions. Only after a long and arduous process – and not always then – is a meeting possible between the new live quality of the actor's actions and the perception of the spectator.

This new organic quality, which derives from a long apprenticeship – defined by Stanislavski and Copeau as 'second nature' – is the consequence of the unease being overcome. It is the paradoxical use of a physiology and of a logic in the space-time in which actors and spectators meet. This extra-daily way of acting and thinking, remote from daily criteria, is an indispensable requirement for the efficacy and justification of the theatre craft.

Working languages

During a session of ISTA, the International School of Theatre Anthropology, we explored the double perspective of presence and *bios*, or scenic life. It was in 1998 in Montemor-o-Novo and Lisbon, Portugal, and our departure point was: that which is organic for the actor/that which is organic for the spectator.

Each theatre tradition has its own working language, which is precise and easy to understand from inside but difficult to explain to others. This applies to big as well as to small traditions, to traditions which are handed down from one generation to another, and to those which consist of a limited number of people sharing a common story and knowledge that will not survive their disappearance. An even more exclusive working language exists: the one which each of us uses while thinking and reflecting upon our own personal way of behaving professionally.

The multitude of these working languages – some codified and some personal, at times secret and at others so explicit that they sound like theories – generates a maze of terms and shadows that conceals the concreteness of experience. Nevertheless, by scraping the surface of the words, of the images and the metaphors, we confront recurring principles and an awareness shared by theatre people of diverse and distant origins.

Let us see how Charles Dullin reflects upon 'presence', one of the terms so often used in Theatre Anthropology:

> There are actors to whom we don't listen … They have handsome voices, an impeccable diction, are nice to look at and are entrusted with important roles. When they enter on stage, you are attentive and say 'how beautiful he or she is', but after five minutes your attention is drawn by an unknown actor in a minor role who possesses this marvellous gift: 'presence'. [...]
>
> Be present (whether liked or disliked). Awake interest even through irritation. Even when you want to be unobserved, *fill your own space, making yourself necessary.* [...] *Presence is a discrete quality emanating from the soul. It radiates and imposes itself.* [...] *The actor, when aware of his presence, dares to express what he feels and will do so appropriately because effortlessly: the spectator's attention is captured and he listens to him. This necessary splitting occurs under the effect of a physical sensation that makes us say: 'How terribly I acted tonight, I didn't feel the audience.' For a reason that escaped our will, we were not there, we performed our part more or less well, but we didn't live it. The character's ghost had not followed us when we stepped onto the stage, and we searched for it in vain during the whole act.* [...] The actor's art is something of a mystery. Its success does not depend only on study, preparation, intelligence and will. Even the person who is perfectly expert on the questions concerning our art, with an admirable body and a superb voice, can be an abominable actor. This idea is expressed in a thousand ways in our scenic jargon. The great Mounet-Sully said, 'This evening, the divinity has not descended.' An instinctive actor of melodrama said: 'The role was not in my shoes.' The vain actor will say, 'What a dull audience tonight!' Someone else, coming off the stage, will clear his throat, touching the vocal chords. The only certainty is that *all of them* [...] *need this presence which does not depend solely on them.*
>
> (Dullin 1946: 87–88; my translation)

The metaphors of 'organicity' and 'presence' are not to be found in the working languages of other traditions. But all have other metaphors to indicate this quality in the actor.

In cultures where trance is a common and recognisable event, it is usual to turn to the vocabulary of possession. Augusto Omolú, from the Afro-Brazilian dance originating from the Candomblé, speaks of *axé*, a subtle energy that stems from the Orixás, the divinities who embody different manifestations of the forces in nature.

A day at ISTA

► The day's activities started at dawn in silence. The first sounds were a song or a melody by one of the masters or by a whole group in the open air while the sun was rising. Fiat Lux at 'Finis Terræ', Montemor--o-Novo (Portugal, 1998), with a song by Augusto Omolú and his ensemble (dance of the Orixás, Brazil). Sunrise at 'Tagore' in Haus Neuland, Bielefeld (Germany, 2000) with a song by Akira Matsui (noh theatre).

▶ Each ISTA session tried to recreate a performers' village where masters and participants shared the same spartan conditions in total isolation. New names for working venues and groups were coined for every session. This map from the ISTA in Bielefeld (2000, Germany) indicates the working groups, the sleeping quarters as well as the closed and open-air working venues by names of colours, poets and playwrights.

Open programme in Bielefeld:
1–3 September: Open Symposium on Theatre Anthropology
Closed programme at Haus Neuland:
6.15–6.45 Awakening (time of silence)
6.45–7.00 Gathering, at Tagore
7.00–7.30 Breakfast
7.45–9.00 The view of the spectator (scrutinising an actor's performance), at Mistral
9.00–11.00 Dramaturgy of a performance tradition, at Mistral
11.00–12.15 Before the Law (group work)

12.15–13.00 Lunch
13.00–15.00 Exchanges and barters
15.00–16.30 Thinking feet and acting voices (approaches to physical and vocal training)
17.00–18.30 Theatre Anthropology with Lluís Masgrau; Dramaturgy of the Grotesque with Ron Jenkins and Nando Taviani
18.30–19.30 Supper
19.30–21.30 Other points of view (the dramaturgy of the author, of the actor, of Iranian Teazieh, etc.), at Mistral

▶ Londrina, 1994; Bonn, 1980. The participants worked with the masters: through foreign forms and patterns they acquired awareness of the recurrent technical principles. [1] Swasthi Withjaja Bandem; [2] Katsuko Azuma; [3] Sanjukta Panigrahi.

2

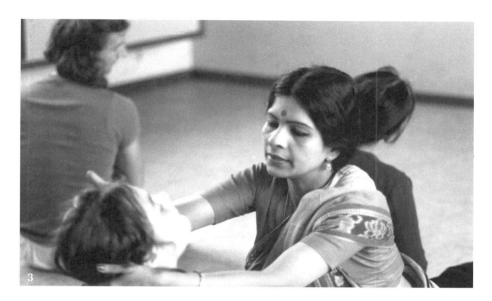

►► Volterra, 1981. The masters gave working demonstrations. Here, I Made Pasek Tempo shows his first learning day. The pupil who assumes the basic position is his daughter. The participants (who are invisible in the foreground) and the masters (seated at the back) watch. From left: Katsuko Azuma and her ensemble (nihon buyo) and Ingemar Lindh (Decroux tradition).

► Londrina, 1994. Tjokorda Istri Padmini (Bali) and Augusto Omolú (Brazil) improvising together.

►► Volterra, 1981. During the pauses there were dialogues and briefings for a new demonstration: Dario Fo and Eugenio Barba together with Katsuko Azuma and Sanjukta Panigrahi.

► Copenhagen, 1996. Luis de Tavira (Mexican director and theorist), Kirsten Hastrup (Danish anthropologist), Mbongemi Ngema (South African playwright) and Jerzy Grotowski, during the three-day symposium in collaboration with the University of Copenhagen, Institute of Anthropology, led by Kirsten Hastrup.

►► Copenhagen, 1996. Dario Fo, translated by Ronald Jenkins, analyses the dramaturgical composition of one of his monologues from *Mistero Buffo*. Seated on the right, Richard Schechner and the Dutch anthropologist Johannes Fabian seem to enjoy the demonstration.

▶ Krzyżowa, 2005. Eugenio Barba in dialogue with a group of participants about the actor's dramaturgy.
▶ ▶ Lisbon, 1998. Scholars discuss around a table. From left: Nando Taviani (with cap), Jean-Marie Pradier, Marco De Marinis, Rina Skeel, Nicola Savarese, Mirella Schino (in white), Clelia Falletti (in black).

► Montemor-o-Novo, 1998. Exchanges took place in small groups, often established spontaneously. Here, Kanichi Hanayagi and Sae Nanaogi are answering questions about some technical aspects of nihon buyo.

Omolú says he is not sure whether in his dance that evening he will receive *axé*. The transformation does not depend on him, it is 'something' that arrives without him playing any part. *Axé* is bestowed. Then Augusto has the distinct sensation of manipulating something unknown, as though he has penetrated into an area within his body that encloses mysterious forces.

In Korea, where the shamanistic culture is still alive, the term *shinmyong* denotes the entering of the spirit into a human being. The same term is applied to the actor when he attracts the attention of the spectator.

Balinese performers speak of *taksu*, literally, 'the place which receives the light'. The actor is illuminated by 'another' energy that works on the spectator. A sort of divine inspiration takes possession of the performer escaping his control. As with *axé* and *shinmyong*, *taksu* too is not decided by the actor. He can only note, 'this evening there was *taksu*' or 'this evening there was no *taksu*'.

In Bali, the feeling that the performer's change of energy constitutes a different quality of life is articulated in various ways. *Ngidupan* (or *menjiwai*) means 'to give life'. *Hidup* is 'life'. If *hidup* is absent, then the performer (or his performance) is *matah*, 'unripe', 'lacking the right taste'. The term 'ripe' as opposed to *matah* does not exist. *Wayah*, 'old', is used, not in the sense of decrepit or weak, but of vigour and vital force. Paradoxically, they say that the sun is old at noon, young at sunset. *Wayah* is 'embodied knowledge'. *Sampun wayah* is a dance that does not give the impression of being 'unripe' or 'undecided'. The Balinese master I Made Djimat affirms that a school can teach how to dance correctly, and yet the performers may be unable to *ngidupan*, 'to give life' to their performance. An actor can dance in a correct way without being *wayah*. As Charles Dullin said: presence (or organic effect) does not depend on technical skill.

In Japan, the term *mi-juku*, 'unripe', is used to indicate the performer who is not mature. Like the Balinese *matah*, the term *mi-juku* is applied to the performer who has not incorporated a dance to the point of giving it life. In Japan too they are aware that an actor may be technically perfect, and nevertheless lack *iki iki*, the quality of dazzling the spectator. *Iki iki* means 'vivid', 'brilliant', 'shining'.

Sanjukta Panigrahi, the great odissi dancer who was one of the founders of ISTA, recognised this recurring image in the working languages of different traditions. In Oriya, her own language, a performer is considered *kacha*, 'unripe or raw', as opposed to *pakka*, 'the ripe performer who rivets the spectator'.

Levels of organisation

Let's return to our handful of European theatre reformers, who were so fascinated by Asian theatre, and to the time in which they were living. At the beginning of the twentieth century, a revolution of the invisible was taking place. The importance of hidden structures was disclosed in physics as in sociology, in psychology as in art or myth. A similar revolution also happened in theatre, with the peculiarity that the invisible structures, in this case, were not something to be discovered in order to understand how reality functioned but rather something to be recreated on stage to give an effective quality of life to scenic fiction. A performance, like a living organism, is a complex entity composed of different levels of organisation, each of them autonomous and simultaneously interacting with the other.

The invisible 'something' that breathes life into what the spectator sees is the actor's subscore. The subscore is not a hidden scaffolding but a very personal process, often impossible to grasp or verbalise, whose origin may be a resonance, a motion, an impulse, an image, a constellation of suggestive words or a text. This subscore that belongs to the basic level of organisation supports still other levels in the performance. These levels extend from the effectiveness of the presence of the individual actor to the interweaving of their relationships, from the use of space to dramaturgical choices. The organic interaction between the different levels brings out the meaning that the performance assumes for the spectator.

The subtext – as Stanislavski called it – is a particular type of subscore. The subscore does not necessarily consist of the unexpressed intentions and thoughts of a character, of the interpretation of his motivations. The subscore may consist of a rhythm, a song, a certain way of breathing or an action which is not carried out in its original dimensions but is absorbed and miniaturised by the actor who, without showing it, is guided by its dynamism even in immobility.

In theatre, the revolution of the invisible marked the age of exercises. A good exercise is a paradigm of dramaturgy, i.e. a model for the actor. The expression 'dramaturgy of the actor' refers to one of the levels of organisation of the performance or to one aspect of the dramaturgical interweaving. Indeed, in every performance, there are numerous dramaturgical levels, some more evident than others, and all of them necessary for the recreation of life on stage.

But what is the essential difference between an exercise – which I would define as a 'paradigm of dynamic dramaturgy' – and dramaturgy in the traditional sense: comedy, tragedy or farce? In each case, it is a question of a well-contrived web of actions. But whereas comedies, tragedies, and farces have a narrative form, exercises are a dynamic form, energetic patterns with no plot. Exercises are small labyrinths which the actors' body-mind can explore and rediscover anew again and again in order to incorporate a paradoxical way of thinking, thereby distancing themselves from their own daily behaviour and entering the domain of the stage's extra-daily behaviour.

The single exercise is not so different from a *kata* in Japanese theatre. But, unlike the *katas*, which acquire a meaningful function in the performance, exercises are like amulets which the actor carries around, not to show them off but to draw from them certain qualities of energy out of which a second nervous system slowly develops. An exercise is made up of body-memory. An exercise becomes memory that acts through the entire body. And the hidden information that the actors have incorporated through the exercises impregnates their 'design of movements' (Meyerhold) or 'score' (Stanislavski was the first to use this term).

Exercises teach how to work on what is visible through repeatable dynamic forms. These forms are narratively empty. At the beginning they are filled with the concentration necessary for the successful execution of each single phase. Once the exercises have been mastered, they either die or they are filled by the capacity for improvisation. This capacity consists in varying the execution of their diverse phases, the images behind them (for example, to move like an astronaut on the moon), their rhythms (to different music), the chains of mental associations.

In this way, a subscore develops from the score of the exercise.

The value of the visible (the score) and the invisible (the subscore) generates the possibility of making them carry on a dialogue, creating a space within the design of movements and their precision. This dialogue between the visible and the invisible is precisely that which the actor experiences as inner life and in some cases even as self-knowledge. And it is what the spectator no longer perceives as interpretation but as the experience of an experience.

At the beginning of the twentieth century, when Stanislavski, Meyerhold, and their collaborators invented exercises to train actors, they gave birth to a paradox. Their exercises were something quite different from the training followed by students at theatre schools. By tradition, actors practised fencing, ballet, singing and, above all, the recitation and acting of particular fragments of classical plays. The exercises, on the other hand, were elaborate scores, codified down to the smallest detail and an end in themselves. All this is evident when we scrutinise the oldest of the exercises passed down to us, those which Meyerhold conceived and called Biomechanics and whose aim was to teach 'the essence of scenic movement'.

Even with a limited knowledge of Asian acting forms, Meyerhold and Stanislavski could perceive intuitively the connection between the actor's fixed patterns (*kata*, exercise, score) and the kinaesthetic and affective consequences they could produce in the perception of the spectators. Hence their interest and gratitude in meeting Sada Yacco, Hanako or Mei Lanfang, not only as great artists but also as models of an acting path which they were trying to open for their own actors.

The shock

Sometimes I try to imagine Stanislavski's and Meyerhold's shock on seeing Asian performers for the very first time. An inconceivable theatrical reality must have overcome them, like an avalanche. I try to remember similar reactions in my own life: the first time I saw Brecht's Berliner Ensemble in Berlin in 1960, my first long night of kathakali in Kerala in 1963, or Grotowski's *The Constant Prince* in 1965. Most of the details are gone today. What still remains indelible in my very bone marrow is the real feeling of an encounter with myself and at same time the sensation of a craftsman-like complexity that only years of practice made me able to grasp and analyse in its components.

A sensorial and sensual avalanche hit Stanislavski and Meyerhold when experiencing Sada Yacco's and Hanako's performance. Were they struck by the story, by the suggestive beauty of the movements, or by the associative and emotional consequences (or animal and divine force) that these performers were awaking in them as spectators? In the aftermath, they must have been thinking about the clear yet flowing somatic ideograms, the simultaneous multiplicity of information springing forth from different parts of the performer's body – the eyes, the hands, the gait, the tensions in the spine – and pondering on form, rhythm and flow. They must have asked themselves how the technical premises for such results could be laid down for other actors too.

It may seem that I am ascribing to the reformers questions and thoughts that they never formulated. But by about 1905 Meyerhold was already applying one of his many great discoveries: the separation of the pattern of movements from the pattern of words in the actor. The aim was to build rhythms that could not coincide, thus letting the spectator's imagination be exposed to two stimuli, the oral and visual. Stanislavski's and Meyerhold's later practice concentrated on form, information, and rhythm, finding concrete solutions and procedures to make complexity grow organically on stage. Their coherent and lasting exploration, also nourished by Asian theatre, belongs to the Eurasian Theatre's patrimony of technical knowledge, offering a set of objective tools and principles to subsequent generations.

Today we know that form, rhythm, and flow are the names of three diverse perspectives in relation to the performer's action. They do not indicate different technical principles or aspects of the composition. They designate three faces of the same reality. We can distinguish them temporarily and operationally, well aware that this distinction is a fiction which is useful to research.

An improvised or fixed score, a series of exercises or a dance may be treated as:

- a form, a design in space and time resulting from a montage and containing different types of information;
- a scansion and alternation of tempi, accents, speed, and various energy colours and nuances;
- a river bank that allows the energy's organic flow.

The final result makes it impossible to distinguish between the action's flow, rhythm, and shape. In the same way, it is impossible to separate the physical action from the mental, the body from the voice, the word from the intention, the performer's pre-expressive level from his expressive efficaciousness, and the actor's dramaturgy from that of a fellow-actor or the director.

A performance must be an organic totality that makes sense, as Jim Brandon said yesterday.[13] At the beginning of the twentieth century, the reformers were empirically discovering and mapping the level of organisation of the actor's presence, of the *bios* of his smallest actions. The Asian actor became for them a model to study and an example to emulate. Their endeavours succeeded and contributed to the explosion of the theatrical system that had existed in Europe since the Renaissance. This 'big bang' scattered the unitary European theatre tradition and generated a multiplicity of small nomadic traditions which were no longer attached to a culture or a society but were embodied by performers and directors who moved from place to place, motivated by curiosity, a spirit of adventure, financial gain, and artistic ambitions, or merely forced by History to migrate. These small nomadic traditions, with their specific visions and practices (Stanislavski, Meyerhold, Copeau, Artaud,

---

[13] Editor's note: Barba refers to Brandon's intervention at the symposium 'Theatre East and West: Revisited'.

► Eugenio Barba's copy of Leonard Pronko's book *Theater East and West* published in 1964.

Brecht, Grotowski, etc.) threw theatre into modernity. A plurality of small traditions is today the only choice for anyone, anywhere, who takes the first steps into a profession where individual urges and technical insight grow into a performance aimed at confronting History.

Books that follow the route of the birds, small traditions, and a flower

A few days before leaving for this conference in Pomona, I was looking for a book in my library. 'Eugenio Barba, Oslo, October 1964' was written on its first white page. It was a maze of underlinings, erasures, notes, highlightings. These were made during my repeated reading of the book at different times. Even my handwriting changed as the years went by. It was like a many-coloured palimpsest, with red, green, blue and black pen and pencil strokes. Sometimes in the margin was written the word *bzdura* – which in Polish (my first professional language) means, 'Nonsense!' Sometimes, a series of exclamation marks were ringed in a circle. Certain paragraphs had not been taken into consideration on the first reading, then on the second were surrounded by question marks which had then been cancelled on the third.

I have read and re-read *Theatre East and West* by Leonard Pronko (1967) which arrived in my library in the same month and year of Odin Teatret's beginning. This is a book with wheels, one that has travelled around and that has made my head and fantasy travel with it. It has brought me here, to this very conference, and the exercises which Julia Varley was showing you before.[14]

Theatre East and West helped me to understand that theatre can be done in two ways: by those who perform it and by the rare few who are able to write it down. But these signs on the paper are incandescent, releasing the living spirit of past experience and dormant knowledge. Incandescent books, and the theatre they evoke, cross borders just like the small traditions embodied by men and women. Sometimes they fly following the route of the birds. Like strolling actors they are always on the move.

Therefore Leonard, permit me to let an actor, Julia Varley, tell with the language of the birds, how your book came into my hands and has accompanied me in my journey through the small tradition to which I belong.

Julia Varley performs a sequence of bird sounds and movements, ending with an interpretation of this poem from her performance *The Castle of Holstebro* (1990):

> Some say love, it is a river that drowns this tender reed.
> Some say love, it is a razor that leaves this soul to blood.
> Some say love, it is a hunger, an endless aching need.
> I say love, it is a flower, and you – it's only seed.

---

[14] Editor's note: In the symposium in honour of Leonard Pronko, Odin Teatret actress Julia Varley presented a work demonstration including several exercises from her training.

All theatre is made of dance

In the text 'The Book of Dances', we have seen how Barba was attracted and inspired by actors/dancers from the different Asian theatres. Here, in a sort of epilogue, he reflects upon dance, considered not as a performative genre but as a borderless 'geological' layer shared by both theatre and dance.

This text, first published in 1996 with the title 'Drama's Hidden Depths' (UNESCO Courier, 49 (1), pp. 16–19), was later included in the programme of Odin Teatret's Doña Musica's Butterflies *(1997) with the definitive title 'All Theatre Is Made of Dance'.*

In certain manifestations of Asian and African culture as well as in its Caribbean and American diaspora, the gods are made of the substance of dance. We can't simply say that the gods dance. The dances are the subtle matter, on the border of the material and the immaterial world, through which the power of the gods is represented. Dance is the vehicle that brings human beings close to the gods.

Theatre, too, is made of the substance of dance. Jacques Copeau, who, together with Stanislavski, was one of the inspirations for the renewal of Western theatre in the twentieth century, affirmed that dance is the essence of drama. Similarly, Meyerhold held that the actors must learn the laws upon which dance is built as a base for their acting.

Dance without music

There are divisions which are like wounds. Such is the one splitting the territory of the performing arts, separating with rigid borders dance from theatre. This separation is a product of European conventions of the last centuries. In most of theatre history and in the reality of experience, such a rigid distinction does not exist. It didn't exist in ancient Greek and Roman theatre, on the Elizabethan stage and in the commedia dell'arte, nor does it exist in the traditional forms of Asian theatre, nor in the practice of those actors who know they are dancing even if they conceal it beneath an interpretation that has nothing to do with the genre 'dance'.

Nor is dance 'naturally' dependent on music. In an anonymous booklet published in Italy in 1607, *Discorso contro il carnevale* (Taviani 1969: 70–81), a mental experiment was proposed in order to demonstrate the diabolic character of dance. The booklet was a ferocious pamphlet against carnivals by a man terrorised by the idea of disorder. The author suggested that one should look at a roomful of men and women dancing and pretend not to hear the music. One can then observe the artificial movements, note the contortions people make as they touch each other, take each other by the hand, lean towards each other, search for each other, lose each other. They don't look like civilised men and women. They are grotesque, jerky, affected or obscene. One might think they are mad. Unbeknown to themselves, they are in the hands of the Devil.

I think this is an excellent exercise for directors and actors. If, when we switch off the music, dance only gives rise to forced, exaggerated or jerky movements, it means that it is not springing organically from the body but is an attempt to impose mechanically the music on the body. When dance is organic, it contains its own music. It does not matter whether the music is silent or provided from the outside for the enjoyment of the spectator.

Performers trained in Asian theatre genres can dance without music and their action doesn't lose its organicity; it is not less attractive to the spectator. Add music, singing, the poetry of words, and the fantasy of narration, and the performance becomes richer and more complete. But even without all this, enacted in its nakedness, the action retains its force and life.

This applies not only to performers from the traditional Oriental theatres. The mimes from the Decroux school, the actors from Odin Teatret or the Théâtre du Soleil, and ballet dancers who are accustomed to music even during their training, know how to dance without a melodic accompaniment, following the inner organic music of their own physical actions. The same ability characterises all those who struggle for a scenic presence through the training of precise physical actions. Stanislavski explained how actors could compose their own dance, working on the character and the situations suggested by a text.

Film allows us to see this skilful, silent dancing in the Biomechanical exercises of Meyerhold's actors or the training of Rena Mirecka and Ryszard Cieślak from Grotowski's early Theatre Laboratory in Opole.

In addition to the rhythm of song, of a musical instrument, or a drum, there is a dynamo-rhythm constituting the music of the body. In all these examples we don't observe the genre 'dance' but the dance of the body-in-life. The word 'life' is not used gratuitously. It indicates that elementary level of performative behaviour which does not mean anything but is pure and simple presence. It is neither expression nor communication, but it is what makes both possible. It is the shared ground of actors/dancers, their pre-expressive level.

Falsity and fiction

Theatre and dance form one single vast territory. This can be explored both from the viewpoint of the geographer interested in neighbourhoods, contiguous zones and mixed panoramas, as well as from that of the geologist wanting to explore the underground layers common to regions which, on the surface, are divided and different.

It is the geologist's approach that attracts me. I am interested in the deep dance, hidden in all performers when their presence is efficient. I try to discover the waves of a rhythm or of a powerful action which is retained in the depths of the body even if it barely moves, or behaves 'normally'.

When actors retain the energies that infuse life into their scenic presence, when they do not dance overtly, something dances within them. Without this deep dance, there is no efficient actor. There would be only falsity; we would lack true fiction.

In theatre, the opposite of falsity is fiction, that is, art.

Whatever acting style an actor chooses, realistic or not, it is necessary that every action is real. An actor must act the fiction and not pretend to act. An action is real only when the slightest movements are rooted in the torso, involving the whole body, and not in a part of it, such as the hands, the eyes or the mouth. This integrity, which springs from the body-mind, this unity of the organism-in-life, is what I call 'dance'. When the hidden dance becomes explicit and develops itself freely in space, then it also becomes dance according to the conventions of performance genres. Then words and silence may no longer be sufficient, and rhythm, drums, and music are required to create a dialogue.

As a spectator, I live a particular experience every time I observe an actor who knows how to reach down to the sources of scenic life. It doesn't matter whether it is a comedy, a tragedy or a sad drama with no hope, where the truth of our meaningless destiny is revealed in all its icy sterility. As soon as my attention moves towards the actor's body, then life triumphs. When

I release myself from the grip of words and plot, facial mimicry, hand gestures, and concentrate on observing the actor's torso and feet, I can see the dance hidden beneath the veneer of acting. The subterranean dragon of life surfaces, revealing its symptoms even when they are barely perceptible. Sometimes its presence emerges in an explosive way, and then, with or without music, we all recognise that theatre is made of dance.

The memory of past centuries hands down to us similar images. At the end of the darkest and most ferocious plays, after reducing to ashes the illusions of the optimistic spectators, after revealing the bestiality that lurks beneath the noble words of knights and the great people of this world, after showing how love can be a bitter struggle, Shakespeare's actors suddenly abandoned the fiction of their characters and began to dance to the lively music of a jig. Then the spectators realised that, despite appearances, the actors had been dancing throughout the play.

IV

Cohabitation:
The performers' village

► I Wayan Bawa in *Medea's Marriage* (2008), directed by Eugenio Barba. I Wayan Bawa is one of the performers in Odin Teatret's *Flying* (2016).

The Romanesque method

Here Barba explains his way of working with performers from different traditions to create a performance in which each of them keeps their own style. Entitled Theatrum Mundi, *in the beginning it was a structured succession of scenes from different theatre traditions, and it concluded the public sessions of ISTA, the International School of Theatre Anthropology. During the Copenhagen session in 1996, the performance acquired a dramaturgical life of its own with the title* The Island of Labyrinths. *Thus,* Theatrum Mundi *became an ensemble with an autonomous activity outside ISTA.*

    After The Island of Labyrinths, *other productions were created according to what Barba calls 'the Romanesque method'. The establishing of Theatrum Mundi marks the moment when ISTA turns into an environment of theatre cohabitation which Barba likes to call 'the performers' village'. This text was first published in 1996 in Portuguese as 'O método românico'* (Cadernos de espectáculos, 2, pp. 21–22).

Nowadays, actors with different conventions and techniques meet, weigh each other up, and reciprocally stimulate each other. It can also happen that different traditions collaborate on the same stage.

A performance that combines diverse artists and genres can come about in many ways. The artists can abandon the style of their own tradition and, together with the others, find a common style. Or else they can assume the style of a foreign tradition in order to give new vigour to the work they are presenting. Greek texts can be interpreted by Japanese actors who draw on kyogen or noh, and texts by Shakespeare can be recited in French by actors who take their inspiration from a scenic knowledge of kabuki. Asian or African actors can migrate towards the traditions which were founded at the Moscow Art Theatre or the Berliner Ensemble; and European or American actors/dancers can become experts in Balinese theatre or kathakali.

Whatever is learnt from other traditions may be faithfully reproduced, or concealed as a secret nourishment, or displayed as a suggestive reference or a homage.

Each one of these methods can be excellent. Together they constitute a range of choices that need not preclude one another but can coexist. They may apply as much to the formation of the actor as to the composition of a performance.

For the performances of the Theatrum Mundi Ensemble, I follow another principle: each artist faithfully preserves the characteristics specific to his or her own style, integrating them into a new context.

With the diverse theatre/dance masters who for many years have collaborated with me at ISTA and with Odin Teatret's actors, we have established an intermittent ensemble. We have given it the same name as the performance, which, since 1981, has concluded the various sessions of ISTA: *Theatrum Mundi*, the theatre of the world.

It is intermittent because it meets only on exceptional occasions. It is a true ensemble because it is characterised by a continuity in its work, by a collection of shared experiences, by the familiarity and the solidarity that distinguish theatre artisans when they toil together towards a common aim.

► Bologna, 2000. Scenes from *Ego Faust* by the Theatrum Mundi Ensemble. [1] Sasakimi Hanayagi and Christina Wistari; [2] Torgeir Wethal (Faust) and Kanichi Hanayagi (Gretchen); [3] Roberta Carreri and I Wayang Djimat with Christina Wistari and Julia Varley in the background.

▶ ISTA Bologna, 1990. Rehearsing Theatrum Mundi. From left: Kanho Azuma, Desak Made Suarti Laksmi, I Nyoman Catra (kneeling), Sanjukta Panigrahi, Eugenio Barba, Julia Varley (seated), I Made Pasek Tempo, Ni Ketut Suryatini, and Kanichi Hanayagi.

We employ a dramaturgy that is based on the intertwining of autonomous styles. The intertwining, as well as the development of the plot, are both my responsibility as director. What is created by the actors belongs to their cultural identity and is not encroached upon by the *mise-en-scène*.

I have called this way of working: 'the Romanesque method'. In Europe, in the Middle Ages, the builders of churches in the Romanesque style (so called because it was common in the regions where the language of Rome was spoken) practised the art of montage. The craftsman's knowledge of how to sculpt a capital, or shape a column of precious marble, had been lost. Nor were there the financial and technological resources available to extract and transport the marble. The ecclesiastical architects therefore chose to use rough or carved stones, fragments of statues, Ionic, Doric or Corinthian capitals, odd columns which they found in various deserted buildings of the ancient Roman Empire. These miscellaneous fragments were reassembled into a new unity, amidst the patches of light and the pools of shadow in the churches and cathedrals where people prayed in front of bread and wine.

The scenic traditions of the actors and actresses who come together in the Theatrum Mundi Ensemble are by no means abandoned styles. But my method of proceeding is similar to that of the ecclesiastical architects of the Romanesque style. I do not interfere with the fragments. I choose them and make connections between them.

A performance composed of fragments remains fragmentary, or else it digs a path towards a deeper unity. In order to reach this point, you have to work within the domain of technique at a pre-expressive level. Thanks to this work, the actions of the actors can interact and so create a context.

In the course of such a process, the nature of the fragments changes. Those that started off as corners of separate worlds become necessary parts of a story which neither I nor the actors would have been able to foresee.

In this way, stories and characters from far away have, before our very eyes, drawn a veil of appearances and illusions that populate *The Island of Labyrinths*.[15]

---

[15] Editor's note: The text was written in 1996, when *The Islands of Labyrinths* was created. The later productions created with 'the Romanesque method' are *Four Poems for Sanjukta* (1998), *Ego Faust* (2000), *Ur-Hamlet* (2006) and *The Marriage of Medea* (2008).

Sanjukta

This text was written after the death of Sanjukta Panigrahi on 24 June 1997. It is a homage to this great Indian dancer and an evocation of Barba's association with this exceptional artist over a period of twenty years. It was published for the first time in 1998 as 'Sanjukta Panigrahi: 1944–1997' (The Drama Review, 42 (2), pp. 5–8).

Sanjukta Panigrahi was not only a great artist; she embodied a many-faceted knowledge. She mastered the performer's work on herself and knew how to lead the spectator's gaze, attention, and imagination. She was able to compose the dramaturgy of a piece and knew the technique to make words and music collaborate with actions. She created choreographies for herself alone or for a group. She was an experienced teacher and a clever ensemble leader and had learnt the difficult art of conjugating management with ethical rigour.

This vast knowledge had not just been handed down to her. She had herself partially invented it. Above all, she had imbued it with her values and with her own ways of perceiving both the aristocratic and the humble nature of art. I have seen her, already exhausted, embark on a train journey from Bhubaneswar lasting more than twenty-four hours, together with her husband Raghunath and her accomplished musicians. In spite of tiredness, she refused to cancel or postpone her tour. Far away, spectators were waiting for her, people for whom she represented a value. She felt a responsibility towards them.

Sanjukta Panigrahi, who had matured while surrendering herself to the demanding discipline of some of the greatest gurus of her time, was the daughter and the queen of a long tradition. She was deeply religious. For this too I admired her although I would hardly call myself a believer. In practice, we believed in the same things. The country of theatre, of which we were both citizens, possesses this peculiarity: what counts is what we believe we must do, not what we say we believe.

Sanjukta's knowledge stemmed also from encounters. The encounter with Kelucharan Mahapatra, who was her guru until her death; with Rukmini Devi to whose school she was sent to study at the age of eight; with Raghunath

▶ Holstebro, 1994. Sanjukta Panigrahi and Eugenio Barba at Odin Teatret's thirtieth anniversary. In the background, Frans Winther and Kai Bredholt.

Panigrahi, the great singer and composer who became her husband and irreplaceable artistic collaborator. Each of these encounters was a struggle and a love. At the end of the 1970s, Sanjukta had reached her summit. Nothing, within her style of odissi dance, could challenge her. It was then that with timid steps and bold heart she threw herself into the International School of Theatre Anthropology (ISTA) adventure. She had the courage to face a theatrical universe and a way of thinking and working that were foreign to her.

The courage of the encounter consists in advancing into a territory that does not belong to us but to which an inner mute force wishes to belong. Thus, step by step, we become citizens of a country wider than the one that saw our birth.

Just as she dressed privately only in Indian clothes and never gave in to other fashions, similarly, in her artistic life, Sanjukta did not like to mix different styles. But she had discovered how to let them establish a dialogue. This was the attitude that we always followed at ISTA, of which Sanjukta was a founder in 1979. We became aware that we could compose performances in which masters from Asian, Afro-Brazilian and Western styles could come together in a unitary result. They did not homologate their styles but intertwined them into a dialogue, each preserving the identity of their own craft and artistic tradition, without changing so much as a step or a look with respect to their incorporated scenic behaviour. It was an embroidery where diverse threads shaped a work born out of the concern to safeguard diversity. For these new works we coined a term from Latin, an ancient language which is no longer spoken: *Theatrum Mundi*, the theatre of the world.

In ISTA, we had found a level of organisation that we called 'pre-expressive'. This level is the technical foundation: the common principles from which the unmistakable peculiarities of the single genres and artistic individualities grow. Thus, digging down to the pre-expressive level, we succeeded in uniting the diverse scenic identities, avoiding syncretism and confusion. At the beginning, *Theatrum Mundi* was the name we gave to the masters' working demonstrations during the ISTA sessions. Artists from various traditions presented themselves one beside another for comparative purposes. Later, they interwove scenes, creating dialogues. Finally, Theatrum Mundi became an ensemble whose members were spread throughout all continents and who periodically came together to perform as a permanent company with a common patrimony of experience and a repertoire.

In the Theatrum Mundi Ensemble, Sanjukta and I had established the relationship that bonds the actor to the director. Such a relationship is difficult to explain: it is made of distance and intimacy, and it is impossible to say who leads and who is led. Similarly, no one can say who is the author of the work that in the end sees the light. Such a relationship is kept alive by details. It is similar to love, because 'love and art amplify small things', as Goethe said (1988: 907).

Goethe wrote these words in the poem 'Euphrosyne', in 1797, the night he learnt of the death of the actress Christiane Becker-Neumann, who had collaborated with him at the Weimar theatre. It happens that poetry builds a room full of echoes around us.

Christiane was much younger than Goethe; therefore, her death was for him yet another demonstration of the cruelty of human destiny. In his poem, he writes of how the ghost of the actress visits him after sunset on a mountain path, in the mists of an arid icy landscape. They talk all night. When dawn approaches, they take a final leave of one another. Christiane whispers to him: 'Even a great talent is followed by another which is greater. Don't forget me! [...] Don't let me go back to the world of the shadows deprived of fame!' (Goethe 1988: 909–10; my translation).

Sanjukta Panigrahi would never utter such a sentence. She didn't believe in fame as a way to escape the injustice of death. Nor did she believe death was an injustice. Her name does not need my help to be remembered. Nor could I ever forget it.

Frozen words and mythology

This text was written in 2013 at the request of Jonah Salz as an appendix to A History of Japanese Theatre, *of which he was the chief editor, to be published in 2016 by Cambridge University Press.*

My first contact with a Japanese theatre was in 1964: a book in French, Zeami's *La Tradition secrète du nô* (1960), translated by René Sieffert. It was one of those texts where words are frozen and only many years later thawed into life within me, acquiring a sense that matched my professional experience.

At the time, Japanese theatres – as well as those from other Asian countries – were totally disregarded in Europe. Almost no books or other sources of information were available about them, and we came across them only as footnotes in historical books concerning legendary tours in Europe before the Second World War.

Only in 1972 did I have the opportunity to see the whole panoply of Japanese theatres – noh, kyogen, kabuki, and post-shingeki. Odin Teatret, in a pioneering and rather monumental initiative, had invited to Holstebro such masters as Hisao and Hideo Kanze, Mannojo Nomura, Sojuro Sawamura, and Shuji Terayama with their ensembles – more than seventy artists. For over a week they gave performances and demonstrations on their apprenticeships and particular techniques. It was an overwhelming encounter. However, I felt I could not adapt what I had seen to my personal practice.

I don't speak Japanese, and my possibility of dialogue with Japanese performers about their technique was non-existent. My knowledge of the various Japanese acting genres remained bookish and intellectual. Then I met Katsuko Azuma, who opened my eyes. She introduced me to her living technique and her professional ethos. And she did this in such a way that what for me was previously abstract insight began to have a relevance to my personal practice and questioning.

During Odin Teatret's tour in Japan in 1980, university professor and theatre director Moriaki Watanabe took me to watch Katsuko Azuma, a nihon buyo dancer, teaching children and shingeki actors who wanted to become

► ISTA Seville, 2004. Eugenio Barba and noh performer Akira Matsui in animated discussion while an imperturbable Jonah Salz translates.

►► ISTA Wrocław, 2005. Akira Matsui (noh), Julia Varley (Odin Teatret) and Augusto Omolú (Afro-Brazilian dances of the Orixás) improvise during the symposium on Theatre Anthropology.

familiar with her style. This close contact lasted only a few hours, but I feel irremediably in love with Katsuko's spine: I was enthralled by the way her torso was radiating energy in spite of stillness. She didn't speak English, and I had to rely on the generous availability of Moriaki Watanabe. The consequence was that I invited them both to the first session of ISTA, the International School of Theatre Anthropology, which was to take place a few months later in Germany.

At ISTA, day and night, for two whole months, I was able to ask her questions, make her repeat a short sequence over and over again, a few gestures or just a transition from one movement to another, admire her in the power of a full performance with costume and orchestra, then see the same dance in jeans and a shirt with no musical accompaniment. Thus I began to discern the technique at work which was hidden from the eyes of the spectators. Most important of all was Katsuko's openness as she explained to me her working terminology and repeatedly showed me how it was applied in practice. Moriaki Watanabe was invaluable not only as translator but also as an expert in modern theatre, pointing out similar or equivalent expressions in Western theatre.

It was Katsuko Azuma who, during the three first sessions of ISTA, gave me an empirical knowledge of her technique, developing my capacity for seeing. In 1983, during a two-month stay in Tokyo, she took me to her classes of kyogen with Mannojo Nomura, to watch classes of martial arts, the tea ceremony, Shinto rituals and, above all, to follow her work with her master Tokuho Azuma. I still remember her, in spite of her age and expertise, washing the floor before dancing for her master.

I owe Katsuko Azuma and Moriaki Watanabe my first knowledge in detecting the technical scenic anatomy of a Japanese performer underneath the seductive skin of the performance. I consider Katsuko Azuma one of the founders of ISTA and one of my main sources for Theatre Anthropology. In the following years, other artists shared their experience with me and helped me sharpen this particular way of watching a performer from the perspective of recurring technical principles: Kazuo Ohno and Natsu Nakajima from butoh, Kosuke Nomura from kyogen, Kanichi Hanayagi and his fellow-performers from nihon buyo, Tadashi Suzuki and Shogo Ota from shingeki or post-shingeki, and, more recently, Akira Matsui from noh, who, besides teaching at the last three ISTA sessions, was one of the protagonists in *Ur-Hamlet*, a performance which I directed with more than 100 performers and musicians from many genres and countries.

I feel I owe much to Japanese theatre in general, and particularly to those artists who shared with me their tradition and personal technique. When I founded Odin Teatret in 1964, we were a group of amateurs longing for technical knowledge. Not only Zeami's frozen words but also famous *onnagatas* and images from *ukiyo-e* nourished my imagination and were turned into exercises and themes for improvisations for my young inexpert actors. Personal creativity is always fostered by personal mythology. And Japan's culture and theatre have no doubt had a significant place in mine.

The geography of illusions

Evoking travels, collaborations, and encounters with theatre artists, books, and films from China, Barba wonders about his feeling of insubstantiality with regard to geographical, national, and cultural categories. Barba sees theatre as an invisible geography of values embodied in individuals, meetings, and relationships. In the latter part of his life, it is this geography that determines and affects the ties with his Asian collaborators. This text was first published in 2006 in Hong Kong (Dramatic Arts, 19, pp. 4–9).

I watch the bustle of people from the dozens of ethnic communities in the restless Hong Kong. Is this town Chinese, Asian, cosmopolitan, Eurasian?

In this metropolis, with its singular history, a normal theatre tour turns into a reflection on cross-cultural connections, syncretism or the significance of traditions. What does it mean to say that a performance is 'Chinese'? Many are the languages, cultures, and histories that are included under the name 'China'.

Even 'Danish', 'Italian' or 'European' do not indicate something precise. These words are grammatically useful, but they don't point out a common identity. A country may have the same language or legislation. Sometimes the illusion of a unitary whole stems only from the state's name and borders. If someone were to affirm that Odin Teatret reflected a 'Danish identity', both my actors and I would be dumbfounded. Yet this doesn't prevent us, at times, from referring to others as typically American or Japanese.

The less we know of a nation or a culture, the more they seem to us to be endowed with a collective identity. We see them from afar, and the profile traced by their borders seems to present a face and an individuality. The cultural identity, the genius loci, the soul of a place or a country, the spirit of an epoch or a civilisation are products of distance. They acquire consistency in books, anecdotes, memories, generalisations. As soon as we approach them, they fade away like a mirage.

When I started writing, the first image that flashed before my eyes was an old film, a melodrama cradled by a song that still resounds in my ears. The real city is here in front of and around me. Yet a sentimental fable weighs on my thoughts as does the hectic city that surrounds me with its enigmas and calls.

Hong Kong seemed so far away, in 1956, when I arrived not by plane but from the sea. I told myself, it's another world, just as today I tell myself that the whole world is the same. Has it changed during these years, between one century and the next? Or is it just an optical illusion that makes past differences, with their brighter colours, appear greater? The enchantment of the exotic has vanished, revealing what it has always been: a spectacle that we prepare for ourselves, using geographical distance as a tool. A conjuring trick.

There was once, in Hong Kong, the young attractive widow of a Chinese general. She was Eurasian, half English and half Chinese. She had studied medicine in China and in Europe. The Second World War was just over, and the young widow cared only about her patients. She wanted nothing to do with love or passion.

We know what happens when such a character appears in one of our fables, ancient or modern, Eastern or Western, classical or popular. The Hong Kong doctor meets an American journalist. At their first date they go to dine on a junk in Aberdeen Bay, under a full moon at the end of the year. They look for auspices in the clouds and the starry sky.

The film continues. We see the doctor's hospital on a hill and a solitary tree in a vast lawn on the top. There the doctor and the journalist embrace. They get together and make love in luxurious hotel rooms. It is a passion without doubts and shadows, so happy that it doesn't even end when the beloved journalist departs and later news arrives of his death in the Korean war. The doctor's love resembles that tree on the hilltop, illuminated by loneliness and pain. A solar darkness, a radiant mourning: a many-splendoured thing. No tears. A butterfly with iridescent wings flies about as when happy memories break into our pain.

The actors are Jennifer Jones and William Holden, the film is from 1955. I saw *Love is a Many-Splendoured Thing* in Norway, when I first arrived as an immigrant. When, some months later, I embarked as a sailor to see the world, I too wanted to dine on that junk in the enchanted bay. Aberdeen was one of the places I wished to touch, together with an Indian temple at the outskirts of Calcutta.

'To touch' means to be free of the illusion that it may become a habit, an appointment to be renewed on each return. Many were my travels to Hong Kong, also when no longer a sailor. I often visited my brother who lived there for several years. I had started to do theatre, and Asian theatres were close to me. I felt more at home in them than in many European ones. But I never set foot in Aberdeen Bay again.

Until the day when, during Odin Teatret's tour to Hong Kong in November 2004, I decided to see it again. The first time I saw the bay, it looked enchanted as in the fable of the film. The second time, almost forty years later, the world had changed. So had I. Yet the loss of the enchantment didn't distress me.

I had learned to break the magic wand that creates a geography of illusions around me. We attribute spirits and breaths that are ours to particular places. Such places help us to define ourselves. Their beauty and power are vital illusions. They possess the fascination of the centre. If we are not ready to withdraw from them, sooner or later they will disenchant us.

There is no better context than Hong Kong to become aware of this. Today, in 2004, I wander in this crowd of differences, in this alluring and disconcerting labyrinth of houses and districts, of highways, tunnels, and skyscrapers, of modernity and relics of the past, without trying to understand or to grasp its nature or soul. I only trace the threads that tie me to a handful of people who, though unwittingly or anonymously, helped me find the path that is mine

There was not a single performance anywhere in Hong Kong. Only the small Cattle Depot Theater was hosting a project entitled *I perform* realised by the Theatre Training and Research Program (TTRP), the original institute created in Singapore by Kuo Pao Kun and Thirunalan Sasitharan. The TTRP presented five short plays. An Indian from Kerala, son of an imam, enacted his double paradoxical condition: a Muslim among Hindus and an actor who had broken with his own culture. A brilliant performer from Shanghai told, in the formalised style of Peking Opera, about a mother, who, during the period of one-child politics, cripples the foetus of her first-born in order, legally, to have a second one. The other three plays were written and interpreted by actors from Macao, Hong Kong, and Taiwan. Common to all of them was the question 'What is our centre?' In other words, what does it mean to be a Chinese from Hong Kong, Taiwan or Macao, where, until a couple of years ago, Portuguese was the official language, the religion Catholic and the main building the cathedral? Prevented from following the long monologues for obvious linguistic reasons, the performance made me slip back in time. I recalled my own explorations, my separation from the models of my culture, my desire to discover and my need to create an environment where I could recognise and chisel my professional identity. I longed for a bartering place with artists from distant cultures: experienced actors/dancers and beginners, musicians, people of the practice and people of the book, historians and theorists, neuro-psychologists and biologists. I reminisced about the origins of ISTA, the International School of Theatre Anthropology.

Also, Peking Opera artists had to live in this performers' village. It was 1980. In communist China, still suffering from the effects of the Cultural Revolution, the various forms of traditional opera were dismantled. I went to Taiwan.

In Taipei, four theatres regularly presented Peking Opera, and every Sunday the national television showed one performance. The four theatres were supported by the military: the army, the navy, and the air force.

For some weeks, starting at dawn, I followed the training at the Fu Hsing School. The commitment of the students – ten-year-old children – and the teachers' concerned yet rigorous attitude reminded me of the ballet school of the Royal Theatre in Copenhagen: the same relationship between teachers and pupils, the same dedication, patience, and care to details. Many of the considerations that inspired Theatre Anthropology – these pragmatic reflections about the basic principles of the performer's technique – initiated here, observing these young boys and girls doggedly repeating strenuous physical exercises and acrobatic sequences. Their distant objective was to capture the spectators' attention without the help of scenography or an understandable text.

The teachers strove to answer my eccentric questions: Why did they tighten a scarf around students' midriffs? What were they thinking when, in the middle of a scene, they suddenly froze in a posture of immobility? On what did they concentrate their gaze or their breath? Why did they constantly choose a difficult balance? What criteria and terms did they use when judging the technical performance of an actor?

What does it mean to be Taiwanese? My memory retains, above all, this question from those days in Taipei in 1980. It was not I who asked it. It emerged suddenly, and for no reason, in my conversations with actors and directors, who – disinterested in their traditional theatre – had studied in the USA. Beside all the insecurities and problems of our craft, they added yet another: how to re-establish the lost contact with the intimacy of their centre, how to express their particular Taiwanese identity, thus emancipating themselves from the models learned abroad.

I chewed over their question, filtering it through my experiences and constraints. How many illusions, and how strange the geography of our personal destinies! I was a southern Italian, had studied in Poland, made theatre in Denmark and had come to Taiwan in search of a professional know-how that helped me to individualise my path. My interlocutors from Taiwan were indifferent to my interest in their traditional theatre. It didn't satiate their hunger, and, therefore, they left for the USA. Some of them were children of the Chinese who had escaped from the mainland after the victory of the Communists, others were Taiwanese. Like me, they had crossed the sea and, in a universe foreign to their culture, had gone in search of a technical knowledge that could appease the questions of the soul.

What does it mean to be Taiwanese? And how do you create performances that express this being, this 'essence'? Their question was identical to the one I heard among Latin American theatre people in the 1970s, when Odin Teatret began to travel regularly in their continent. What does it mean to be Peruvian? What are the specific features of Colombian theatre? How does the cultural identity of a Paraguayan actor manifest itself? The obsession of a centre, of a cultural identity, an identical invariable core that stresses our diversity, would also spread in Europe about ten years later as a reaction to the changes caused by the European Union and to the immigration of ethnic and religious minorities.

When, in 2002, I visited Taipei with Odin Teatret, no Peking Opera theatre was left. The Sunday television show had also been cancelled. The old people who enjoyed it were dead or close to death, and the young were not interested.

The spectators reacted with bursts of laughter at the wisecracks of the young artists from the TTRP from Singapore. I sat mute and motionless, apparently disinterested. Yet their performance had shaken me and had thrown me into a labyrinth of memories and questions. Labyrinths, with their walls and complicated geometries, with their apparent intelligence and wickedness, teach us to watch our steps, to unravel the threads and find our bearings. The threads are always relationships, human beings, values passed on by a person dear to us.

Why was I attracted by traditional Chinese theatre? Without doubt because of Mei Lanfang, of what I had read about him, of the emotional impact that his art, his artistic reforms, and the coherence of his life caused in me. Mei Lanfang was one of the totems of this theatrical clan to which I felt I belonged. I considered him as an ancestor in my genealogy that I succeeded patiently in conquering through so many efforts, pilgrimages, books, encounters, and disenchantments.

But also the young people who asked themselves 'Who am I?' belonged to my clan. They too had left their home, the material one and the one of their beliefs and traditions, and had hit the road. The earth is round, and we are always the East for somebody else.

One more thread, one more face and voice: Kuo Pao Kun. In 1999, the playwright and director Kuo Pao Kun stayed for a couple of weeks at Odin Teatret in Holstebro. He wanted to get to know our working rhythm and activities. He had in mind a project which he had been cherishing for years: a sort of theatre laboratory, the Theatre Training and Research Program, which he created the following year in Singapore together with T. Sasitharan. The TTRP's purpose was to bring together theatre artists from the whole of Asia to exchange experiences, learn their reciprocal traditional techniques and become familiar not only with Western methods but also with the variety of styles from their own continent. A couple of years after giving life to his dream, Kuo Pao Kun died.

Kuo Pao Kun and I met daily at Odin Teatret, often by chance, in our library, in the kitchen or in a corridor. After a few formalities, we exchanged comments, reflections, biographical information, bewilderments, and certainties. I was impressed by his voracious curiosity, barely veiled by a patina of politeness, and by the pertinence of his questions. He was intrigued by the mystery of Odin Teatret's duration and my lifelong collaboration with the same core of actors. His life, so similar to that of many of my Latin American and European friends, recalled the destiny of one of the fetishes of our common theatrical beliefs: Bertolt Brecht. As a child, Kuo Pao Kun, together with his family, left his native Hebei, in China, to settle in Singapore. He studied in Australia, travelled throughout Asia, was arrested for his political ideas, his passport was seized, and he was stripped of his Singapore citizenship. He never ceased writing, directing, educating one generation after another of actors and directors, discovering untraditional places to turn into theatrical venues. Thus, an abandoned electric plant became a Home for the Arts: the Substation. At the end of his life, awards and acknowledgements were showered upon him. His adversaries were forced to bend in front of his enduring coherent action.

As a teenager, his father sent him to Hong Kong to keep him away from politics. It was in 1957, just one year after my visit to this city and its enchanted bay. We might have crossed one another in the streets, both of us so sure of our ideas and with our hunger for life and change. We met now, old enough to appreciate the virtues of doubt and even more the certainty that it is not necessary to hope in order to undertake. Theatre can shake the conscience of a handful of individuals and the habits of the profession and of society provided we don't play according to the rules but make our own rules with the determination to impose them within our life span.

► Taipei, 2008. Eugenio Barba speaking to the Nankuan Opera performers during a rehearsal of *Daily Life in a Besieged Country*. Behind him, his assistant Pierangelo Pompa and Wu Wen-tsui.
►► Julia Varley and Lin Ya-lan during a rehearsal.

To look from afar, while keeping our distance, allows us to generalise proficiently and to put order into our mental schemes. But this harmless 'objective' procedure, which ought to organise, becomes a tool of chaos if we have the illusion that these generalisations are founded on reality. Or if we ask what our European, Asian or African identity is, what we have to do to embody and develop it or what threatens to pollute it.

These were my reflections while I moved in the streets and districts of Hong Kong, a city which, the more I imagine I know it, the more I realise how unfamiliar I am with it. My thoughts concern that special geography that ignores boundaries and is made up of movement and bonds. What seems certain in the static geography – ethnical affiliations, nations, cultural identities – becomes movable and passionate in the mind's geography. The mind's geography is not irrational; it speaks a language that only an inner hunger can decipher. Our spectators, spread everywhere, are a tangible part of this geography. Our colleagues and our craft are the country in which we sink our roots.

To see how a city changes induces a special emotion. I tell myself: 'Hong Kong is no longer the same.' I speak about myself, about my dismay in noticing how I have changed with the changing times. I think, *this city had a soul and has lost it.* It is not true. I speak about my soul, whatever this word means. I hint, turning my gaze elsewhere, to my unavowed fear that time, just as sand running through an hourglass, carries away something precious that gives a sense to my being, that which I call 'the essential': the centre of my mind's geography.

How many times have I visited this city in the past fifty years? Fifteen, twenty, perhaps more. But it is the first time I am here with Odin Teatret.

From where do these hundreds of spectators emerge, silently waiting in the immense lobby of the Cultural Centre to be introduced into the particular space of our performance? Young and elderly people, solitary men and women, couples, small groups, casually as well as formally dressed. Who are they, what do they do for a living, how were they informed of our presence here, what do they know about Odin Teatret, why do they want to see this Danish group? What does theatre represent for them? A pastime? A tunnel through which to escape from their island? A vital need or just one of their interests, like golf or the new fusion gastronomy?

Only very few people greet me at the end of the performance. In Europe, Latin America, Canada or the USA it is different. The spectators recognise me, not as the director but as the person who welcomed them, accompanying them to their places. When leaving, they come back to me, and I can often foresee their reactions. Some just utter a 'thanks for the performance'. Others lose themselves in a tide of words, imagining that their disconnected sentences explain the tumult the performance aroused in them. A few, in silence, shake my hand and withdraw furtively, their eyes shining with tears.

Here, in Hong Kong, the spectators' behaviour is different. Nobody approaches me, and the few people I know nod politely and avoid me. Only the mute figure of Gloria Lam is eloquent. Motionless in her stylish Chinese dress, an impenetrable expression on her face, her long black hair reflects the lights of the ceiling: she embodies the image of a spectator who is remote from the preoccupations of my theatre. Yet it is her immobility and silence as a spectator who has seen our performance every evening that touch me and speak to me, not her presence as Manager of the Leisure and Cultural Services Department.

I think I know what is happening inside her. Ethnic and cultural differences are empty and well-sculpted shells in which our intimate personal diversity lets our voices and turmoil reverberate. A performance composes music of echoes and frescoes of sensations which are compressed inside these shells, dissolving in the spectator's centre. Some threads, some lifelines intertwine for a short moment and perhaps form a knot. Here, in the unique memory of the spectator, theatre discovers one of its centres.

Theatre allows us to experiment in how to use illusions without illusions using us. To make performances means to live on enchantment, to create archipelagos of tragic or grotesque fairy islands, mirrors of the world as we know it, or worlds as dissimilar from reality as a fantastic delirium. Islands in which we can orient ourselves or labyrinths where nothing is certain. But after every enchantment, the magic wand has to be broken and thrown away, every evening, after the last scene. We let our performance grow into a sacred tree, and then we fell it. But from its branches, dark seeds sink into the depths of the spectator and germinate, sometimes leaving him or her mute and motionless.

We build small worlds with laws, confinements, noble and inexorable values. The more inexorable, the more we know that they are fictive. To do and to undo: in theatre, this spiritual exercise becomes craftsmanship and subversion.

Odin Teatret's performance was entitled *Within the Skeleton of the Whale* (1997). In Holstebro, immediately after finishing it, I said to myself: it is unintelligible. Instead, it has shown an astonishing aptitude to travel far away from the context in which it was born. Not because it is easily understood but because wherever it goes this performance makes no claim to be understood.

It explicitly manifests its vocation to remain 'foreign'. It doesn't tell a story and doesn't convey messages. Just like a live organism, it has an inner logic of its own, it pulsates, acts and changes even when it has no intention of becoming recognisable. When this performance is totally alive, the quality of its difference becomes so allusive and elusive that each spectator reacts with his own head, that is, with the weight and the strength of his own difference.

In Hong Kong, I discovered that our performance is just as foreign here as in Holstebro, the small town in Denmark where we have our home.

When I arrived in Holstebro from Norway with my actors in 1966, we settled on foreign ground. We are still together – we who come from a dozen different countries – after a life passed in shifting working rooms and travels, deeply rooted in our Danish houses yet aware of that truth which is so easy to forget: we are in a place, we are not of that place. It is enough to add the word 'time' to 'place', and theatre materialises.

Theatre, by its nature, is foreign, whether it wants it or not, whether it knows it or refuses to know it. This characteristic of its nature becomes evident when travelling. The tours with Odin Teatret, often far from our country and continent, made me discover that we are foreign not because we come from different parts of the world and speak different languages but because we are prey to the geography of the mind. Countries' frontiers fade, and the mutable interlacements of relationships and passions take the upper hand.

These are not fantasies or abstractions, but practical facts. When a theatre is on tour, the roles are reversed. We, the foreigners, become the hosts in the small space of our performance. We welcome the spectators, who, for an hour or so, become 'foreigners' on a visit. They are confronted, in a more or less accentuated way, with something that originates from another history and another geography. They enter, take their place, observe, at times like simple tourists, curious, open-minded or animated by an arrogant superiority complex, admiring or indifferent. This happens, to a greater or lesser degree, also when the majority of the spectators consider the theatre that hosts them as a local theatre. The sense of intimate distance is more explicit and noticeable when a theatre comes from a faraway country. But it is always the same relationship between 'foreigners' that comes into play, here dissimulated, there disclosed.

Threads are important. They are tenuous, deceptive, imperceptible, tempered by the years or the intensity of an encounter. Together they build a net. This net is a country. No geographical map can show or describe it. We live in a geography of threads, bonds, knots. The threads are people, meetings, relationships, passions.

► Wuzhen, November 2014. Eugenio Barba as Honorary President of Wuzhen Theatre Festival delivers the closing speech, translated by the Festival's Artistic Director, Stan Lai.

►► Shanghai, November 2014. Professor Lou Wei appoints Eugenio Barba Honorary Professor at Shanghai Theatre Academy.

Some threads are books, places, figures lost in time: Cao Xueqin and his novel *The Dream of the Red Room*; the school of Liyuan, the mythical Pear Garden; the slender Mei Lanfang as he lives in my fantasy together with his intellectual brother Qi Rushan who died in exile. Other threads are shorter or longer collaborations, fleeting circumstances, lightning encounters or recurrent dates: Tsao Chun-lin and Lin Chun-hui, who accompanied me during the foundation of ISTA; Mei Baojiu, Mei Lanfang's son, who filled our theatre in Holstebro with his father's aura; Pei Yanling's unforgettable warrior; Ushan Shii's touching performances directed by Peng Ya-ling; Verena Tay's solitary commitment; Ong Ken Sen with his existential revolt; Chun Mingder 'Taimu' and his students who crossed the sea to see Odin Teatret; Wu Hsing-kuo and Li Hsio-wei and their powerful Contemporary Legend Theatre.

When I met Huang Zuolin in Germany in 1988, the life of this pioneer started flowing in front of my eyes: his beginnings as an amateur, the studies with Michel Saint-Denis in London, the discovery of Brecht, the return towards his centre in which Shakespeare and the traditions of kunju and huaju cohabited, strengthening each other reciprocally. Huang Zuolin's presence materialised in Hong Kong from the pages of *Shashibiya*, Li Ruru's book on Shakespeare's artistic vicissitudes in China (2003). Above all, this book appealed to me because of the author's sensibility and biographical vicissitudes in a painful epoch.

An opportunity exists to live with Odin Teatret, to take part in its training, to see all its performances and become acquainted with our group dynamics and the organisation of its local and international activities. It is the Odin Week Festival, an annual gathering lasting ten days in Holstebro. A few years ago, a director from Shanghai participated. Before leaving, he said to us, the people of Hong Kong, where I now work, must see your performances.

For three years we didn't hear from David Jiang. Then an invitation arrived from the Leisure and Cultural Services Department of Hong Kong. David is the thread that has guided our theatre through many difficulties to this impressive building in Kowloon, which is mirrored in the sea and hosts *Within the Skeleton of the Whale*. Pure coincidence? But this thread expands and is multiplied. A few months later, four actors from Hong Kong collaborated with Odin Teatret during the Festuge, Holstebro's Festive Week. I remember one of them, at night, in our silent theatre, decorating letters of greeting to be offered at dawn to our town's bakers, together with hot coffee and cakes from different cultures during a 'theatrical visit'.

Action belongs to us, not its fruit. What we have to do, we must do without questioning. It belongs to the quest towards our centre. This can also be one of the aims of theatre which knows that it is pretence, and does not pretend to know.

The steps on the river bank

Here Barba looks back to his long connection with India. During the phase of dialogue that made the development of Theatre Anthropology possible, it was the technical know-how of any tradition that captured Barba's interest. In the subsequent period of cohabitation, the essential value is the personal relationship with the master who embodies the tradition. The text was first published in 1994 in English (The Drama Review. 38 (4), pp. 107–19).

The poet is sick. He is put ashore in Brindisi and carried on a stretcher over the Apennine Mountains to Naples to die (I am talking of Hermann Broch's novel *The Death of Virgil*). Just after disembarking, he notices a dark-skinned youth with luminous, impertinent eyes. He thinks he recognises him. But then he realises that he has never seen him before. And yet he knows him intimately.

During this last journey, Virgil – the wise poet who had also learnt magical and secret arts from the elders of his people, the Etruscans – meditates on what he has achieved during his life.

What purpose was served by telling the story of Aeneas who left the burning city of Troy carrying an old man on his shoulders and leading a child by the hand?

When he awakes from his drowsiness, Virgil looks around him and encounters those luminous and impertinent eyes. The youth continues to follow him, at a distance, laughing, with the swift movements of an intelligent or mischievous child. In the end, just as he is sinking into the last sleep, Virgil realises that the dusky child is himself when he was still far from being the famous and satiated man he has become.

The road of dreams

Drammensveien was the third street name I learnt when, in 1954, I left my country, Italy, and settled in Oslo, Norway. The first was Bogstadveien, where I had a job in a workshop as a welder; the second was Damfaret, where

I lived; the third was Drammensveien. I later discovered that Drammen was a town about forty kilometres from Oslo and so Drammensveien was simply 'the road to Drammen'. But Drammen sounds rather like *drömmen*, which, in Norwegian, means dream.

I had the idea that Drammensveien meant 'the road of dreams', also because on the same road there was the university library where I used to seek refuge every day after work, at about five in the afternoon.

I knew nobody in Oslo, I didn't speak Norwegian, and I had no desire to spend my free time in the cafés where foreigners met to chat together in their own language. So I went to the library, 'the house of dreams', I found books in Italian, and I read.

The Italian books were soon exhausted, so I started on the French ones. I could not speak French at that time, but I had studied it in school, and, with some difficulty, I could read it. I did not choose but took out books one after another, as I came across them. One day, I happened upon a book by Romain Rolland entitled *La Vie de Ramakrishna*. I discovered that in the nineteenth century in Bengal a peasant's son had become a monk, a devotee of Kali, and had a series of enlightenments. He brought about a revival of religious devotion at a time when Bengal was undergoing an intense philosophical, literary, political, and social reawakening inspired by Ram Mohum Roy and three generations of the Tagore family. The last of these, the great poet Rabindranath (Nobel Prize winner in 1913), was about twenty years younger than Ramakrishna.

Ramakrishna had spent most of his life in a temple a few kilometres from Calcutta. Apart from Hinduism, he had experienced other religious forms, causing a scandal when – himself a priest of Kali, the Mother – he had practised Muslim devotion. During another period, he immersed himself in the sayings of Christ. He said that different religions were like people with different languages drawing water from the river: they all used a different word to indicate what was in their pitcher; the pitchers too were all different, but their content was the same.

I was nineteen years old, indifferent to religion, already agnostic. I couldn't explain it, but I had an overwhelming desire to go to Dakshineswar, to that temple on the banks of the Ganges which had been built for Ramakrishna by a rich widow of a low caste. I yearned to set foot on those steps which, according to Romain Rolland, Ramakrishna descended every morning to reach the river and perform his ablutions. On 'the road of dreams', my dream was to go there.

I had no money. In 1955, going to India seemed an impossibility. The dream of those steps in Dakshineswar, which I cradled within me, warmed me in the greyness of the Scandinavian winter.

In the 'house of dreams', a librarian became my friend. He was a painter. In the mornings, he painted, and then, when the light faded, he earned his living in the library. One day he asked me if I would like to earn a little extra money as a model for a painter friend of his. Thus I found myself in the studio of Willi Midelfart, one of Norway's known painters. His studio was enormous, the back wall totally covered by books. I had to remain in a pose, but I could talk or read.

I owe most of my intellectual awareness to this elderly, cultured artist who had been in Paris in the 1920s and Moscow in the 1930s. While he painted me, he commented, explained, related the book I was reading to other books, other names, other historical events. And I went back to the library, conscious that the books were the bricks of an enigmatic building, a labyrinth whose living thread was hidden beneath the printed words.

One day, I spoke of Ramakrishna to Willi, and I asked if he knew of him. Of course! And he told me of his disciples, of Vivekananda who had been quite the opposite of Ramakrishna, extrovert, intellectual, committed to action, much travelled in the West. I also told him of my dream. He replied that every year on 26 December he was invited to dinner by Wilhelm Wilhelmsen, the Norwegian shipowner. The names of his ships had a common characteristic: they all began with the letter 'T'. He said he would tell him about me.

On the morning of 29 December, Willi phoned me. I was to contact the shipowner's offices because there was a possibility of a job. On 5 January 1956, it was snowing when I boarded a ship, the Talabot, bound for the East, as engine boy.

The theatre did not enter my mind. For me, the Orient was strange religions and philosophies. No, theatre did not exist for me.

We passed through Suez and arrived in Aden. I received a parcel. It came from Willi and contained three books. I don't remember the first one. The second was Céline's *Journey to the End of the Night*. The third was *Man's Fate* by Malraux, the description of a revolt in China in 1927 that culminated in a massacre carried out by the army of Chiang Kai-shek. That was the other face of the East, the fierce face of history.

The Talabot sailed on to Colombo, Madras, Chittagong. Then Calcutta. One morning, very early, I went to Dakshineswar. I saw the steps. My feet touched them. I too descended them to the river's edge. That's all.

Then I went back to the greasy work in the ship's deafening engine room and the seasickness of the return voyage on rough monsoon seas.

A footnote in a theatre history book

I had gone to India by sea for the first time in 1956. I returned there overland in 1963 with Judy (later we were to marry). She drove our second-hand Land Rover, as I didn't know how to drive. I read – perhaps as a counterbalance to the monotony of the Iranian desert – Gibbon's *Decline and Fall of the Roman Empire*. This time, I really was searching for the Indian theatre. I wanted to learn something professionally useful.

At that time I was working with Grotowski. They were the darkest and most precarious years for his theatre, which was almost unknown and always on the point of being suffocated by the communist censorship in Poland. Being a foreigner, I was freer than a Pole to travel abroad, spreading information and establishing contacts which might make it a little less easy for the Polish bureaucracy to eliminate the tiny theatre laboratory in Opole.

In June 1963, the UNESCO's International Theatre Institute (ITI) held its international congress in Warsaw. The Polish hosts had made sure that in the programme of events not even the slightest hint was made of the existence of Grotowski. Grotowski and I discussed how to break this silence. He went with his theatre to Łódź – only a couple of hours away from Warsaw – to perform Marlowe's *Dr Faustus*, which had just had its premiere in Opole. I went to Warsaw and mingled with the delegates of the ITI congress. I succeeded in convincing a number of them to travel with me to Łódź to see *Dr Faustus*. The performance was a shock for them, and the next morning, in the congress hall, Grotowski's name was on everyone's lips. There was much praise for the Polish authorities for supporting such a theatre. They were astounded but put a good face on it.

Judy worked as a secretary in the ITI, and that was how we met. I had told her that I wanted to go back to India, but overland this time. 'I have a car', she said. 'Let's go', I replied. A month later, during the summer holidays, we set out together.

Being used to the space-time of European travel where I could go from one capital to another in a few hours, India for me was like falling into a bottomless well. It took us three days to reach New Delhi, which, on the map, seemed only a short jump from Pakistan's border. There, at last, I would be able to get to know Indian theatre.

The people I approached told me I should meet Ebrahim Alkazi. He was a well-known personality and taught at the National School of Drama. There, to my great surprise, I listened to something that was not so different from what was being taught at the Warsaw theatre school. Ebrahim Alkazi had lived for a long time in Egypt. He had a profound knowledge of British theatre and was making his name as an innovator by introducing the visions of Stanislavski and the actors' studio.

Then someone said to me: 'Why don't you go to Bombay? Adi Marzban is there; he is a playwright who produces some interesting theatre'. Again, day after day of driving. But also in Bombay, among plays taken from the British tradition and popular theatre, the outlook was not very stimulating for a young man who was impatient and hungry for professional secrets.

Someone suggested, 'You must go south. There you will find something that is really unique.' He assured me that kathakali would not disappoint me. He was from Kerala.

And so Judy got back behind the steering wheel of the Land Rover. After a seemingly endless journey down through the whole of India, we arrived in Kerala to be faced with the problem of tracing kathakali. Finally, in Trichur, in a bookshop owned by Kerala's former Minister of Culture, they told us of a kathakali school in a village called Cheruthuruthy.

At last we arrived. We were allowed to stay in the hospital in a somewhat isolated bungalow, which, if I remember rightly, was previously meant for lepers.

I went to the kathakali school Kerala Kalamandalam. The teachers were not in the least interested in my presence. I was a burden, and my questions were seen as pedantic and boring, a pure waste of time. Underneath the patina of an elementary courtesy to guests, the teachers made no effort to hide the annoyance they felt towards me. The memory of those weeks at the kathakali school still has a bitter flavour, although I cannot today blame the teachers. My prejudices collided with theirs. From my side, I could not help also seeing in the school an image of routine, with the masters seated, beating out the rhythm, in an attitude which to me could either be one of patience or of resignation. And the students repeated the same handful of exercises. Exactly the opposite of what in my imagination during those years I idealised as sacred or necessary theatre.

But something of great importance became deeply engraved in my memory: the silence and attitude of the nine-year-old students who began their training at dawn.

There is an essential difference between the theatre you begin to practise as an adult and that whose apprenticeship begins in childhood. The children are projected into a context that gives them a value, into a tradition that transcends them and which at first they do not grasp but, little by little, they incorporate. They feel they represent something that is beyond them, a higher meaning.

I thought of myself and my colleagues at the Warsaw theatre school, impatient and full of justifications, with our own secure ways of looking at, explaining, and discussing theatre. *How difficult it is*, I pondered, *to love art in oneself and not oneself in art, according to the precepts of Stanislavski, when you begin as an adult, already formed.*

In Cheruthuruthy, the value of the theatre did not lie in what the children may say, believe or dream. It was as though they were carrying on their frail shoulders, sometimes with difficulty, sometimes light-heartedly, the image of a tradition that they might later interpret and transform but that was not theirs to dispose of as they wished.

For me, kathakali was those small boys whose work I followed daily, with whom I chatted, and who answered my complicated questions courteously or with an embarrassed smile.

There were few kathakali performances at that time of year. During the three weeks of my stay in Cheruthuruthy, I only saw a couple, lasting the whole night. I sensed a dilation of time, full of penitence for me, sitting for hours on a rush mat, in that big open space, among mothers and children chattering and eating, with hawkers moving around and snoring men. And all the while, on the stage, the actors' flame continued to burn, indifferent to indifference, without any sacred aura.

I came from the experience with Grotowski in Opole, where, from 1961, I participated in the invention of a new theatre identity, trying to restore the sacredness of this art. Yet here, in Kerala, the sacred became calm and serene irreverence. I think that more even than the beauty of the performance, it was my incapacity to understand that surprised me. Why was I so fascinated when I neither understood the story performed by the actors, nor its religious meaning? What was it that kept me spellbound in this atmosphere similar to that of an Indian railway station that contradicted all my ideas about theatre and its sacredness?

Leaving the Kathakali Kalamandalam, I wrote these lines of thanks in its guestbook:

> To the Secretary, Kalamandalam,
> Cheruthuruthy
>
> Dear Sir,
>
> I had not the occasion last night at the performance to thank you for all the kind help you have given me during my stay here. To you, and to the Superintendent, and to all the boys who were so willing to be of service, I would like to express my gratitude and sincerest thanks.
>
> My visit to Kalamandalam has greatly helped me in my studies and the research material I have collected will surely be of the greatest assistance to those people working at the Theatre Laboratory in Poland. Many thanks once again,
>
> Yours sincerely,
>
> Eugenio Barba
>
> (Schechner 1983: 147)

I signed this message of thanks on 29 September 1963, at the end of my three weeks' stay. I had forgotten this formal note until in 1984 I had the surprise of finding it on page 147 of Richard Schechner's *Performative Circumstances from the Avant Garde to Ramlila* (1983) published in Calcutta by Seagull Books who, incidentally, have the same emblem as the Moscow Art Theatre.

Schechner read my words in the school visitors' book when he went to the Kathakali Kalamandalam in 1972. He quoted them as a reminder of how a twenty-seven-year-old Italian passed on the news of the kathakali exercises to a young Polish director of barely thirty, Jerzy Grotowski, who incorporated them into the actors' training at his Theatre Laboratory of the 13 Rows in Opole.

That letter of so many years ago is merely a footnote in the history of theatre research in the second half of the twentieth century, in the chapter on the beginnings of Grotowski's career, before *The Constant Prince* (1965) and *Apocalypsis cum figuris* (1968), before the Poor Theatre and fame. It could also be a way to introduce the story of Odin Teatret as Eurasian Theatre.

The legacy

On my return to Europe, I wrote about kathakali in some French, Italian, Danish, and American journals. My essay generated an interest that, throughout the following years, made Cheruthuruthy into an almost obligatory goal for a certain kind of theatre people.

But it is not important who was first off the mark and why. Nor is it important whether or not there are inaccuracies in my articles about kathakali and its history. Even less is it worthwhile asking oneself what one can take from kathakali, its training and its performing technique.

What is important is that which belongs neither to kathakali nor to me, and which, in quite another context, in forms which are incomparable, still guides me when I question myself about the meaning of theatre.

What appears in front of me is not a technical precept or an answer made up of words but the precious image of those children who at dawn practised their exercises without the presence of any teacher. And I repeat to myself the words which I have constantly whispered to my actors: 'What you must do, you must do. And don't ask why, don't ask why.'

Do I really like to work with performers from other traditions? The real collaboration actually begins when I forget about traditions, about geographical and cultural distance and all the differences in the personality in front of me.

Traditions do not exist. Just as ideas and religions do not exist. Only the people embodying them are real. Fidelity to tradition and the desire to preserve its purity can be a powerful guide when there is a personal vision. But they become a burden on others when they turn into orthodoxy. Then the past suffocates the germs of life and the dead bury the living.

After so many years of working together, I often forget that Sanjukta Panigrahi is Indian, that she dances in the odissi style, that she excels in this genre. And I believe that she sometimes manages to forget that I am a Westerner, a European, an Italian.

There are some old photographs of Sanjukta as a child. Underneath the costumes and the dancer's make-up, you can discern the expression that particularly beautiful children often have, who, if they don't encounter something much greater than themselves, risk becoming arrogant. That young girl certainly did not find it easy to obey. For this reason, her artistic humility is precious. Those photos of Sanjukta as a child remind me of the ones which I myself took at Cheruthuruthy, depicting the skinny bodies of the kathakali pupils doing their exercises.

When I first met Sanjukta, she was already famous in India. She had founded a style and had made it known outside her home region. But there is something recognisable in those people who have been used to getting up early and working alone, with no one to watch them, no one to rebuke or praise them. Those who have passed through such an experience that distils the meaning of doing theatre into silent actions, are compatriots, whatever their culture and tradition. If we call this ethics, then we risk turning it into theory or rhetoric.

Looking back, I ask myself what it was that so struck me about Romain Rolland's book on Ramakrishna. The author didn't indulge in powerful images and suggestive language. He didn't oppose the narrowness of scientific reason to the boundless horizons of the spirit. He didn't confront India with Europe, the East with the West. He dealt with the extraordinary experiences of his protagonist with the same vivid practicability and the same good sense that he applied to the description of nature or the history of modern India. He spoke of the muscles and nerves involved in ecstasy. He showed Vivekananda touching the muscles of his aspiring pupils before admitting them to spiritual training.

And, above all, he insisted upon the concept of realisation. He denied that there was any point in distinguishing between the real and the ideal. Ramakrishna was a realiser, a doer.

In that book, there was a primitive photograph accompanied by a note presenting it as an exceptional document. Unwittingly, I have re-evoked this image in some of my productions. The photo showed a few men dressed in white, crouched on the floor against a large window which was covered by a straw mat and through which the scorching sun was beating. Ramakrishna was standing in the centre, thin and bearded, like a sick man tottering as he attempts to walk, or one who has had too much to drink. One arm was raised, while the other hand, on a level with the heart, formed the mudra which in dance represents the bee sucking nectar from a flower. Beside him, a robust man was ready to support him. The scene gives the impression of simple family happiness, a gaiety without festive frills, among people who are able to let themselves go and are not afraid if a companion seems to hover on the verge of madness. Ramakrishna – from what I could make out in the dim light – was laughing. The caption said that the photo portrayed the exact moment when the holy man passed into *samadhi*, ecstasy, during a *kirtan*, a session of religious songs and dances.

This way of representing light through the most humble of actions is what Ramakrishna, the kathakali children, Sanjukta and India have all taught me. And I rediscover it in the attention to technical accuracy and the tension of the visions among the women and men who populate Eurasian Theatre.

When I speak of Eurasian Theatre, I am not thinking of theatres within a geographical space but of a mental dimension, an active idea that has inspired the theatre of our century. This concept encompasses the experiences which, for all artists, whatever their cultural background, constitute the essential

Reproduction Tod. Schlemmer

RAMAKRISHNA, parmi ses disciples

La photographie, très rare, a été prise à l'instant précis où il passait dans le SAMADHI (extase). Un de ses disciples s'est levé, pour le soutenir.

Romain Rolland, Vie de
Ramakrishna, Paris, Stock, 1930
[lot (imprimés)] fin le 14 181 c 183

▶ Ramakrishna falling into *samadhi* (ecstasy).

points of reference for their theatre practice: from Ibsen to Zeami, from the Peking Opera to Brecht, from the mime of Decroux to noh, from kabuki to Meyerhold's Biomechanics, from Delsarte to kathakali, from ballet and modern dance to butoh, from Artaud to Bali, from Stanislavski to *Natyashastra* and butoh.

We could say that Eurasian Theatre represents a common country: that of our craft, of our professional identity. Or else it is a legacy, that which remains and can be shared equally – regardless of our national origins – in that country of transition which is theatre.

Eurasian Theatre

*For Barba, the definition 'Eurasian Theatre' serves to conceptualise the characteristics and the value of his association with Asian artists. In the context of this book, it represents a conclusion. Barba has changed the final part to strengthen this value. It was first published in 1988 in English (*The Drama Review*, 32 (3), pp. 126–30).*

The influence of Western theatre on Asian theatre is an acknowledged fact. The important effect that Asian theatre has had and still has on Western theatre practice is equally irrefutable. But a feeling of uneasiness remains: that these exchanges might be part of the supermarket of cultures.

Dawn

Kathakali and noh, *onnagata* and Barong, Rukmini Devi and Mei Lanfang – they were all there, side by side with Stanislavski, Meyerhold, Eisenstein, Grotowski, and Decroux when I started to do theatre. It was not only the memory of their theatrical creations that fascinated me but, above all, the detailed artificiality through which they attained an actor-in-life.

The long nights of kathakali gave me a glimpse of the limits which the actor can reach. But it was the dawn that revealed these actors' secrets to me, at the Kalamandalam school in Kerala. There, young boys, hardly adolescents, monotonously repeating exercises, steps, songs, prayers, and offerings, crystallised their ethos through artistic behaviour and an ethical attitude.

I compared our theatre with theirs. Today, the very word 'comparison' seems inadequate to me since it separates the two faces of the same reality. I can say that I 'compare' Indian or Balinese, Chinese or Japanese traditions if I compare their epidermises, their diverse conventions, their many different performance styles. But if I consider that which lies beneath those luminous and seductive skins and discern the organs that keep them alive, then the poles of the comparison blend into a single profile: that of a Eurasian Theatre.

► Cheruthuruthy, Kathakali Kalamandalam, 2013. An apparently confused Barba tries to orientate himself in the place he visited fifty years ago and which has now become a university college.

Anti-tradition

It is possible to consider the theatre in terms of ethnic, national, group or even individual traditions. But if in doing so one seeks to comprehend one's own identity, it is also essential to take the opposite and complementary point of view and think of one's own theatre in a transcultural dimension, in the flow of a tradition of traditions.

All attempts to create 'anti-traditional' forms of theatre in the West, as well as in the East, have drawn from the tradition of traditions. Certain European scholars in the fifteenth and sixteenth centuries forsook the performance and festival customs of their cities and villages and rescued the theatre of Athens and ancient Rome from oblivion. Three centuries later, the avant-garde of the young Romantics broke with the classical traditions and drew inspiration from new, distant theatres: from the 'barbarous' Elizabethans and the Spaniards in the Golden Century, folk performances, the commedia dell'arte, 'primitive' rituals, medieval mystery plays, and Asian theatres. These are the images

▶ Holstebro, 1994. Sanjukta Panigrahi and Kazuo Ohno improvising during Odin Teatret's thirtieth anniversary.

that have inspired the revolutions of the anti-traditional Western artists in the twentieth century. Today, however, the Asian theatres are no longer approached through tales but are experienced directly.

Every ethnocentricity has its eccentric pole that reinforces it and compensates for it. Even today, in the Asian countries, where often the value of autochthonous tradition is emphasised as against the diffusion of foreign models and the erosion of cultural identity, Stanislavski, Brecht, agitprop, and 'absurd' theatre continue to be means of repudiating scenic traditions which are inadequate to deal with the conditions imposed by recent history.

In Asia, this breach with tradition began at the end of the nineteenth century. Ibsen's *A Doll's House*, the plays of Shaw and Hauptmann, the

► ISTA Copenhagen, 1996. At the end of the session, Jerzy Grotowski was invited on the stage, and all masters celebrated him with a collective improvisation together. Here, Steve Paxton (Contact improvisation, USA) with I Made Djimat (Bali).

theatrical adaptations of Dickens's novels or of *Uncle Tom's Cabin* were presented not as simple imports of Western models but as the discovery of a theatre capable of speaking to the present.

In the meeting between East and West, seduction, imitation, and exchange are reciprocal. We in the West have often envied the Asians their theatrical knowledge, which transmits the actors' living work of art from one generation to another. They have envied our theatre's capacity for confronting new subjects and the way in which it keeps up with the times. Such flexibility allows for personal interpretations of traditional texts that often assume the energy of a formal and ideological conquest. In the West, stories that are unstable in every aspect but the written; in the East, a living art, profound, capable of being transmitted and involving all the actors' and spectators' physical and mental levels but anchored in stories and customs which are forever antiquated. On the one hand, a theatre which is sustained by *logos*. On the other, a theatre which is, above all, *bios*.

Why

Why, in the Western tradition, as opposed to what happens in Asia, has the actor become specialised: the actor/singer as distinct from the actor/dancer and, in turn, the actor/dancer as distinct from the actor/interpreter?

Why, in the West, do actors tend to confine themselves within the skin of only one character in each production? Why do they not explore the possibility of creating the context of an entire story, with many characters, with leaps from the general to the particular, from the first to the third person, from the past to the present, from the whole to the part, from persons to things? Why, in the West, does this possibility remain relegated to storytellers or to exceptions such as Dario Fo, while, in the East, it is characteristic of every traditional theatre and their actors, both when they act/sing/dance alone and when they are part of a performance in which the roles are shared?

Why do so many forms of Asian theatre deal successfully with that which in the West seems acceptable only in opera which uses words whose meaning the majority of the spectators cannot understand?

Clearly, from the historical point of view, there are answers to these questions. But they only become professionally useful when they stimulate us to imagine how we can develop our own theatrical identity by extending the limits that define it against our nature. It is enough to observe from afar, from countries and customs which are distant, or simply different from our own, to discover the latent possibilities of a Eurasian Theatre.

The performers' village

The divergent directions in which Western and Asian theatres have developed provoke a distortion of perception. In the West, because of an automatic ethnocentric reaction, ignorance of Asian theatre is justified by the implication that it deals with experiences that are not directly relevant to us, too exotic to be usefully explored. This same distortion of perception idealises, and thus evens out, the multiplicity of Asian theatres or venerates them as sanctuaries.

ISTA, the International School of Theatre Anthropology, has given me the opportunity to gather together masters of both Asian and Western theatres over a period of many years. Here we compared the different results and working processes of actors from various genres and reached down into a common technical substratum: the level of pre-expressivity. This is the level at which the actors engage their own energies according to an extra-daily behaviour, modelling their 'presence', their *bios*, in front of the spectator. At this pre-expressive level, the principles are similar, even though they nurture the enormous expressive differences that exist between one tradition and another, one actor and another. They are analogous principles because they are born of similar physical conditions in different contexts. They are not, however, homologous, since they do not share a common history. The application of these similar principles often results in a way of thinking that, in spite of different formulations, permits theatre people from the most divergent traditions to communicate with each other.

The work with Odin Teatret has led me, by means of practical solutions, not to take the differences between what is called 'dance' and what is called 'theatre' too much into consideration; not to accept the character as a unit of measure of the performance; not to make the actor's gender coincide automatically with that of the character; to exploit the sonorous richness of languages and their emotive force, which is capable of transmitting information above and beyond their semantic value. These characteristics of Odin Teatret's dramaturgy and of its actors are equivalent to some of the characteristics of traditional Asian forms, but those of Odin were born of an autodidactic training, of our situation as foreigners and of our limitations. This impossibility of being like other theatre people has gradually rendered us loyal to our diversity.

For all these reasons, I recognise myself in the culture of a Eurasian Theatre today. That is, I belong to the small and recent tradition of a theatre group which has autodidactic origins but grows in a professional 'village' where kabuki actors are not regarded as being more remote than Shakespearian texts, nor the living presence of an Indian dancer less contemporary than the American avant-garde.

Thought-in-action

It often occurs in this village that the actors (or a single actor) not only analyse a conflict, let themselves be guided by the objectivity of the *logos* and tell a story but dance in it and with it according to the flow of the *bios*. This is not a metaphor. Concretely, it means that the actor does not remain bound to the plot, does not interpret a text, but creates a context, moves around and within the events. At times, the actor lets these events carry him, at times he carries them, while at other times he separates himself from them, comments on them, rises above them, attacks them, refuses them, follows new associations or leaps to other stories. The linearity of the narrative is shattered by constantly changing the point of view, dissecting the known reality and interweaving objectivity and subjectivity, expositions of facts and reactions to them. Thus, the actor embodies the freedom and the leaps of the thinking process, guided by a logic which the spectator cannot immediately recognise.

That which has often caused misunderstandings about Asian theatres, has confused them with archaic rituals or has made them appear as perfect but static forms is in fact that which brings them closest to our epoch's most complex concepts of time and space. These theatres do not represent a phenomenology of reality but a phenomenology of thought. They do not behave as if they belonged to Newton's universe; they correspond to Niels Bohr's subatomic world.

Tradition and founders of traditions

When we speak of culture, the subject of identity is always at the centre of our discourse. Our ethnic identity has been established by history. We cannot shape it. Personal identity is formed by each of us on our own, often unconsciously. We call it 'destiny'. The only profile on which we can work consciously as rational beings is the profile of our professional identity.

It is possible to develop a professional identity that can grow in contact with other cultures, also at the intra-cultural level, allowing for the discovery and absorption of that which is different, even in our own culture. For the European reformers of the twentieth century, some of the events belonging to their history were fundamental for revising their practice: classical Greek theatre, the commedia dell'arte, and different types of popular performances, alive today or extinct, accepted or marginalised.

It is through exchange, rather than isolation, that a culture can evolve and transform itself organically. The same process applies to actors. However, in order to make an exchange, you must offer something in return. Therefore, one's historical-biographical identity is fundamental when confronted with its opposite pole, the meeting with 'otherness', with that which is different. This does not mean the imposition of one's own horizon or way of seeing but rather a displacement that makes it possible to glimpse a territory beyond one's known universe.

Defining one's own professional identity implies overcoming ethnocentricity to the point of discovering one's own centre in the tradition of traditions. Here, the term 'roots' becomes paradoxical: it does not imply a bond that ties us to a place but an ethos that permits us to change places. Or, better, it represents the force that causes us to change our horizons precisely because it roots us to a centre.

This force is manifest if at least two conditions are present: the need to define one's own tradition for oneself and the capacity to place this individual or collective tradition in a context that connects it with other, different traditions.

It is not the traditions that choose us but rather it is us who choose them. An American can become a Buddhist and a Maori an excellent opera singer. Traditions preserve and hand down a form, not the sense that gives it life. Each of us must define and reinvent that sense for ourselves. This reinvention expresses a personal, cultural, and professional identity.

Traditions stratify and refine the knowledge of successive generations of founders and allow every new artist to begin without being obliged to start from scratch. Traditions are a precious inheritance, spiritual nourishment, roots.

But they are also a constraint. There is no identity without a struggle against the constraint of the forms inherited from 'tradition'. Without such a struggle, artistic life collapses. In art, the spark of life is the tension between the rigour of the form and the rebellious detail that shakes it from within, forcing it to assume a new significance, an unfamiliar aspect.

The actor who does not belong to a codified scenic tradition often risks feeling disinherited, rootless and without concrete points of reference to disobey. Those who do not have a tradition often idealise it and refer to it with a superstitious belief as though it could bestow a meaning on their work.

The tradition of traditions

A spirit of revolt and a longing for a set of values has permeated the theatre of the twentieth century. At a hasty glance, the distinction between tradition and founders of traditions is equivalent to that between classical schools and innovators, the orthodox and the rebellious, the Asian actor/dancer hidden beneath a golden costume and the restless and eclectic experiments of contemporary performers. But it is not like that. Even the most rigid tradition only lives on through reinvention by its interpreters. And the more subtle and imperceptible these reinventions seem, the deeper they run.

► Calicut, 2013. Swami Gurukal, Ravi Gopalan Nair, and Barba in the Industhan Kalarippayattu.

►► Holstebro, 2013. Parvathy Baul teaching during the Transit Festival. She is one of the performers in Odin Teatret's *Flying* (2016).

In daily practice, 'tradition' is the same as 'knowledge' or, rather, 'technique', a far more humble and effective word. Technique does not define us but it is the necessary instrument for overcoming the borders that confine us. Technical knowledge allows us to encounter other forms and introduces us to the tradition of traditions, to those principles that constantly recur beneath the differences in style, culture, and personalities.

The goal is not to identify oneself with a tradition but to build a nucleus of values, a personal identity, both rebellious and loyal to one's own roots. The way to achieve this is always through a minutely detailed practice that constitutes our professional identity. It is competence in one's craft that transforms a condition into a personal vocation and, in the eyes of others, into a destiny that is a legacy and a tradition.

It is for us to decide which history we belong to professionally and who are the ancestors in whose values we recognise ourselves. They may be from distant eras and cultures, but the meaning of their work is the legacy to be safeguarded and transmitted. Each one of us is the offspring of someone's work. Each one of us moves forward, leaving behind a past which we have chosen for ourselves.

POSTSCRIPT

Two pairs of eyes

This foreword by Barba to Li Ruru's The Soul of Beijing Opera: Theatrical Creativity and Continuity in a Changing World *(2010: xi–xiv) wanders far from the historical facts that the author reconstructs. But this text is a valid postscript to this book since it synthesises the intellectual and emotional significance of Barba's long-lasting relationship with Asian traditional theatres and their performers.*

Is traditional Chinese theatre really so distant from ours? Are the differences that distinguish us really as significant as they seem? Is what we have in common really common to both of us? Are we speaking of the same things when we speak of the same things, and speaking of different things when we speak of different things?

Reading the script of Li Ruru's book *The Soul of Beijing Opera: Theatrical Creativity and Continuity in the Changing World* (2010), I felt as if I were two people, as if two different pairs of eyes were looking at the lines and the chapters. The first glance enjoyed the variegated landscape of the theatre, which, since my youth, I have known and loved under the name of Peking Opera. The second continually made comparisons – behind that landscape – with the European theatre. It's a split that is typical of cross-cultural vision. We can't escape assessments and comparisons: us versus them. It's hard to break out of this exotic and familiar vice.

For us theatre practitioners in Europe, traditional Chinese theatre has long been a legend. Then it became an apparition. Finally it materialised in real encounters. In the beginning of the twentieth century, a few major artists of the Great Reform of the European stage experienced Mei Lanfang's visit to Russia: an important episode in the history of our theatre but also a tale that has become one of the founding myths of the Eurasian Theatre.

The Eurasian Theatre is neither a style nor a geographical extension. It is a way of seeing, a mental category – or rather an attempt to overcome the distinction between us and them. It implies the historical fact that since 1900 theatre people all over the world orientate themselves within the horizon of a shared theatre culture including performance genres both with European and Asian roots. This constellation of imagined knowledge and real know-how has guided all those who have reflected upon the craft and the art of the actor – from Stanislavski to Brecht, from Meyerhold to Grotowski, from Copeau to Artaud and Decroux.

Why did the most creative European artists, those who were most dissatisfied with their own tradition and obsessed by the future, turn with voracity towards the Asian theatres, towards their ancient forms that belonged to backward epochs? Why did they consider them up to date? Was it only because they were refined models of performances that rejected realism?

'This is not the only reason', answers my friend Nicola Savarese. And he adds,

> Think about the reaction of the poet François Prévert and his colleague Claude Roy when they saw the Peking Opera in Paris in 1955. 'This', they said, 'is the theatre of the actor who has not forgotten anything.' François Prévert explained: 'After all, what is a circus acrobat? An actor who has forgotten in which play he is acting. What is a dancer? A singer who has forgotten that she knew how to sing. And what is an actor? A dancer who has forgotten that he knew how to dance. The Chinese actor, on the other hand, is one who has forgotten nothing.'

This may be so, but how can we explain that artists such as Brecht and Meyerhold, revolutionaries, secret anarchists who were always hostile to the bourgeois mentality and art, admired Chinese theatre which was an expression of a feudal culture, based on violence and revenge, on war and the repression of women? Georges Banu, another of my friends, replies,

> For the same reason that theatre people in China and Japan accepted the realistic and imprecise European way of acting, and acknowledged the 'spoken' theatre, deprived of song and dance, importing the plays of Ibsen and Beckett, that raised the problems of contemporary men and women and expounded the anguish and the uncertainty of the future in their tragic nakedness.

Georges Banu is a professor at the Sorbonne in Paris and a collaborator of Peter Brook. Nicola Savarese is a scholar of Renaissance theatre and of Asian theatres, one of the founders of the International School of Theatre Anthropology (ISTA) and co-author with me of *A Dictionary of Theatre Anthropology: The Secret Art of the Performer* (2005).

I ask them, 'Then, according to you, in the twentieth century, was there a kind of complementarity established between theatres of a European tradition and Asian classical theatres?' Savarese and Banu answer almost with the same words:

You may call it a division of tasks or an exchange between equals. Both acknowledged their own weaker sides without inferiority complexes. From the Europeans, Asians could learn how to face, on stage, the problems and contradictions of modern times. From the Asians, Europeans could learn how the actor could rediscover an effective language, able to capture the attention of the spectators and make them dream.

Still today, in Western books, we see photos with captions such as 'A Peking Opera actor in the role of an old man' or 'An actress of the Chinese classical theatre as the mythical character of the Monkey King'. But in the same books we don't see 'A German actor in the role of Oedipus', 'A Russian actress in the role of Liubov' or 'A European dancer in the role of Gisele'. There are Christian names and last names. They are not characters, they are people.

Instead, the actors of the Asian traditional theatres often appear without a name, as if the actor as a person didn't exist and only his or her appearance was important. It's true that in many cases the mask or the make-up make quite different faces look almost the same, but this doesn't justify a generic way of looking that takes into account only the forms and not the people embodying them. Is it laziness? Our tendency to generalise? An unintentional colonialist attitude? It is interesting to reflect on the fact that the only type of European theatre for which we adopt a similar attitude is commedia dell'arte. This has long been considered a form of fanciful yet inferior theatre, belonging to the popular traditions, where the individuality of the actors doesn't count but only the permanent presence of the masks.

Jingju, noh, commedia dell'arte, kabuki or gambuh are names of great living traditions which, when you look at them from afar, are often treated as fossils. But they are the result of struggles and continuous tensions between traditionalists and innovators. They are not only forms but also theatre languages, continuously changing, with their rules and recognisable peculiarities, and with the inexhaustible mutability of every living language.

I like books in which the winds of the theatre are not cancelled by distance, where I can distinguish not only the genres, conventions and rules of various theatres but also the exceptions, the rebellions and the profiles of the individuals who prevent the forms from always being predictable. Where personal passions don't get buried in a language of sand. I like meticulous and precise books, but those where the precision is disarranged by the disorder of individual histories.

For these reasons, although coming from a foreign theatre, I was happy to introduce Li Ruru's journey into the noble regions of jingju. That which from afar appeared like a dream landscape, a real utopia of the theatre, reveals itself to me as a garden of heresies and discoveries.

I said before that I read the text of Li Ruru's book with two different pairs of eyes. To each of them I had given a name: René and Victor. There is a book of great significance for the European understanding of the Chinese civilisation. It was published in France in 1921. The author had died in 1919, exhausted not from his long wanderings in the Far East but from the First World War which was fought in Europe. It's a strange, unfinished book, halfway between a novel and an *impression de voyage*. The title is the name of a person, *René Leys* (1971). The author is Victor Segalen, a medical officer in the French Navy and a poet. The two different pairs of eyes are those of René and of Victor, the character and the author. The understanding of Chinese civilisation happens through the crossing and the contrast of these two gazes.

This posthumous book relates a day in June 1911 when Victor and René watch a performance of jingju in the capital. René has lived in Beijing for many years. He knows how to judge the different degree of skill of each individual actor, appreciates the way he overcomes the difficulties of the physical and vocal score and notices the least uncertainty and inaccuracy. He goes into ecstasy while watching the actors' summit of virtuosity where technique disappears and turns into a rare spiritual experience.

Victor has only just set foot in China. He sees quite another performance – incomprehensible stories – but he senses flashes and flickerings that cross the space and shake it. Human bodies show him changing passions, sublime loves and sadistic martyrs, bodies unable to keep their feet on the ground, thrown into space like branches truncated by the wind, that suddenly fall into an exhausted stillness and at once dart away and explode. He sees swords that don't scatter blood but create vortexes and hurricanes. Unveiled by the theatre, for a few instants he succeeds in perceiving the reality that our illusions hide from us.

All this is technique, training, make-up, costumes, words, and songs amalgamated in plots of feelings. The rigorous scaffolding that René is able to see behind the wonders of the performance is only fiction. But it is also what Victor sees: the fiction that falls, revealing a bareness that attracts us and pushes us away. In other words: Truth.

In the French forest of Huelgoat, ancient oaks and huge round stones seem to have been placed in the most improbable spots by the hands of giants or the spells of magicians. We are in Brittany, in one of the many geographical zones denominated *finis terrae*, a place where Earth ends. Once, the Knights of the Round Table had ridden through this forest and become lost in it.

There Victor Segalen went for a lonely walk on the morning of 21 May 1919, taking with him a small provision of food. He accidentally hurt his leg. Two days later, he was found, having bled to death at the foot of a tall tree, a copy of Shakespeare's *Hamlet* by his side. He had searched for Buddha on long sea voyages across the Far East. Instead, he encountered him during a solitary stroll a short distance from the hotel where his wife was anxiously awaiting him for supper.

▶ Istanbul, 1959. Eugenio Barba.

'The slap of a stone on the water. It had my name engraved on it
and floated like a tiny island. It moved away and in its wake shimmered
four words: disappeared in the East.'

(Burning the House: A Director's Origin)

Bibliography

BALÀZS, Béla. 1980. *Scritti di teatro: Dall'arte del teatro alla guerriglia teatrale* (Texts on Theatre: From Theatre Art to Guerrilla Theatre), ed. by Eugenia Casini Ropa, trans. by Eugenia Casini Ropa and Edoarda Dala Kisfaludy (Florence and Milan: La Casa Usher)

BARBA, Eugenio. 1965a. *Alla ricerca del teatro perduto* (In Search of a Lost Theatre) (Padua: Marsilio)

— 1965b. *Kírsérletek színháza* (In Search of a Lost Theatre) (Budapest: Színháztudományi Intézet)

— 1979. *The Floating Islands* (Holstebro: Drama)

— 1981. *Il Brecht dell'Odin* (The Odin's Brecht) (Milan: Ubulibri)

— 1986. *Beyond the Floating Islands*, trans. by Judy Barba (New York: Performing Arts Journal Publications)

— 1995. *The Paper Canoe: A Guide to Theatre Anthropology*, trans. by Richard Fowler (London and New York: Routledge)

— 1999. *Land of Ashes and Diamonds: My Apprenticeship in Poland, followed by 26 Letters from Jerzy Grotowski to Eugenio Barba*, trans. by Eugenio Barba and Judy Barba (Aberystwyth: Black Mountain Press)

— 2004. *La terra di cenere e diamanti: il mio apprendistato in Polonia seguito da 26 lettere di Jerzy Grotowski a Eugenio Barba* (Land of Ashes and Diamonds), 2nd edn (Milan: Ubulibri)

— 2005. 'La conquista della differenza' (The Conquest of Difference), *Teatro e Storia*, 25: 271–90

BARBA, Eugenio and Ian Watson. 2002. 'The Conquest of Difference: An Electronic Dialogue', in *Negotiating Cultures*, ed. by Ian Watson et al. (Manchester: Manchester University Press)

BARBA, Eugenio and Nicola Savarese. 2005. *A Dictionary of Theatre Anthropology: The Secret Art of the Performer*, 2nd edn, trans. by Richard Fowler and Judy Barba (London and New York: Routledge)

BRANDON, James R. 1978. 'Form in Kabuki Acting', in *Studies in Kabuki: Its Acting, Music and Historical Context*, ed. by James R. Brandon, William P. Malm and Donald Howard Shiverly (Honolulu: The University Press of Hawaii)

BRECHT, Bertolt. 1964. *Brecht on Theatre*, ed. and trans. by John Willett (London: Methuen)

— 1967. *Buch der Wendungen* (Book of Changes), in *Gesammelte Werke*, vol. V (Frankfurt: Suhrkamp)

— 1975. *Scritti teatrali* (Texts on Theatre), vol. II, trans. by Carlo Pinelli, Mario Carpitella, Emilio Castellani, Paolo Chiarini, Roberto Fertonani and Renata Mertens (Turin: Einaudi)

CRAIG, Edward Gordon. 1962. *On the Art of the Theatre* (London: Mercury Books)

DAUMAL, René. 1970. *Bharata: L'Origine du théâtre, la poésie et la musique en Inde* (Bharata: The Origin of Theatre, Poetry and Music in India) (Paris: Gallimard)

DECROUX, Etienne. 1985. *Words on Mime*, trans. by Mark Piper (Claremont: Mime Journal)

DULLIN, Charles. 1946. *Souvenirs et notes de travail d'un acteur* (An Actor's Memories and Working Notes) (Paris: Odette Lieutier)

EISENSTEIN, Sergei. 1971. 'Til Pærehavens troldmand' (The Sorcerer from the Pear Garden), *Teatrets Teori og Teknikk*, 15: 52–57

GOETHE, Johann Wolfgang von. 1988. *Sämtliche Werke* (Collected Works), chief ed. Karl Richter, vol. 4.1, *Wirkungen der Französischen Revolution 1791–97* (The Effects of the French Revolution), ed. by R. Wild (Munich: Carl Hanser)

GROTOWSKI, Jerzy. 1968. *Towards a Poor Theatre* (Holstebro: Odin Teatrets Forlag)

LEITER, Samuel L. 1991. '*Kumagai's Battle Camp*: Form and Tradition in Kabuki Acting', *Asian Theatre Journal*, 1 (8): 1–33

LI, Ruru. 2003. *Shashibiya: Staging Shakespeare in China* (Hong Kong: Hong Kong University Press)

— 2010. *The Soul of Beijing Opera: Theatrical Creativity and Continuity in a Changing World* (Hong Kong: Hong Kong University Press)

MEYERHOLD, Vsevolod. 1969. *Meyerhold on Theatre*, ed. and trans. by Edward Braun (New York: Hill & Wang)

PATANJALI. 1962. *Yoga Sutras: Kriya yoga and kaivalya yoga*, ed. by S.V. Ganapati (Madras: Hindi Prachar Press)

PRONKO, Leonard. 1967. *Theatre East and West: Perspectives towards a Total Theatre* (Berkeley: University of California Press)

RUFFINI, Franco. 1980. *La scuola degli attori* (The School of Actors) (Florence: La Casa Usher)

SAVARESE, Nicola. 1980. *Il teatro aldilà del mare* (The Theatre beyond the Sea) (Turin: Studio Forma)

SCHECHNER, Richard. 1983. *Performative Circumstances from the Avant Garde to Ramlila* (Calcutta: Seagull Books)

SCOTT, Adolphe Clarence. 1959. *Mei Lan-Fang, Leader of the Pear Garden* (Hong Kong: Hong Kong University Press)

SEGALEN, Victor. 1971. *René Leys* (Paris: Gallimard)

TAVIANI, Ferdinando. 1969. *La fascinazione del teatro* (The Fascination of Theatre) (Rome: Bulzoni)

TOPORKOV, Vasili. 1979. *Stanislavski in Rehearsal: The Final Years*, trans. by Christine Edwards (New York: Theatre Arts Books)

WILLETT, John. 1967. *The Theatre of Bertolt Brecht: A Study from Eight Aspects* (London: Methuen)

YOUNG, Stark. 1930. 'Mei Lan-fang', *Theatre Arts Monthly*, 14 (4), 295–308

ZEAMI, Motokiyo. 1960. *La Tradition secrète du Nô* (The Secret Tradition of Noh), ed. and trans. by René Sieffert (Paris: Gallimard)

— 1984. *On the Art of Nō: The Major Treatises of Zeami*, ed. by J. Thomas Rimer, trans. by Yamazaki Masakazu (Princeton: Princeton University Press)

APPENDIX

BY LLUÍS MASGRAU

Facts and statistics about Eugenio Barba's and Odin Teatret actors' collaboration with performers from traditional Asian theatres

These statistics offer an overall vision of the relationships of Barba and his actors with Asian performers. The document shows clearly the various aspects and the specificity of this relationship in the theatre culture of the twentieth and twenty-first centuries. Two of these aspects are especially relevant: on the one hand, the length of the period (more than fifty years) and the regularity of this relationship; on the other, the variety of traditional Asian theatre genres it encompasses.

The document includes work meetings both in Asia, Europe and other parts of the world. Odin Teatret's tours in Asia are only included when there has been a working meeting with a traditional theatre performer.

To complete the information I have also included field work on Asian martial arts and some modern stage forms such as butoh, post-shingeki or the renovation of traditional Chinese theatre developed by Wu Hsing-kuo and his Contemporary Legend Theatre in Taiwan.

This document has been drawn from three sources: Odin Teatret Archives (OTA), Barba's passports from 1983 until today (essential to reconstruct the dates of his travels) and various meetings with Eugenio Barba and Julia Varley, whom I thank for their patience. Without their help this document would not have been possible.

Given the quantity of the data and the period of time covered in the document, on a few occasions it has not been possible to specify the date or other details of meetings.

DATE	PLACE	THEATRE TRADITION	PERFORMERS	ACTIVITIES
1963 3–29 September	Cheruthuruty (India)	Kathakali	Kerala Kalamandalam students	Eugenio Barba field work
1972 15–20 September	Holstebro (Denmark)	Noh	Hisao Kanze, Hideo Kanze and their ensemble	Seminar about Japanese theatre organised by Odin Teatret
		Kabuki	Sojuro Sawamura	
		Kyogen	Mannojo Nomura	
		Post-shingeki	Shuji Terayama and his Tenjo Sajiki troupe	
1973 February	Denpasar, Ubud, Batubulan and Saba (Bali, Indonesia)	Balinese theatre	I Cde Gusti Raka Saba, I Made Bandem	Eugenio Barba field work at ASTI School
1974 February	Denpasar and Saba (Bali, Indonesia)	Balinese theatre	I Cde Gusti Raka Saba, I Made Bandem	Eugenio Barba field work at ASTI School and Saba
(until 1989)	Saba and Denpasar (Bali, Indonesia)	Balinese theatre	Several performers	Institute of Theatre Anthropology and Archeology in collaboration with Ferruccio Marotti
17–21 April	Holstebro (Denmark)	Balinese theatre	I Made Djimat, I Made Pasek Tempo	Seminar about Balinese and Javanese theatre organised by Odin Teatret
		Javanese Theatre	Sardono Waluyo Kusumo	
1976 2–7 March	Holstebro (Denmark)	Bharathanatyam	Shanta Rao	Seminar about Indian theatre organised by Odin Teatret
		Kathak	Uma Sharma	
		Kathakali	Krishna Namboodiri	
		Odissi	Sanjukta Panigrahi, Raghunath Panigrahi	

Date	Location	Theatre form	Artist	Description
1977 28 August – 6 September	Bergamo (Italy)	Noh (Japanese theatre)	Hideo Kanze	International meeting of theatre groups
		Kathakali	Krishna Namboodiri	
		Balinese theatre	I Made Bandem, Swasthi Widjaja Bandem	
1978 January–March	Ubud and Tampaksiring (Bali, Indonesia)	Balinese theatre	Agung Rai, Ni Ketut Suryatini, I Made Pasek Tempo	Iben Nagel Rasmussen, Toni Cots and Silvia Ricciardelli practical studies
	Kerala (India)	Kathakali	Krishna Namboodiri	Tom Fjordefalk practical studies
21–27 October	Herning (Denmark)	Odissi (Indian dance)	Sanjukta Panigrahi	Eugenio Barba and Sanjukta Panigrahi collaborate in a workshop
21–28 May	Ayacucho (Peru)	Butoh	Isso Miura	International meeting of theatre groups
1979 October	Tokyo (Japan)	Kyogen	Mannojo Nomura	Eugenio Barba field work
October	Toga (Japan)	Modern Japanese theatre	Tadashi Suzuki	
December 1979 – January 1980	Denpasar, Ubud and Tampaksiring (Bali, Indonesia)	Balinese theatre	I Made Pasek Tempo	Eugenio Barba field work to prepare the 1st ISTA session at ASTI School and in Tampaksiring together with Toni Cots
1980 May	Tokyo (Japan)	Nihon buyo	Katsuko Azuma	Eugenio Barba field work to prepare the 1st ISTA session
September	Taipei (Taiwan)	Peking Opera	Tsao Chun-lin, Lin Chun-hui	Eugenio Barba field work at the Foo Hsing Opera School to prepare the 1st ISTA session

Date	Location	Genre	Performers	Notes
1–31 October	Bonn (Germany)	Balinese theatre	I Made Pasek Tempo, I Wayan Suweca, I Wayan Punia, I Gusti Nyoman Tantra, I Dewa Ayu Ariani, Desak Ketut Susilawati, Desak Putu Puspawati	1st ISTA session
		Odissi	Sanjukta Panigrahi, Raghunath Panigrahi	Sanjukta Panigrahi works with Roberta Carreri
		Nihon buyo	Katsuko Azuma	Katsuko Azuma works with Roberta Carreri
		Peking Opera	Tsao Chun-lin, Lin Chun-hui	
5–9 November	Holstebro (Denmark)	Balinese theatre	I Made Pasek Tempo, I Wayan Suweca, I Wayan Punia, I Gusti Nyoman Tantra, I Dewa Ayu Ariani, Desak Ketut Susilawati, Desak Putu Puspawati	ISTA session
		Odissi	Sanjukta Panigrahi, Raghunath Panigrahi	
		Nihon buyo	Katsuko Azuma	Katsuko Azuma works with Julia Varley
		Peking Opera	Tsao Chun-lin, Lin Chun-hui	
13–16 November	Porsgrun (Norway)	Balinese theatre	I Made Pasek Tempo, I Wayan Suweca, I Wayan Punia, I Gusti Nyoman Tantra, I Dewa Ayu Ariani, Desak Ketut Susilawati, Desak Putu Puspawati	ISTA session in collaboration with Grenland Friteater
		Odissi	Sanjukta Panigrahi, Raghunath Panigrahi	
		Nihon buyo	Katsuko Azuma	
		Peking Opera	Tsao Chun-lin, Lin Chun-hui	

Date	Place	Genre	Performers	Notes
20–27 November	Stockholm (Sweden)	Balinese theatre	I Made Pasek Tempo, I Wayan Suweca, I Wayan Punia, I Gusti Nyoman Tantra, I Dewa Ayu Ariani, Desak Ketut Susilawati, Desak Putu Puspawati	ISTA session in collaboration with Teater Sharazad
		Odissi	Sanjukta Panigrahi, Raghunath Panigrahi	
		Nihon buyo	Katsuko Azuma	
		Peking Opera	Tsao Chun-lin, Lin Chun-hui	
1981 April	Tokyo (Japan)	Nihon buyo	Katsuko Azuma	Eugenio Barba field work to prepare the 2nd ISTA session
5 August – 7 October	Volterra (Italy)	Balinese theatre	I Made Pasek Tempo, I Ketut Tutur, I Gusti Nyoman Tantra, I Wayan Lantir, I Nyoman Punia, I Made Terika, Anak Agung Putra, Ni Wayan Latri, Ni Nyoman Suyasning	2nd ISTA session
		Odissi	Sanjukta Panigrahi, Raghunath Panigrahi	
		Nihon buyo	Katsuko Azuma, Mari Azuma	
		Kyogen	Kosuke Nomura	
1983 29 October – 20 December	Tokyo (Japan)	Nihon buyo	Katsuko Azuma, Tokuho Azuma	Eugenio Barba field work
		Kyogen	Mannojo Nomura	
		Butoh	Kazuo Ohno, Natsu Nakajima	

1984 January	Bhubaneswar (India)	Odissi	Sanjukta Panigrahi	
27–31 May	Jerusalem (Israel)	Butoh	Natsu Nakajima	Roberta Carreri works with Natsu Nakajima
6–16 December	Tokyo (Japan)	Nihon buyo	Katsuko Azuma	Eugenio Barba field work
		Kyogen	Kosuke Nomura	
16–20 December	Taipei (Taiwan)	Peking Opera	Tracy Chung, Yvonne Lin, Helen Liu	Eugenio Barba field work
1985 12–26 April	Blois and Malakoff (France)	Odissi	Sanjukta Panigrahi, Raghunath Panigrahi	3rd ISTA session
		Nihon buyo	Katsuko Azuma	
		Kyogen	Kosuke Nomura, Ryosuke Nomura, Akiyaso Hirade	
25–29 November	Peking (China)	Peking Opera	Mei Baojiu	Eugenio Barba field work to prepare the 4th ISTA session
		Hebei Opera	Pei Yanling	
28 November – 8 December	Tokyo (Japan)	Nihon buyo	Katsuko Azuma, Kanho Azuma, Kanichi Hanayagi	
8–20 December	Denpasar (Bali, Indonesia)	Balinese theatre	Swasti Widjaja Bandem, Ni Putu Ary Widhyasti Bandem, Desak Made Suarti Laksmi, Ni Made Wiratini	
21–30 December	(Kerala, India)	Kathakali	M.P. Sankaran Nomboodiri, K.N. Vijayakumar	
1986 17–22 September	Holstebro (Denmark)	Balinese theatre	Swasti Widjaja Bandem, Ni Putu Ary Widhyasti Bandem, Desak Made Suarti Laksmi, Ni Made Wiratini	4th ISTA session

Date	Place	Genre	Participants	Event
		Peking Opera	Mei Baojiu, Tracy Chung, Yvonne Lin, Helen Liu,	
		Hebei Opera	Pei Yanling	
		Odissi	Kelucharan Mahapatra, Sanjukta Panigrahi, Raghunath Panigrahi, Gautam (gotipua)	
		Kathakali	M.P. Sankaran Namboodiri, K.N. Vijayakumar	
June–July	Tokyo (Japan)	Nihon buyo	Katsuko Azuma, Kanho Azuma, Kanichi Hanayagi	Katsuko Azuma works with Roberta Carreri
	Tokyo (Japan)	Butoh	Natsu Nakajima	Natsu Nakajima works with Roberta Carreri
	Yokohama (Japan)	Butoh	Kazuo Ohno	Kazuo Ohno works with Roberta Carreri
1987 17–24 February	Tokyo (Japan)	Nihon buyo	Katsuko Azuma, Haruchiho Azuma, Kanichi Hanayagi	Eugenio Barba field work to prepare the 5th ISTA session
24 February – 5 March	Denpasar (Bali, Indonesia)	Balinese theatre	I Made Pasek Tempo, I Made Bandem, Swasti Widjaja Bandem, Desak Made Suarti Laksmi, I Nyoman Catra	
1–14 September	Salento (Italy)	Balinese theatre	I Made Pasek Tempo, I Made Bandem, Swasti Widjaja Bandem, Desak Made Suarti Laksmi, Ni Ketut Suryatini, Ni Nyoman Chandri, I Wayan Rai, I Nyoman Catra, I Ketut Kodi, Tjokorda Raka Tisnu	5th ISTA session

Date	Place	Tradition	Participants	Notes
13–22 December	Calcutta (India)	Odissi	Sanjukta Panigrahi, Raghunath Panigrahi, Gangadhar Pradhan	
		Nihon buyo	Katsuko Azuma, Haruchiho Azuma, Kanichi Hanayagi	
		Martial arts in theatre traditions of China, Japan, Sri Lanka, India and Indonesia		Eugenio Barba at the International Festival and Seminar on Theatre, Dance and Martial Arts organised by Padatik
December	Bangkok (Thailand)	Khon	Several teachers from the National Theatre School	Julia Varley field work
	Gurayaur (India)	Kathakali		
	Irinjalakuda (India)	Kutiyattam	Two Chakyar brothers	
25–30 December	Trivandrum (India)	Kalarippayattu (martial art)	Sopanam Company Director: K.N. Panikkar	
1989 9–17 December	Tokyo (Japan)	Nihon buyo	Katsuko Azuma, Kanho Azuma, Kanichi Hanayagi	Eugenio Barba field work to prepare the 6th ISTA session
17–30 December	Denpasar (Bali, Indonesia)	Balinese theatre	I Made Pasek Tempo, I Made Bandem, I Gde Gusti Raka Saba, I Nyoman Catra, Desak Made Suarti Laksmi	
1990 28 June – 18 July	Bologna (Italy)	Balinese theatre	I Made Pasek Tempo, Desak Made Suarti Laksmi, Ni Ketut Suryatini, Ni Nyoman Chandri, I Wayan Rai, I Nyoman Catra, Tjokorda Raka Tisnu, Ida Bagus Nyoman Mas, Tjokorda Istri Putra Padmini, I Wayan Berata	6th ISTA session

Date	Place	Form	Performers	Notes
1992 2–8 March	Padova (Italy)	Odissi	Sanjukta Panigrahi, Raghunath Panigrahi	1st session of University of Eurasian Theatre
		Nihon buyo	Kanho Azuma, Kanichi Hanayagi, Senkai Azuma	
		Butoh	Natsu Nakajima	
10–30 March	Holstebro (Denmark)	Odissi	Sanjukta Panigrahi, Raghunath Panigrahi	Rehearsals for *The Jungle Book* with Odin Teatret actors
4–11 April	Brecon and Cardiff (Wales, United Kingdom)	Balinese theatre	Desak Made Suarti Laksmi, I Gusti Ayu Srinatih, I Ketut Partha, I Ketut Suteja	7th ISTA session
		Odissi	Sanjukta Panigrahi, Raghunath Panigrahi	
		Nihon buyo	Kanichi Hanayagi	
1993 4–27 January	Bhubaneswar (India)	Odissi	Sanjukta Panigrahi, Raghunath Panigrahi	Kai Bredholt and Jan Ferslev field work
22–30 May	Fara Sabina (Italy)	Odissi	Sanjukta Panigrahi, Raghunath Panigrahi	2nd session of University of Eurasian Theatre
10 August – 10 September	Holstebro (Denmark)	Odissi	Sanjukta Panigrahi, Raghunath Panigrahi	Rehearsals and performances of *The Jungle Book* with Odin Teatret's Iben Nagel Rasmussen, Jan Ferslev and Kai Bredholt *Shakuntala*, directed by Eugenio Barba
28 December – 9 January 1994	Denpasar (Bali, Indonesia)	Balinese theatre	Swasti Widjaja Bandem, Ni Nyoman Chandri, Ni Ketut Suryatini, Desak Made Suarti Laksmi	Eugenio Barba field work to prepare the 8th ISTA session

Date	Place	Type	Performers/Masters	Notes
1994 10–16 January	Tokyo (Japan)	Nihon buyo	Kanichi Hanayagi	8th ISTA session
16–24 January	Denpasar (Bali, Indonesia)	Balinese theatre	Swasti Widjaja Bandem, Ni Nyoman Chandri, Ni Ketut Suryatini, Desak Made Suarti Laksmi	
11–21 August	Londrina (Brazil)	Balinese theatre	Swasti Widjaja Bandem, Desak Made Suarti Laksmi, Tjokorda Raka Tisnu, Tjokorda Istri Putra Padmini, Ni Nyoman Sedana, Ni Nyoman Chandri, I Gede O Surya Negara, Ni Ketut Suryatini, I Ketut Suteja, Ida Bagus Nyoman Mas, Ni Warastrasari Dewi Bandem	
		Odissi	Sanjukta Panigrahi, Raghunath Panigrahi	
		Nihon buyo	Kanichi Hanayagi, Shogo Fujima, Sae Nanaogi	
30 September – 3 October	Holstebro (Denmark)	Odissi	Sanjukta Panigrahi, Raghunath Panigrahi	'Tradition and founders of traditions': symposium to celebrate Odin Teatret's 30th anniversary
		Butoh	Kazuo Ohno, Natsu Nakajima	
1995 19–27 January	Batuan and Ubud (Bali, Indonesia)	Balinese theatre	I Made Djimat, Cristina Wistari	Eugenio Barba and Julia Varley field work to prepare the 9th ISTA session
9–21 May	Umeå (Sweden)	Balinese theatre	I Made Djimat, Cristina Wistari, I Wayan Bawa, Ni Wayan Sekarini	9th ISTA session
		Odissi	Sanjukta Panigrahi, Raghunath Panigrahi	
		Nihon buyo	Kanichi Hanayagi	

1996 3–12 May	Copenhagen (Denmark)	Balinese theatre	I Made Djimat, Cristina Wistari, I Wayan Bawa, Ni Wayan Sekarini, I Wayan Naka, Ni Ketut Maringsih, I Nyoman Budi Artha, I Nyoman Jony, Ni Made Sarniani	10th ISTA session
		Odissi	Sanjukta Panigrahi, Raghunath Panigrahi	
		Nihon buyo	Kanichi Hanayagi, Shogo Fujima, Sae Nanaogi	
		Butoh	Natsu Nakajima	
1997 7–11 February	Batuan (Bali, Indonesia)	Balinese theatre	I Made Djimat, Cristina Wistari, I Wayan Bawa	Eugenio Barba and Julia Varley field work to prepare the 11th ISTA session
2–5 March	Batuan (Bali, Indonesia)	Balinese theatre	I Made Djimat, Cristina Wistari, I Wayan Bawa	
1–8 June	Scilla (Italy)	Nihon buyo	Kanichi Hanayagi, Sae Nanaogi	4th session of University of Eurasian Theatre
14–21 September	Seoul (South Korea)	Shamanistic Keorean rituals	Jindo Ssikkim Kut troupe Mik Ok Park, Dae Rye Kim, Sook Ja Chung	Eugenio Barba and Julia Varley field work
1998 August–September	Holstebro (Denmark)	Balinese theatre	I Made Djimat, Cristina Wistari, I Wayan Bawa, I Wayan Naka, I Nyoman Budi Artha, I Nyoman Kopelin, Ni Made Sarniani, Ni Wayan Sekarini, Ni Ketut Maringsih	Rehearsals of Theatrum Mundi Ensemble
		Nihon buyo	Kanichi Hanayagi, Sae Nanaogi, Jutaiichiro Hanayagi	Rehearsals of Theatrum Mundi Ensemble

14–25 September	Montemor-o-Novo (Portugal)	Balinese theatre	I Made Djimat, Cristina Wistari, I Wayan Bawa, I Wayan Naka, I Nyoman Budi Artha, I Nyoman Kopelin, Ni Made Sarniani, Ni Wayan Sekarini, Ni Ketut Maringsih	11th ISTA session
		Odissi	Rina Jana, Raghunath Panigrahi	
		Nihon buyo	Kanichi Hanayagi, Sae Nanaogi, Jutaiichiro Hanayagi	
1999 22–26 September	Holstebro (Denmark)	Balinese theatre	Gambuh Pura Desa Ensemble: Cristina Wistari, Ni Komang Jumiati, Ni Made Sarniani, Ni Wayan Sudiani, Ni Wayan Sekarini, Ni Wayan Nugini, Ni Wayan Agustini, I Wayan Bawa, I Nyoman Terima, I Wayan Purnawan, Dewa Nyoman Sutrawan, I Wayan Mertawan, I Ketut Rida, I Wayan Supir, I Wayan Lesit, Mangku Kumpul, I Ketut Suana, I Wayan Naka, I Ketut Karwan, Dewa Wayan Kandel, I Made Rarem, I Ketut Doble, I Wayan Lambih, I Wayan Rawa, I Made Rena, I Nyoman Geten, I Wayan Salin, I Made Suamba, I Wayan Kader, I Made Kembar	'Tacit Knowledge – Heritage and Waste': symposium to celebrate Odin Teatret's 35th anniversary
		Noh	Kawamura Kanze noh troupe: Noboru Aida, Nobushige Kawamura, Kiichi Tomoya, Yasushiro Odagiri, Akihiro Takao, Kazutaka Kawamura, Kotaro Kawamura	

		Shamanistic Korean rituals	The Jindo Ssikkim Kut troupe, Mik Ok Park, Dae Rye Kim, Sook Ja Chung	
2000 25–27 August	Bologna (Italy)	Balinese theatre	I Made Djimat, Cristina Wistari, I Nyoman Budi Artha, I Wayan Bawa, Ni Ketut Maringsih, I Wayan Naka, Ni Made Sarniani, Ni Wayan Sekarini	*Ego Faust* Theatrum Mundi Ensemble
		Nihon buyo	Kanichi Hanayagi, Sae Nanaogi, Sasakimi Hanayagi	
1–10 September	Bielefeld (Germany)	Balinese theatre	I Made Djimat, Cristina Wistari, I Nyoman Budi Artha, I Wayan Bawa, I Nyoman Kopelin, Ni Ketut Maringsih, I Wayan Naka, Ni Made Sarniani, Ni Wayan Sekarini	12ᵗʰ ISTA session
		Nihon buyo	Kanichi Hanayagi, Sae Nanaogi, Sasakimi Hanayagi	
		Noh	Akira Matsui	
		Kathakali	M.P. Sankaran Namboodiri	
11–20 September	Copenhagen (Denmark)	Balinese theatre	I Made Djimat, Cristina Wistari, I Nyoman Budi Artha, I Wayan Bawa, Ni Ketut Maringsih, I Wayan Naka, Ni Made Sarniani, Ni Wayan Sekarini	*Ego Faust* Theatrum Mundi Ensemble
		Nihon buyo	Kanichi Hanayagi, Sae Nanaogi, Sasakimi Hanayagi	*Ego Faust* Theatrum Mundi Ensemble
2001 18–28 January	Holstebro (Denmark)	Balinese theatre	Cristina Wistari, Ni Nyoman Chandri, Tjokorda Istri Agung	3ʳᵈ Transit Festival

Date	Location	Theatre form	Performers	Event
2002 4–6 April	Claremont (USA)	Noh	Akira Matsui	Work demonstration with Eugenio Barba and Julia Varley
8–14 April	Taipei (Taiwan)	Peking Opera	Hsieh Yei-shya, Tsao Ya-lan, Chiu Fang-hsuan	Eugenio Barba and Julia Varley field work
14–18 April	Ubud (Bali, Indonesia)	Balinese theatre	I Made Djimat and Gambuh Pura Desa Ensemble (*see* 1999)	
2004 15–25 January	Holstebro (Denmark)	Odissi	Ileana Citaristi	4th Transit Festival
		Peking Opera	Hsieh Yei-shya, Tsao Ya-lan, Chiu Fang-hsuan	
		Balinese theatre	Cristina Wistari, Ni Nyoman Chandri	
1–3 October	Holstebro (Denmark)	Peking Opera	Contemporary Legend Theatre Wu Hsing-kuo	Odin Teatret's 40th anniversary
15–25 October	Sevilla and La Rinconada (Spain)	Balinese theatre	Cristina Wistari, I Wayan Bawa, Ni Wayan Sudi	13th ISTA session
		Odissi	Ileana Citaristi	Ileana Citaristi works with Julia Varley
		Noh	Akira Matsui	
1 December – 3 January 2005	Ubud and Battuan (Bali, Indonesia)	Balinese theatre	Gambuh Pura Desa Ensemble (*see* 1999)	Rehearsals of *Ur-Hamlet* directed by Eugenio Barba, with Odin Teatret actors
		Noh	Akira Matsui	
2005 1–15 April	Krzyżowa and Wrocław (Poland)	Balinese theatre	Cristina Wistari, I Wayan Bawa, Ni Wayan Sudi	14th ISTA session
		Odissi	Ileana Citaristi	
		Noh	Akira Matsui	

Date	Place	Theatre form	Artist / Ensemble	Notes
2006 5–26 March	Ubud and Battuan (Bali, Indonesia)	Balinese theatre	Gambuh Pura Desa Ensemble (*see* 1999)	
		Noh	Akira Matsui	
25 March – 3 April	Taipei (Taiwan)	Peking Opera	Hsieh Yei-shya	Eugenio Barba and Julia Varley field work
11 – 20 April	Ubud and Battuan (Bali, Indonesia)	Balinese theatre	Gambuh Pura Desa Ensemble (*see* 1999)	Rehearsals of *Ur-Hamlet* directed by Eugenio Barba, with Odin Teatret actors
		Noh	Akira Matsui	
15–19 June	Ravenna (Italy)	Odissi	Tiziana Barbiero, Luigia Calcaterra	8th Eurasian Theatre University
9–24 July	Ravenna (Italy)	Balinese theatre	The Gambuh Pura Desa Ensemble (*see* 1999)	*Ur-Hamlet* directed by Eugenio Barba, with Odin Teatret actors
		Noh	Akira Matsui	
25–31 July	Holstebro (Denmark)	Balinese theatre	Gambuh Pura Desa Ensemble (*see* 1999)	
		Noh	Akira Matsui	
1–15 August	Helsingør (Denmark)	Balinese theatre	Gambuh Pura Desa Ensemble (*see* 1999)	
		Noh	Akira Matsui	
2007 22–28 January	Holstebro (Denmark)	Wayang kulit Balinese theatre	Ni Nyoman Chandri	5th Transit Festival
		baul song and dance (India)	Parvathy Baul	
		Balinese theatre	Cristina Wistari	
17 March – 6 April	(Bali, Indonesia)	Balinese theatre	Gambuh Desa Batuan Ensemble* (*see* 1999)	Rehearsals of *The Marriage of Medea*, directed by Eugenio Barba, with Odin Teatret actors Julia Varley and Tage Larsen

* Previously known as the Gambuh Pura Desa.

Date	Location	Theatre form	Company / person	Activity
1–8 December	Taipei (Taiwan)	Nankuan Opera	Chou Yih-chang and Gang A Tsui Theatre	Rehearsals of *Daily Life in a Besieged Country* directed by Eugenio Barba, with the participation of Julia Varley
8–19 December	Ubud and Batuan (Bali, Indonesia)	Balinese theatre	Gambuh Desa Batuan Ensemble (*see* 1999)	Rehearsals of *The Marriage of Medea* directed by Eugenio Barba, with Odin Teatret actors Julia Varley and Tage Larsen
2008 13–15 April	Kaoshiung (Taiwan)	Traditional shadow puppet theatre	Liu Dao-lsun	Eugenio Barba and Julia Varley field work
16–22 April	Taipei (Taiwan)	Nankuan Opera	Chou Yih-chang and Gang A Tsui Theatre	Rehearsals of *Daily Life in a Besieged Country*, directed by Eugenio Barba, with Julia Varley
22–28 April	Ubud and Batuan (Bali, Indonesia)	Balinese theatre	Gambuh Desa Batuan Ensemble (*see* 1999)	Rehearsals of *The Marriage of Medea*, directed by Eugenio Barba, with Odin Teatret actors Julia Varley and Tage Larsen
3–16 June	Holstebro (Denmark)	Balinese theatre	Gambuh Desa Batuan Ensemble (*see* 1999)	Holstebro Festuge (Festive Week) with *The Marriage of Medea*, directed by Eugenio Barba, with Odin Teatret actors Julia Varley, Tage Larsen and Augusto Omolú
2–5 October	Batuan (Bali, Indonesia)	Balinese theatre	Gambuh Desa Batuan Ensemble (*see* 1999)	Eugenio Barba and Julia Varley field work
21 December – 16 January 2009	Batuan (Bali, Indonesia)	Balinese theatre	Gambuh Desa Batuan Ensemble (*see* 1999)	Rehearsals of *Ur-Hamlet*; Eugenio Barba and Julia Varley field work; preparation of a dancing concert, *Manik Suara*, and Topeng version of Shakespeare's *Hamlet*
2009 16–24 January	Taipei (Taiwan)	Peking Opera	Contemporary Legend Theatre, Wu Hsing-kuo	Eugenio Barba and Julia Varley field work
31 May – 23 June	Wroclaw (Poland)	Balinese theatre	Gambuh Desa Batuan Ensemble (*see* 1999)	*Ur-Hamlet* at 'The World as a Place of Truth' International Theatre Festival, organised by the Grotowski Institute
		Noh	Akira Matsui	

			6th Transit Festival
6–16 August	Baul song and dance	Parvathy Baul	
2010 8–12 March / Batuan (Bali, Indonesia)	Balinese theatre	Gambuh Desa Batuan Ensemble (*see* 1999)	Rehearsals of *Ur-Hamlet* Eugenio Barba and Julia Varley field work
16–22 October / Kaoshiung (Taiwan)	Traditional shadow puppet theatre	Liu Dao-hsun	Eugenio Barba and Julia Varley field work
2011 21 May – 27 June / Holstebro (Denmark)	Balinese theatre	I Wayan Bawa	Participation in the Holstebro Festuge (Festive Week) in *Ageless Love*, directed by Julia Varley; preparation and presentation of a work demonstration, *The Total Actor*, in collaboration with Julia Varley
21 December – 3 February 2012 / Batuan (Bali, Indonesia)	Balinese theatre	Gambuh Desa Batuan Ensemble (*see* 1999)	Rehearsals of *Ur-Hamlet*, Eugenio Barba and Julia Varley field work
2012 13–15 March / Pondicherry and Auroville (India)	Kamigata-mai (Japanese dance)	Keiin Yoshimura	Tantidhatri Magdalena Festival with the participation of Eugenio Barba and Julia Varley
	Kathakali	Margi Vijayakumar	
	Ashtanaga Kalam Pulluvan Pattu ritual	Macheri Paambil Padmavathy Ensemble	
	Bhaul song and dance	Parvathy Baul	
15–25 March / Kerala (India)	Ashtanaga Kalam Pulluvan Pattu ritual	Ravi Gopalan Nair; Macheri Paambil Padmavathy Ensemble	Eugenio Barba and Julia Varley field work
	Kutiyattam	Gopalan Nair Venu	
	Muniyattam	Ravi Gopalan Nair	Eugenio Barba and Julia Varley field work
December / Batuan (Bali, Indonesia)	Balinese theatre	I Wayan Bawa	I Wayan Bawa works with Sofía Monsalve

Date	Place	Activity	Performer/Group	Event
2013 19–25 April	Batuan (Bali, Indonesia)	Balinese theatre	Gambuh Desa Batuan Ensemble (*see* 1999)	Eugenio Barba and Julia Varley field work
28 May – 9 June	Holstebro (Denmark)	Kamigata-mai	Keiin Yoshimura	7th Transit Festival
		Baul song and dance	Parvathy Baul	
14–19 June	Fara Sabina (Italy)	Kamigata-mai	Keiin Yoshimura	Teatro Polach Intercultural Laboratory of Theatre Practice
		Baul song and dance	Parvathy Baul	
2014 14–22 June	Holstebro (Denmark)	Baul song and dance	Parvathy Baul	Participation in the Holstebro Festuge (Festive Week) in *The Love Carpet* with Odin Teatret actors Iben Nagel Rasmussen and Elena Floris
22 June	Holstebro (Denmark)	Balinese theatre	I Wayan Bawa and I Nyoman Jony with The Sanggar Seni Tri Suari (Batuan)	Participation in the Holstebro Festuge (Festive Week) in *If the Grain of Wheat Does Not Die*, directed by Eugenio Barba
		Baul song and dance	Parvathy Baul	
		Ashtanaga Kalam Pulluvan Pattu ritual	Macheri Paambil Padmavathy Ensemble	Participation in *Clear Enigma*, Odin Teatret's 50th anniversary
27 June – 6 July	Fara Sabina (Italy)	Kamigata-mai	Keiin Yoshimura	Teatro Potlach Intercultural Laboratory of Theatre Practice
		Baul song and dance	Parvathy Baul	
13–16 November	Shanghai (China)	Cai Zheng Ren, Wu Shuang (*kunqu*), Yan Li (*jinju*)	Shanghai Theatre Academy	ISTA Symposium 'The Performer's Embodied Knowledge'
		Balinese theatre	I Wayan Bawa	

Index of Photographs

PAGE 236
- Unknown photographer.
  From Romain Rolland's book
  The Life of Ramakrishna.

PAGE 239
- Photo by Julia Varley.
  Julia Varley's archive.

PAGE 240
- Photo by Fiora Bemporad.
  Odin Teatret Archives.

PAGE 241
- Photo by Fiora Bemporad.
  Odin Teatret Archives.

PAGE 246
- Photo by Julia Varley.
  Julia Varley's archive.
- Photo by Rina Skeel.
  Odin Teatret Archives.

PAGE 255
- Photo by Ole Daniel Bruun.
  Eugenio Barba's archive.

Index